# Don Cupitt and the Future of Christian Doctrine

Paul's book.

# Don Cupitt and the Future of Christian Doctrine

Stephen Ross White

SCM PRESS LTD

0 334 02563 X

First published 1994
by SCM Press Ltd
26–30 Tottenham Road London N1 4BZ

Typeset at The Spartan Press Ltd,
Lymington, Hampshire
and printed in Great Britain by
Biddles Ltd, Guildford and King's Lynn

# Contents

# Introduction: Cupitt in Context

In common with most areas of human thought and creativity, and in common also with most academic disciplines, the study of theology has witnessed periods both of growth and of stagnation, of inventiveness and of aridity, of change and of conservatism. It has had its times of rich fertility, in which it has challenged men and women to look at their faith in new ways or from a new angle, and its times of barren sterility when it has been content simply to repeat the well-worn platitudes and clichés of a previous age, and in which the faith of the faithful has gradually been deprived of any significant intellectual content, and has, furthermore, lost touch with the world in which it must be lived out. In such ages faith has become a ghetto for those who cannot bear to face the starker realities of life.

The twentieth century has – remarkably, though not uniquely – seen something of both of these directions. In so far as it is even possible to characterize it at this point in time, it would appear to have been a century notable both for its efforts to 'update' theology, and to cling to the past. At one end of the spectrum there has been a widespread revival of various kinds of more-or-less biblical fundamentalism, most dramatically in the United States of America, but of significant proportions in other parts of the world as well. This 'movement' has clung desperately on to the outmoded 'certainties' of a pre-critical and pre-scientific age, and has found itself bedevilled by all the inconsistencies and intellectual contortions which such a position almost inevitably entails, and which James Barr in particular has delineated so clearly and dissected so clinically.[1]

At the other end of the spectrum the watchword – indeed often the rallying-cry – has been the cruelly overworked concept of 'relevance'. There has been a widespread conviction that unless faith, and the theology which undergirds it, has something to say to the world in which we live, and about the way in which we live in it, then it has, in fact, nothing to say at all and had better remain silent in the face of other disciplines which have.

This conviction has manifested itself in a myriad different ways around the world as theologians of vastly differing experience and cultural background have attempted to 'translate', or at least re-interpret the Christian message in ways appropriate to their particular context. Some of these efforts have been largely geographical in origin – that is, the content of the theology has been dictated by the exigencies of a specific cultural or political situation within one or more countries. Among such theologies the best known and most widespread is that of Liberation Theology, which after its genesis in such places as Peru in the thinking of men like Gustavo Gutierrez,[2] has found widespread support throughout central and southern America.[3] In many respects, though, the most remarkable attempt to create an indigenous theology has come from Japan, and the pen of Kosuke Koyama. His work has not been so radical and thoroughgoing as that of the Liberation Theologians, but it has involved the creation of a new language of forgiveness in Japanese theological thinking, most notably in his book *Mount Fuji and Mount Sinai*, which explores, among other things, the notion of a theology of forgiveness in a nuclear age.

Other efforts to re-interpret traditional theology have been not so much geographically as socially based – that is, they have taken as their jumping-off point the needs of a particular section of society (as often globally as locally) and sought to develop the gospel message from this standpoint. As an emergent example of this kind of theology one could cite the 'Bias to the Poor' variety of thinking which is gaining currency in England as a result of the efforts of people such as David Sheppard[4] and the thinking behind the Archbishop's Commission's report on *Faith in the City*.

A more fully-fledged example of this kind of theology, however, would be that variety known as Feminist Theology. Within this movement there has been a radical critique of traditional ways of looking at both the Bible and Christian history,[5] and the movement has sought to re-evaluate the biblical evidence on the place and status of women in the eyes of Jesus, and consequently their place and status in the contemporary religious scene. As a theological method it has both sprung from, and in its turn has fed, the wider feminist movement in society, and in this two-way relationship with secular thinking it represents one of the most fruitful interactions between theology and contemporary thinking to have emerged in recent years.

Finally, there have been a number of individual attempts by theologians to relate theology to what they have perceived as the issues which affect the world most profoundly. Among them, one of the most outstanding is the German theologian, Jürgen Moltmann. He has rightly diagnosed a disjunction between the impassive, impassible God of traditional orthodoxy, and the all-too-real suffering and evil and death which afflict the world. For him – as I suspect for many others less able than he to articulate their position – there is something almost obscene in the idea of a God who creates a world such as this with all its suffering, and is then able to be totally unaffected by it. So he has re-interpreted the traditional picture of God in such a way as to lay an emphasis on the capacity of God to suffer, both in the person of Christ, the 'Crucified God',[6] and in himself. In such a way God is, whilst not diminished, yet made 'one' with his creatures in sympathy and in compassion, indeed even in experience, though not – in good orthodox fashion – in nature.

Of these various attempts at re-defining the traditional categories of theology very few have, until recently, been rooted within the framework of 'mainstream' Western Christianity, and this has suffered in consequence. For peoples and nations in various parts of the world, for many of the world's poor and oppressed, and for many women the world over, Christianity has acquired a new richness and depth as it has finally begun to speak to what these people themselves perceive as being their needs. By contrast, the rest of Western theological thinking has remained relatively static, confining itself to the traditional ways of thought and using traditional language and concepts in somewhat well-worn ways. Certainly these have been re-interpreted in some cases, but they have not been re-defined in the same way as they have in, say, Feminist

Theology or Liberation Theology; nor have they been given a new or challenging relationship with the world at large.

Thus it is that for many – if not indeed for most – Western Christians today, there is a vast gap between faith and life, between theology and secular thought, between worship and the world. In their everyday lives Christians – like everyone else – live in a technological, scientific world: a world of computers and electronics, of psychological and sociological ways of thought. Once in church, however, they are presented with the largely mediaeval concepts and categories of faith and expected to make sense of these for themselves, without re-interpretation or re-definition, in a world which itself seems light years away from that which framed these ways of thinking. No wonder the twentieth century has seen a widespread loss of faith, and has been and still is a time of much confusion even for those for whom 'faith' still has some content and meaning.

If this situation is to be remedied, and if the Christian faith is to speak anew to the bulk of Western Christians in the same way as it now does for other groups, then there clearly must be attempts to re-define or re-translate the Christian faith into terms intelligible in the modern age. This, I would suggest, is a task which needs to be undertaken on two levels: the pragmatic, and the strictly theological.

In an ideal world there is no doubt that the strictly theological thinking would come first and then find itself being worked out in coherent and consistent pragmatic terms. As reality and ideals coincide all too rarely, however, it is hardly surprising that the two undertakings have necessarily proceeded side by side with one another, and have evolved a rather 'leap-frogging' mode of progress. As yet the two would not seem to have interacted to any substantial extent, but one would expect this to happen in the fullness of time. At present, therefore, exponents of Christian praxis such as Paul Rowntree Clifford[7] and – less so – Margaret Kane[8] are working in something of a theological vacuum, and whilst they may be able to contribute towards a reorientation of Christian living in the world, they are not able significantly to re-interpret or revitalize the categories and concepts of faith itself.

Thus there is a vital need also for a far-reaching theological re-think in Western Christianity. To say this is not to deny the fact that for the last one hundred years or so there have been periodic efforts to 'update' the Christian faith or to accommodate it to the latest developments in – usually – scientific thinking. These efforts have borne fruit in some of the most outstanding theological thought in the period, most notably of all perhaps, the *Lux Mundi* group in 1889,[9] and the *Soundings* group in 1962.[10] The shortcoming of all such efforts is, however, that they have been partial rather than systematic, addressing themselves only to selected issues rather than to the problems facing theology as a whole. Similarly there have been several searching re-examinations of particular doctrines within the Christian faith. By their very nature these discussions have usually been controversial, and have perhaps generated more heat than light. Such, in retrospect, was the case with the publication of the famous – or infamous – collection of essays entitled *The Myth of God Incarnate*.[11] The other major defect with this collection, and with other similar debates about particular doctrines, is not so much their fragmentary nature in taking one doctrine and not paying sufficient attention to the implications which they may have in other areas of doctrine, but rather their somewhat rarefied nature. It is all very well – and doubtless very necessary – to discuss in suitably learned fashion the *pros* and *cons* of the incarnation, but it is equally important to assess the effect of this in more concrete terms. In other words, it needs also to be established what difference any particular way of thinking will, by implication, make to the terms and ideas in which we actually express and practise our faith. What will it mean for worship? For our ideas of salvation and redemption? For the way in which we perceive God? For the way in which we relate to him? These and other similar questions are usually answered all too inadequately in the more abstruse discussions of doctrine.

So there is a need for a theological 'method' which unites the strengths of these various approaches and also attempts to set its theological thinking in the context of Christian practice, both within the church itself and in terms of the living out of its understanding of the Christian faith in the world. This task, though vast and daunting, has been, with varying degrees of success, attempted by theologians who have been, of necessity, radical in their approach. In his recent book *Tradition and Truth*, David L. Edwards attempts to do justice to the thinking of seven of the most significant of them. Perhaps the theology which is the most well worked-out and coherent among them is that of Bishop John Robinson, but in many ways the most remarkable, the most radical, and the most stimulating of them is Don Cupitt.

Cupitt, I believe, stands in the midst of this widespread theological ferment which I have outlined, and is attempting to achieve the kind of theological re-statement and re-definition for which I have argued there is so great a need. He is also a theologian whose work deserves more academic attention than it has so far received. He has been dismissed or condemned for the extreme and often unorthodox nature of his views in recent years, and this has obscured the fact that whether or not one agrees with all of his conclusions, nonetheless he is addressing the issues which genuinely *matter* at the present time, and is attempting with sincerity and intellectual honesty both to ask and to answer some of the crucial questions about the status of the Christian faith in the late twentieth century.

More than this though, his work is of particular interest – and perhaps too, of particular importance – for a number of reasons. Unusually amongst theologians, his work has been marked by a continuous development of thought, although the pace of this development has by no means always been constant. There was a long period during which the changes, outwardly at least, were slow, and in which some new directions are visible only in retrospect, and this has been followed since the early 1980s by a period of rapid and accelerating change, as the implications of insights gained in the earlier years have been more thoroughly worked out. Yet, in spite of this rather uneven rate of progress there is, in Cupitt's thought, a very definite onward movement which can be traced from the beginning of his career to the present day. Each new work has built on what has gone before, and his theological offerings have not, on the whole, been piecemeal ones, but very definite individual steps towards the construction of a major theological thought world. Such a unity of thought is, in itself, enough to set Cupitt apart from many other theologians, but the internal coherence of his work has another strand to it, namely that he has himself, albeit briefly, reviewed his own previous thinking from time to time and commented on how he sees the various phases of his own pilgrimage and work fitting together. Thus several of his earlier books have been given a new Preface for a Second Edition,[12] in which he has attempted to set the book firmly in the context of his own development. In doing this, and more generally in thinking and writing in such an internally unified manner, Cupitt gives us a valuable record of one individual's changing thought which amounts almost to a theological auto-biography from the perspective of someone who is trying honestly to work out what it means to be a Christian in the late twentieth century.

This fact too is cause for taking Cupitt very seriously indeed. One of the criticisms which has often been levelled against him – and one which I would partially echo – is that his work does not touch the concerns, the questions, the doubts or the worries of the vast bulk of people. It does not speak either to, or on behalf of, that being to whom all things everywhere are referred – the man in the street. Undoubtedly this is true, and it may well also be regrettable, although one suspects that the fault lies as much with the man in the street who never, it seems, troubles himself to think much about anything, as it does with Cupitt, who perhaps does not trouble himself to speak to such a man! This once admitted, however, it remains true that Cupitt does speak for a larger class of people than is usually recognized. Scott Cowdell remarks that Cupitt appeals especially to 'disaffected Christian intellectuals',[13] and it may be that this is a more substantial group than even Cowdell would care to acknowledge. Certainly it is for them that Cupitt primarily speaks, but his thinking may also strike a chord with anyone who has troubled himself to ask even a few of the fundamental questions about religion in general and the Christian religion in particular. There is, then, an important sense in which Cupitt's own clearly recounted theological and spiritual quest is a product of, and for, its time. Like other such quests in previous ages it may become dated with the passing of the years, but it deserves to be treated with great respect and seriousness in its own age.

In the course of it, Cupitt has also faced explicitly the task of coming to terms with many of the most important and influential thinkers of the past two hundred years or so. His work has something of a panoramic quality, in that it takes in, and attempts to take account of the influence of a wide variety of disciplines. He draws most notably on philosophy, psychology and sociology, as well as on theology. Admittedly it must be allowed that his presentation of other people's ideas is not always entirely free from bias or even prejudice. One frequently feels that he has been less than just to ideas and individuals with whom he disagrees, and has not always presented arguments entirely fairly. But perhaps it would not be realistic to look for such Olympian detachment on every occasion, for after all, Cupitt is concerned to present an argument of his own and to present it as persuasively and cogently as he is able. Again, whether or not one agrees with Cupitt's use of arguments and ideas in any particular instance, it is nonetheless refreshing to find a theologian who is willing to look again at our intellectual heritage and to re-evaluate it and use it in the service of his own creative and compelling contribution to theology.

In the light of these various considerations it will have become clear that I regard Don Cupitt as a major and somewhat neglected figure in the current theological landscape. To date there have been, apart from reviews and other minor pieces, occasional refutations of his work, most notably by Keith Ward[14] and Brian Hebblethwaite,[15] and two recent extended studies by David L. Edwards[16] and Scott Cowdell.[17] With the exception of these offerings, Cupitt's work has been received with a deafening silence by the theological establishment. One could imagine three possible reasons for such a silence. By some he will have been dismissed as being too eccentric and radical to merit any serious or sustained attention. Others may be too alarmed at the prospect of what may emerge once the Pandora's Box which Cupitt has given the theological world is fully opened; others again are presumably applying the principle of Gamaliel and fervently hoping that Cupitt-style radicalism will turn out to be 'not of God' and will thereby go away of its own accord.

For whatever reasons it may have arisen, this silence is, I believe, misplaced. Cupitt may be radical to an extreme degree, but he is engaged in the time-honoured task of the serious theologian – namely, that of attempting to relate the areas of personal faith, intellectual discovery, and the world in which these must live, in a manner intelligible to, and believable by the temper and mind-set of his age and culture. As Cupitt himself has said, it is time alone which will measure the success or failure of his endeavours,[18] but that does not absolve the rest of the theological world from the task

Isle of Man Section 13

Bessler - 13 page 182

| | |
|---|---|
| Personal Name: | Critchley, Simon, 1960- |
| Type of Material: | Book (Print, Microform |
| LC Control Number: | 99487855 |

=============================================

| CALL NUMBER: | BJ319 .B467 2000 |
| | Copy 1 |
| -- Request in: | Jefferson or Adams Bl |
| | Rms |
| -- Status: | Not Charged |

---

| CALL NUMBER: | BJ319 .B467 2000 |
| | Copy 2 |
| -- Request in: | Jefferson or Adams Blc |
| | Rms |
| -- Status: | c.2 Temporarily Shelve |
| | or Area Studies Read |
| | Not Charged |

of instigating that process of critical evaluation which, continuing over a generation or two, itself constitutes the judgment of time.

Clearly then, there is room for further contributions to the debate which Cupitt is attempting to instigate. Within this debate, this study is initially an attempt to outline Cupitt's contribution to theological thought. The first part, therefore, is in the nature of a survey. The second part, however, is more critical and evaluative in approach. Having argued for Cupitt's stature as a theologian, it must be admitted that I by no means always agree with his conclusions, nor even necessarily with the premisses from which those conclusions are derived. The second part of this study will therefore be devoted to the perceived problems and shortcomings of Cupitt's method and conclusions, and I shall argue that, first, certain of these can be constructively challenged, and that secondly, rational and coherent alternatives can be put forward to some of the questions Cupitt raises and the views he expresses, and that these alternatives and – an admittedly fairly liberal – orthodoxy based on critical realism, are not mutually exclusive.

Cupitt, then, is a major theologian whose radicalism must be seriously reckoned with. In company with other radical theologians he has opened the way forward to a new kind of theology. The world he has shown us is one which theology must enter if it is to retain any semblance of intellectual respectability, but at the same time it may justifiably be asked whether, in the search for a 'post-modern' theology, the pendulum has not swung too far towards radicalism. It will be my contention that the time is ripe for more orthodox theologians to rise to Cupitt's challenge, to accept the freshness of his thinking with gratitude rather than to brand him as a heretic, but at the same time to challenge him in return and to offer answers to his very real and pertinent questions from a position which is more consonant with the best of the Christian tradition in which, sometimes despite appearances, both Cupitt and the rest of us stand.

# Part One

# Cupitt and his Development

# I

# Roots in Orthodoxy

## I

As Don Cupitt himself observes in his foreword to Scott Cowdell's study,[1] most of the fairly scant critical attention which has been paid to him has been in the form of refutations.[2] The result of this is that all too little attention has been paid to the development of Cupitt's thought. A wide variety of people have taken it upon themselves to criticize his more recent – and more radical – thinking, without pausing to consider how and why he has reached his present views. To a certain extent Scott Cowdell has succeeded in filling this lacuna through his own study. In it he considers in some detail the various stages of Cupitt's development both in its earlier and its later phases. He does this by following the admirably clear schema which he sets forth in his own introduction to the book.[3] There still remains, however, one notable omission in this, as in all other considerations of Cupitt to date. For neither Cowdell, nor anyone else, has yet paid sufficient attention not only to tracing the path of Cupitt's move away from 'orthodoxy', but also to outlining the forces, and in particular the objections to orthodox thinking, which have propelled him down this path.

These objections to orthodoxy are important not only in them-selves, as influences and indeed as major factors in Cupitt's theological pilgrimage – since it is very often his objections and dissatisfactions with received tradition which have impelled him onward to new positions – but they are also important when it comes to assessing the value of Cupitt's thought, and in particular to establishing what contribution, if any, he may have made to the major theological issues of the late twentieth century. Until the present time most critical opinion on Cupitt has simply pronounced judgment on the totality of his theological thinking: it has taken his conclusions in isolation and lauded or execrated him accordingly. This seems to me to be a short-sighted and unhelpful approach to an individual whose thought is as developmental and sequential as Cupitt's is. I remarked in the Introduction to this study that Cupitt addresses some of the central problems and issues facing theology today, and to this I would add that one can respect and appreciate, and also assimilate into one's own thinking, many of the problems with orthodoxy which Cupitt raises without necessarily agreeing with all of his conclusions. In terms of the fruitfulness of his work for generating further thought, the premises of his arguments are as important – if indeed not more so – than the conclusions which he derives from them. To neglect his dawning and growing perception of the problems raised by orthodoxy is at best to attempt to live in a long-vanished world of primal innocence, and at worst wilfully to ignore the very issues with which theology must grapple if it is to retain its intellectual and spiritual integrity for the future.

For a large part of his career, however, Cupitt's orthodoxy was not seriously in question. In the early 1970s he was hailed even in the august pages of the *Church Times* as a 'stalwart believer',[4] and for a number of years he was seen as being more concerned with the restatement and re-interpretation of traditional doctrines and ideas than with their rejection or replacement by any new form of belief.

In view of the remarkable disparity between the early and the later Cupitt it is instructive to consider, at least briefly, the background of his early thinking in order to see more clearly the nature of the starting point of his theological peregrinations.

Cupitt has always had a keen eye for change in his own position, and he is delightfully honest about his own perception of himself. Writing in 1979, when he was on the threshold of a period of intense ferment and rapid change in his thinking, he said of an early essay entitled 'What is the Gospel?':

> When I wrote it in 1964 I was one of those serious hyper-orthodox young men who arise in each generation to dismay their elders and betters (just as today, replicas of what I was, they have arisen to reproach me).[5]

However, even at this early stage in his career, this 'hyper-orthodox young man' could still balance the scales with a healthy dose (arguably, in retrospect, an overdose) of scepticism. Again he writes of himself:

> If one accepts the scientific outlook one must reject anthropomorphic and interventionist ideas of God. The world about us is continual natural process, without any hidden wire-pulling. My own background is in natural science, empiricist (and more recently, post-Kantian) philosophy, and in the old long-secularized industrial England. Though temperamentally very religious, I have never looked for or believed in miracles, answers to prayer, particular providences or the 'supernatural' in the popular sense.[6]

For the most part, though, his earlier years – certainly up to and including *The Leap of Reason* in 1976, and even *Jesus and the Gospel of God* in 1979 – were years of orthodoxy, sometimes critical certainly, but always broadly compatible with what might be called 'mainstream' theological thinking. This is true both of his approach to particular areas of faith and doctrine such as the person of Christ, or the problem of the objective content of faith, and of his response to several of the major twentieth-century critical weapons against Christianity, most notably the various forms of projection theory which have been advanced.

## II

Thus Cupitt devotes a good deal of attention to the problem of the objectivity of faith even in some of his earliest books, rightly perceiving that one's answer to this question is fundamental to all that comes after it. It is part of the foundation on which any religious superstructure can then be built. Clearly, in the light of his later work it is one of the problems which, in his own words, have 'obsessed me permanently',[7] and it is interesting to find him addressing it as early as 1971 and returning a resoundingly orthodox answer to it. At the end of a lengthy discussion of the 'confessional' nature of belief and whether or not this precludes, or negates the need for, any cognitive aspect to belief, he concludes:

> ... I would still insist that for there to be a cognitive experience of God there must be, as a necessary condition, one or more justifiable beliefs about God. Our analysis of a religious speech act has not obliged us to retract the view that beliefs about God are presupposed in religious utterances. The religious man has indeed a passionate interest in their truth, but that is not to say that they are constituted true by the passion of his interest.[8]

To this he raises the potential objection that it is precisely the 'passion of the interest' rather than 'philosophical analysis' which is and must be the sole arbiter of the truth of religious statements. Such an objection, once admitted, would quite clearly open the door to a much more relativistic and subjective understanding of religious utterances which would then become purely 'confessional' and 'non-cognitive', and Cupitt is very determined indeed that, whatever the difficulties involved, there must remain some cognitive element in belief. In defence of this he argues that although the presence or absence of faith may materially affect what is apprehended, yet faith does not *create* that which it apprehends. Faith is 'in the last analysis receptive'.[9] It can:

> ... only respond to an object which was before it, as being before it, if in some way the prior and surpassing reality of that object can be articulated independently of the passion of faith and then recognized in it.[10]

For Cupitt, at this early stage in his thinking, religious statements do make some cognitive claims about the nature of reality, including inevitably and pre-eminently, the reality of God himself.

Five years later, in what is arguably one of his most sustained and consistently well-thought out books, *The Leap of Reason*, we find him once again devoting a substantial amount of time and attention to this same problem, though now expressed in more general terms as referring rather to the *possibility* of objective religious discourse than to discussing any specific examples of it. His first priority is to establish the 'possibility' of transcendence, rightly leaving to one side in the first instance the question of whether such transcendence is purely subjective or has any objective content. To this end he offers us in Chapter 3 of *The Leap of Reason* a reworking of Plato's allegory of the cave. There are two major differences in this account from that of Plato: 'there is most definitely no chink in the prison wall, and we do not postulate that our prisoner has any extra-ordinary faculties'.[11] Even in this completely enclosed situation, however, Cupitt's prisoner is able to formulate, by that 'leap of reason' from which the book derives its title, at least the possibility of an 'outside', with all the new possibilities which that would entail. As a result he becomes a changed man, and it would be true to Cupitt's account to say that out of the resulting sense of dissatisfaction with what is now perceived as 'here', the spiritual quest is born. At times it appears that Cupitt is in danger of attaching too much significance to this glimpsing of the possibility of the transcendent and to imbue it with at least a putative objectivity before he has developed his own argument to the point where objectivity becomes an issue. Viewed on its own terms, however, and without looking, as yet, outside it, the parable is significant because it opens up the possibility of transcendence even if it does not yet help us to establish whether the 'outside' exists only in the prisoner's own imagination or whether it has any meaningful existence of its own independently of the mind of any observer. As yet this does not matter. It will follow later. For the present, and as the first step in his argument, then, as Cupitt remarks:

. . . if you are prepared to allow that the parable is *intelligible*, then that is something. The prisoner's colleagues would not admit even that much.[12]

Having established this basis for the possibility of transcendence, Cupitt then proceeds in the rest of the book to develop his case for its reality, and to offer at least some suggestions as to its content. To do this, though, he has to establish some defence of his ideas in the face of the twentieth-century bogeyman of relativism which periodically threatens to assail the meaningfulness of almost everything and especially of theology and philosophy. He does this by arguing with devastating clarity that relativism actually contains within itself the seeds of transcendence, at first sight an unlikely notion, but one which he demonstrates by neatly turning the tables upon the supporters of relativism. The crux of his argument is expressed in two admirably short and lucid sentences:

> My reply [to the relativists] has been to disclaim any direct intuition of the absolute, and instead to point out that the statement 'All our knowledge is relative to interpretative frameworks', if something we know for true, is an exception to the rule it states. Precisely because we can grasp what relativism is and asserts, we can transcend it.[13]

The idea of transcendence in general, even if not in specifically religious terms, is therefore seen to be fundamental even to a concept as universally iconoclastic as relativism. Indeed, as Cupitt concludes:

> The idea of transcendence, in this very general sense, is necessary for creative advance in any department of human life and thought whatever.[14]

Relativism having been thus warded off, the final hurdle for Cupitt is to establish the content of a specifically religious transcendence. This, he readily acknowledges, is more difficult, especially in view of the fact that by definition the transcendent is not directly knowable, and in view of the insistence of Christianity – and all other theistic faiths – that the transcendent is, ultimately, in some sense at least, personal.[15]

Cupitt approaches these two related problems in characteristically resourceful fashion. He invokes the idea of five stages in our perception of the transcendent, which may be expressed as establishing firstly its possibility (as in the parable of the cave); secondly its objectivity as an absolute perspective (argued for in his refutation of relativism); thirdly its expression in myth, story, doctrine, morals, symbols and the like; fourthly an iconoclastic negation of the third stage which recognizes the inadequacy of all our efforts to say the unsayable and define the undefinable; and fifthly a final recognition that although the fourth stage with its inbuilt agnosticism is the logical end to our search, yet we must still say something and claim to know something. Thus we live in a state of 'flux and reflux between stages three and four',[16] a position which is somewhat akin to that described by John Macquarrie in his discussion of Absolute Idealism in *Twentieth-Century Religious Thought*.[17]

This rather complicated route by which Cupitt approaches the transcendent is one which acknowledges the very real problems involved in speaking at all of that which is beyond our direct perception, and it is one which wisely admits to a measure of agnosticism whilst still maintaining fully the need to make some approach to, and speak as coherently as possible about the transcendent. There are echoes of St Augustine's bewildered and yet insistent attempt to speak of God in the first book of the *Confessions*, where after numerous attempts to capture the mystery and paradox at the heart of the Godhead he concludes:

And what have I now said, my God, my life, my holy joy? or what saith any man when he speaks of Thee? Yet woe to him that speaketh not, since mute are even the most eloquent.[18]

Full of problems, and demanding a measure of agnosticism as it does, Cupitt's account of our approach to the transcendent does allow him, as the final stage of his argument, to present the case not only for the existence of the transcendent, but for its 'knowability' in personal terms. This he does cogently and succinctly in Chapter 7 of *The Leap of Reason* via the necessary presence of the transcendent in the realm of morality. And morality, being a sphere in which the personal is of prime, if not of supreme, importance, he is able to predicate the existence of a personal quality to the transcendent:

According to my argument, however, to attain an active and non-ascetical moral goodness we are morally obliged to believe in Grace, to regard the transcendent as the source of those supremely precious moral virtues which are necessarily secret. That is, those aspects of moral goodness which we cannot without absurdity think to create in ourselves by conscious and deliberate effort are to be regarded as bestowed by the transcendent. So the way the transcendent is related to our thought is paralleled by the way it expresses itself in the moral life.[19]

The moral qualities he is thinking of are primarily personal rather than abstract – love, generosity, sympathy and the like. And so he draws the conclusion that:

> Theistic ethics is under a moral necessity to ascribe such moral qualities to the transcendent, and so (within its programme) to speak of him as personal and as the final good.[20]

Finally, Cupitt's account of transcendence – and its relationship to relativism, including religious relativism – enables him to emerge from his lengthy and detailed argument to present a remarkably high and orthodox picture of monotheistic faith. In this picture all the relativities and shortcomings of our own perception of God are freely admitted, and the necessary indirectness of our knowledge of God acknowledged. But this is not allowed to obscure the reality or the value of our knowledge of God, nor of the admittedly imperfect religious 'programmes' through which we relate to him. Though our perceptions and ideas of God are *only* our perceptions and ideas of him and must always be acknowledged as such, this does not prevent them from being perceptions of a God who is 'real' in himself. Although we may only know and speak of that reality indirectly and by analogy, we can still vouch for its importance, its effect, and its power in shaping and guiding our lives, and as something – indeed somebody – perceived as a reality 'outside' ourselves. In *The Leap of Reason* Cupitt has succeeded remarkably in synthesizing critical thinking and a religiously significant and fulfilling picture of reality which is compatible with, and indeed creatively restates, the received traditions of the Christian faith.

Alongside this concern with establishing the possibility of objectivity in religious belief and utterance – clearly a fundamental task in the construction of any religious world-view – Cupitt has also devoted himself extensively to specific problems in Christian doctrine. One of the most significant and long-lasting of these has been his attempt to achieve a contemporary understanding of the person and work of Jesus Christ. An early essay in this direction is the latter part of *Christ and the Hiddenness of God*, in which he considers such things as what we may understand by the resurrection, what sense can be made of claims to 'know' Christ, and what knowledge of God may be mediated through Christ. None of these themes needs to be treated exhaustively here, but rather it is sufficient to note that his conclusions in each area are critical rather than sceptical, and lie well within the range of opinion which would be endorsed by most modern theologians. In the case of the analogical knowledge of God which we have through Jesus, and Jesus' own knowledge of God, it is interesting that Cupitt invokes what is essentially an earlier version of his five stages of religious understanding from *The Leap of Reason* outlined above. Jesus' own knowledge of God, and ours through him, is largely, and necessarily, anthropomorphic, but this contains within itself the seeds of its own negation and transcendence, thus pointing beyond itself to a reality beyond our knowing which we must nonetheless relate to and understand in precisely those same anthropomorphic terms which we have just discarded as inadequate. Thus, as in his later account, Cupitt here depicts us as living in a state of 'flux and reflux' between positive anthropomorphism and an image breaking *via negativa*.

So it is that to the question of our knowledge of God Cupitt returns an answer which is at once orthodox and critical, aware of the inadequacy of our knowing, and even of our power of knowing, and yet committed to the value – and the reality – of that knowing:

> If we ask the question, what kind of justification of our analogical discourse about God can there be, the Gospels return a curious answer. They represent Jesus as living out the relation to God through a certain set of anthropomorphic images – and the logic of the images was such that, followed through, they led to their own loss. They were self-transcending. If they are justified it is because they do point beyond themselves, to Calvary and Easter.[21]

A similar blend of honest agnosticism combined with a deep-seated faith which is not indifferent to knowledge but which reaches beyond it, is contained in Cupitt's final remarks on the meaning of talk about Christ with which he concludes the book:

Our argument has led us to this position. Christ now is not indicable, nor can his existence be inferred in a valid argument. Talk of the present Christ could have a reference and does have a use, but that reference cannot be satisfactorily established. The believer gives it an historical reference: Christ is none other than Jesus, exalted as Lord. And he gives it a present use. For the rest, he believes that he knows Christ in the sense that he will recognize him when he sees him, and that he now knows God through him.[22]

Such a conclusion may not be enough to satisfy those of a more fundamentalist temper, but it is not dissimilar to many of the answers which have been given throughout Christian history by those who have gone beyond the 'popular' aspects of faith and grappled with any of the philosophical and metaphysical issues attendant upon theistic belief. He may express himself in different language, but his consistent attitude of devout agnosticism in this book would not have disgraced many of the Church Fathers, or indeed the mediaeval mystics.

Eight years later, in 1979, one can see the same preoccupations at work in *Jesus and the Gospel of God*. In one sense Cupitt's appreciation of Jesus has deepened rather than changed during these years; but in another sense we can see him standing on the threshold of the major changes which were to come during the next two or three years. Even as early as *Christ and the Hiddenness of God*, one can see, in the conclusions quoted above, Cupitt's concern for the 'purely religious' context and content of religious language. It is, for example, the believer who gives any talk of Christ its 'present use'. There is nothing heterodox about this, but it is only a short step from here to a position in which the believer creates *all* religious meaning, and in which the objective content of faith, which Cupitt has been so anxious to safeguard, is emptied out into the bottomless pit of the subjectivity of the individual believer.

It is this 'purely religious' appreciation of faith which has come to the fore in *Jesus and the Gospel of God*. Throughout the book Cupitt argues compellingly for the radical call to faith in God issued by Jesus, a call which turns the believer's world upside-down, and which summons him to faith in a God who is at once ineffable and transcendent, and vividly – almost shatteringly – present in demand and in judgment. Confronted by this call, the believer's response is at once a practical apprehension of the demands of God, and a purely religious appreciation of the reality of God: that is, God is not perceived as a putative metaphysical entity, but as a challenging, potent, awesome and surprising being who demands, through Jesus' call to a radical conversion of life, a definite and uncompromising response of will, mind and heart. This Cupitt sees, and quite possibly rightly, as being a return to the immediacy and urgency of the earliest Christian faith which has been diluted by centuries of comfortable Christendom. So he argues passionately for the need for this rediscovery and of the practical and religious immediacy of God in Jesus Christ:

> To throw off the legacy of Christendom, however, and return to the teaching of Jesus and the primitive faith requires not only that we rescue Jesus from dogmatic captivity, but that we rescue God from metaphysical captivity. The earliest faith was practical and purely religious in its categories, but Christianity gradually became so extensively permeated with dogmatic, philosophical and cosmological ways of thinking that by now many people find it hard to recognize the purely religious as a category at all. Thus in our talk of God the non-religious God of the philosophers has held the field more or less continuously since the thirteenth century, and in spite of numerous valiant attempts a truly religious understanding of God has not yet been restored to general currency.[23]

In view of this dominance of the 'God of the philosophers', Cupitt stresses the need for Christianity to return to its origins in Jesus and the simplicity, directness, and world-overturning surprisingness of his call for response to God:

> . . . the primitive Christian faith, if and when we rediscover it, will also come as a total surprise. What we need today is not the transposition of the remains of Christendom into some liberal or humanist framework of ideas, but something more drastic, a

reaffirmation of the purely religious categories in which Christianity first came into the world.[24]

In all of this, and especially in his call for a return of Christianity to
something of its primitive simplicity and potency, Cupitt is, whilst
deliberately challenging towards and severely critical of cosy
establishment Christianity, still working within the framework of
orthodoxy. The problems inherent in the 'purely religious' use of
language remain, and will lead to an increasing non-objectivity later
on; but for the present, it is interesting to note that even this close to
*Taking Leave of God*, which was published in the following year,
Cupitt, although using concepts which will lend themselves to his
later non-realism, is still maintaining his foothold on what has always
been one of the most dangerous precipices on the path of orthodoxy
– the nature and work of Christ. Although his programme for
Christianity as set out in *Jesus and the Gospel of God* might demand a
great deal of change by the church, yet he could plausibly and
legitimately argue that his radical solution is more faithful to the
origins of Christianity in Jesus and the pages of the New Testament
than is the rather milk-and-water ecclesiastical establishment and
piety which he is criticizing.


# III

Given Cupitt's willingness to argue both for the objectivity and
cognitive content of religious belief, and his efforts to contribute to a
meaningful modern understanding of the person and work of Jesus
Christ, it is hardly surprising either to find him devoting at least a
modicum of attention to the task of defending Christianity against
some of the more far-reaching and fundamental criticisms which
have been levelled at it during the past one hundred years or so, and
also against a number of wider trends in modern thought which he
perceives as reductive of the fullness of the Christian faith.

Of these trends, the most pervasive, and therefore the one which
Cupitt is most concerned to head off, is humanism – interestingly
and ironically in view of the later developments in Cupitt's own
position.

We have seen already, in the discussion of Cupitt's ideas about the person of Christ, how insistent he is that Christianity should not be eviscerated and transformed into 'some liberal or humanist framework of ideas'.[25] He expands this idea in the selection of 'Working Notes' appended to the same book. He notes the feeling of many thinkers – and cites Hans Küng's *On Being a Christian* as an example – that we 'live in a world now permanently non-religious and humanist'.[26] In such a world, the importance which Cupitt attaches to the category of the 'purely religious' and to the transcendent is misguided. Instead, 'Christianity must be presented as the highest fulfilment of humanism'.[27] To this swamping of Christianity by humanism, Cupitt objects, on the grounds that it is both reductive of the content of Christianity, and also little better than a means of self-deception:

> . . . in modern humanist and liberal theology both God and Jesus tend to become mere symbolic reinforcements of a concern for the human in general. Does this not in the end approximate to Comtism – human self-infatuation tricked out in evocative religious metaphors?"[28]

His objection is a cogent one, and has been echoed by other writers. Thus Lloyd Geering shares Cupitt's mistrust of humanism as reductive, and indeed is not willing even to allow that humanism retains any vestiges of religious richness, even in the attenuated form of the 'evocative religious metaphors' which Cupitt is willing to grant it:

> Humanism . . . though widespread today at a superficial level, is somewhat vague, powerless and lacking in the capacity to stir the imagination. Like streams which flow into the desert and disappear into the sand, it tends to ebb away and leave a religious vacuum.[29]

Geering rightly perceives that humanism comes in many shapes and guises, and is incompatible with any more structured and specific form of belief such as Christianity. It is hardly surprising, therefore, that Cupitt, who at this stage in his career shared this perception, should find humanism to be in direct opposition to the radically challenging 'otherness' of the 'God through Christ' oriented theology which he sets out in *Jesus and the Gospel of God*.

However, it is not only trends of thought which threaten the integrity of Christianity. Of equal, if not of greater significance, are the various direct challenges and criticisms which have been levelled at it by other disciplines, especially psychology and sociology. Once again Cupitt is aware of the dangers of reductionism inherent in some of these challenges and criticisms. He singles out for especial attention in at least two books that complex of ideas which has been labelled 'projection theory', and which has impinged upon Christianity both in its psychological and sociological manifestations.

The depth of Cupitt's hostility to this theory, though not the clarity of his critique of it, is evident at a very early stage in his career in *The Crisis of Moral Authority*. In a protracted discussion of the various species of projection theory stemming from Hegel and then Feuerbach, Cupitt singles out Freud's variation of this theme for a particularly stinging rebuttal. There is little considered argument in his treatment of Freud, but a good deal of irritation! He is willing to grant Freud a certain measure of truth in his perception and criticism of the grosser anthropomorphisms of Christianity, especially in its more 'popular' manifestations, but he summarily dismisses the main thrust of Freud's attack on religion with the damning comment that, 'Freud's views on religion are largely sheer prejudice'.[30]

Such a remark may reveal Cupitt's feelings very clearly, and certainly testifies to his desire to rid Christianity of the projectionist spectre, but it does not make any great strides in the direction of providing a sustained and reasoned counter-critique of Freud's views. In this respect he is more successful in the very short and otherwise fairly unremarkable study entitled *The Worlds of Science and Religion*. In this book he takes the trouble to produce a reasoned answer to Freud. Admittedly it is not the only possible answer, but it is a particularly valid one in that it tackles Freud on his own ground and using his own terms of reference. His argument is so concise and incisive that it is worth quoting in full. Having briefly explained how Freud characterizes religion as infantile, primitive and immature, he continues:

To show the richness and ambiguity of religious metaphors, [such as that of the development of the child,] we can easily reply to Freud on his own terms, and argue that the trust we place in science and technology in modern culture is illusory, being nothing but a projection of infantile belief. Modern man's mental age is about seven; he wants his toy-cupboard full of marvellous gadgets, and believes he will be perfectly happy when his environment responds to his every whim. But modern man's gadgets, his greater knowledge, and his technical control over nature have done nothing whatever to alter or diminish the fundamental facts of life, namely, moral evil, suffering, solitude and death. It is time to outgrow utopian fantasies of omniscience and omnipotence, and recognize that we cannot attain final happiness until we come to terms with realities we cannot manipulate. If we read the life of Jesus, or of the Buddha, we may begin to grow up. Science is to religion as infancy to adulthood.[31]

Having thus turned the argument on its head, he comments finally:

Now, keeping strictly within the thought-world of psychoanalysis, this use of the metaphor of outgrowing childhood is surely just as plausible as Freud's, though it suggests a conclusion directly contrary to his.[32]

It is true that Cupitt is, in the interests of polemic, probably overstating his case here, and that there is a *measure* of projection in religion – at least in the specific content of its imagery, even if not in its doctrinal form – but the general outline of Cupitt's case is a telling one, and would find support even among the ranks of psychologists themselves.[33] There is little doubt that, for all its apparent reasonableness, Freud's critique of religion is only one way of interpreting the phenomenon of religion; and Freud himself would seem to have been so immersed in his own theory that he failed to see that it can equally well be used against him in the defence of religion!

From this very brief survey of Cupitt's roots in orthodoxy it is plain that in his earlier years he was attempting to achieve two closely related objectives. Primarily he was seeking to formulate an approach to Christianity which could survive in the modern world.

In order to do this, both the case for theism and specific areas of doctrine such as christology and ethics had to be addressed afresh. Cupitt's restatement of these things represents an essay in creative theology, taking the traditional elements of religion and reworking them in such a way that they take account of the parameters and concerns of modern thought. Alongside this, however, runs the necessity, in an increasingly hostile world, to carve out a space in which *any* religious apprehension of the world can find expression. Thus he is brought into direct conflict with certain trends and ideas such as humanism and projection theory, in the face of which it is necessary to construct a case for viewing life through a religious perspective at all.

In all of this, perhaps the first thing that strikes one about the early Cupitt is his passionate religious seriousness. There is a sense running throughout all of these early works that this *matters*, that there are real issues at stake, and that the success or failure of a religious outlook in general and Christianity in particular to maintain its credibility and intellectual respectability is an issue of the first magnitude, both for individuals and for society as a whole. Cupitt himself, although his views have changed so greatly, has never been dismissive of his earlier writings. He has never disowned them simply because he has moved on from the positions expressed in them. Thus in a 1985 introduction to *The Leap of Reason*, he said of the book, written nine years earlier:

> . . . when I wrote in *The Sea of Faith* about 'the artist-theologian', I meant that when a religious writer's standpoint changes, he need not and probably must not any longer think of himself as having advanced in a logical and progressive way from one 'position' to another. He has changed, and the change is important; but one should be wary of the assumption that it represents an improvement.
>
> All of which explains why, although my present standpoint is not quite that of this book, nor do I in any way disclaim it.[34]

And one suspects that a part of this refusal to disown even his earliest works stems from a recognition of the seriousness and integrity with which they were written. The views may have changed, but the manifest honesty and integrity of these books have stood the test of time, even in the occasionally self-deprecating mind of the author himself.

It is precisely the seriousness of these early works which renders it unjust and thoughtless to brand the later Cupitt as being purely destructive or simply unreligious. Certainly even in his earliest years as a theologian he was iconoclastic to a degree which many may have found disturbing, but even this iconoclasm was employed with the intention of restoring or maintaining what he perceived as the spiritual and intellectual integrity of the Christian faith. To a large extent his later work, although far more radical, has built on this foundation, and it will be seen that his objections to, and departure from orthodoxy arise not from any disrespect or wilful desire to shock or wound, but directly out of that same religious seriousness which informed his earlier thinking and writing. Just as the early Cupitt felt the need for a dramatic departure from the norms of received piety in *Jesus and the Gospel of God* if Jesus and his message were to speak once more in 'purely religious' terms, uncluttered by the debris of centuries, so too, even in his later books, Cupitt's primary concern has been with the integrity of religion. One may well feel bound to disagree with much of his later thinking, but one cannot but respect his reasons for it, and indeed feel some sympathy with many of the criticisms which he levels at conventional orthodox piety and theology. Underlying the extreme shift of position, there is a continuing concern with the quest for coherence in religion and with a sense of its importance, for better or for worse, in the shaping and guiding of people's lives. Thus in the seriousness with which the early Cupitt defends a more orthodox position are to be found the seeds of the passion with which the later Cupitt departs from it in the interests of his own personal religious integrity.

# 2

# Objections to Orthodoxy

## I

By now it should have become clear that Don Cupitt is not merely some kind of middle-aged *enfant terrible* within the church. His earlier writings, with their challenging restatements of orthodox thinking, show him to have understood the tradition in which he stands, and to have perceived the need – widely felt this century – to re-work this tradition in such a way that its truths are expressed in a form that is consonant with a contemporary world-view. Once perceived, this need becomes an imperative one as a result of Cupitt's own religious seriousness discussed at the end of the previous chapter. Cupitt is concerned with the continuing integrity of the Christian faith, and this integrity is imperilled if Christianity is allowed to cling to an outmoded and largely mediaeval understanding of itself.

Cupitt is thus impelled, by his own concern for the Christian faith and by his discernment of the gap between that faith and the twentieth century's understanding of itself and its environment, to attempt a contemporary restatement of what he perceives as the essentials of faith. The extent of his roots in orthodoxy bears witness to his respect for the best of traditional thinking, but inevitably the nature of his task led him – even in its earliest stages – to become dissatisfied with a number of aspects of the Christian tradition, and to question them with increasing force. It is these dissatisfactions and growing objections to orthodoxy which have in turn led Cupitt to formulate his more recent and more radical ways of thinking. One does not necessarily have to agree with Cupitt's own answers to his objections to orthodoxy in order to feel the force of some, if not all, of these objections. The objections themselves may well be cogent ones, even if Cupitt's ultimate response to them is not the only, or even the most satisfactory one. Certainly they are a major reason for Cupitt's movement, at first gradual and then increasingly dramatic, away from orthodox thinking, and as such deserve careful investigation if one is to understand how the later Cupitt has developed out of the earlier one.

Broadly speaking, his objections to orthodoxy fall into three categories, which largely, though not entirely, develop out of one another in a more or less logical progression. Admittedly there are traces of all of them visible at all the different stages in Cupitt's development, but in general terms they do represent an evolutionary series. These three categories are: firstly, specific objections to particular doctrines or areas of Christian thought or practice; secondly, a dissatisfaction with what he perceives as the repressiveness, backwardness and irrelevance of much of church life – a criticism of the institutional and dogmatic aspects of faith; and thirdly, a growing dissatisfaction with the traditional objective content of the Christian faith – a dissatisfaction with realism *per se*.

The first intimations of Cupitt's collision course with orthodoxy, then, concern his objections to a number of specific doctrines and areas of thought and practice. The most central of these is his growing dissatisfaction with the categories of traditional christology. Cupitt's attempts to reformulate the essence of the Christian understanding of Jesus have already been examined in some detail in Chapter 1, but alongside these attempts – which grow increasingly uneasy over the years – there runs a deeply felt uncertainty about the ultimate value of traditional christological methods and categories. There is a sense that a largely classical Greek metaphysic and a twentieth-century mind are mutually incompatible. Neither is Cupitt alone in this among modern theologians. Even so relatively conservative a figure as John Macquarrie is not immune to a degree of uncertainty over how far the gap between the first and twentieth centuries can be adequately bridged:

One would say, however, that these principles [of historical criticism] are nowadays very widely accepted among secular historians, and if they are taken into christology and history is allowed to have the dominant role in christology, then very severe restrictions are laid on what may be claimed for Jesus Christ, and the task of constructing a christology which will both remain loyal to the traditional faith in Christ and will be respectful towards the canons of modern thought becomes very questionable.[1]

It is principally in a number of early essays that Cupitt's initial questionings as to the adequacy of traditional christology arise. In an essay entitled 'The Last Man', which is itself the text of a 1975 radio broadcast, he isolates three issues which have coloured – less than helpfully, he feels – our understanding of the person of Christ. Thus:

> ... Western accounts of Christ have been strongly tied to a particular historical tradition, to a particular model of man, and to a particular kind of dogmatic symbolism. And all three must be set aside.[2]

Briefly, the historical tradition is represented by the view that Christ stands at the centre of all history, both cosmic and universal. These are co-extensive, and therefore Christ 'encompassed and determined the meaning of the whole cosmic process'.[3] This model, says Cupitt, 'has been broken apart by a huge enlargement of our perceptions in many directions'.[4] The doctrine of man is encapsulated in the phrase, 'In Adam all die', and states that it is Christ alone who can redeem man from this bondage to sin and death. This is both too anthropocentric, and too peculiar to only one cultural tradition to be of universal application. The dogmatic symbolism is that which has portrayed Jesus as Son of God, Lord, and a 'uniquely adequate icon or visible embodiment of God in history',[5] and it has led to the over-exaltation and authoritarianism of the church on the grounds that just as Jesus represents God, so the church represents Jesus and shares in his power. This, Cupitt argues, is untrue to the real nature of Jesus and results in a frequent abuse of spiritual authority such as that instituted by Constantine and his successors in order to reinforce their own authority as emperors.

Of the three issues, it is this last one which Cupitt sees as being the most serious. And he argues for its inaccuracy in portraying Jesus on the firmest grounds possible, namely, the witness of the New Testament:

In the earliest gospels Jesus is portrayed as one who prays to God rather than is God, and whose relation to God is one of faith rather than identity. He suffers, he is tempted, he experiences storms of indignation, exultant triumph, joy and despair. He is not at all a stately icon of God. There is nothing impassive about him. He is not so much one who embodies God, as one who with the whole of his passionate nature witnesses to God.

So I would wish to set aside later interpretations of Jesus, and words like 'Son' and 'Image', and start again with the Jesus of history, an eschatological prophet, whose finality lies not so much in what he is as in what he bears witness to, and the way he bears witness to it.[6]

In Cupitt's view it is the church, and not God, which has accorded Jesus a divine status. Such a status is incompatible with the Jesus of history, and faced with the choice between the divine Son of God and a radical eschatological prophet, Cupitt has no hesitation in preferring the latter on the grounds of its faithfulness to scripture. In this there is certainly a break with orthodoxy, yet it must be allowed that Cupitt's primary reason for it is precisely in order to allow the all-important message of Jesus, the prophet and man of God, to speak with the same freshness today as it did nearly 2,000 years ago.

This theme of the church's exaltation of Jesus to foster its own ends is one which Cupitt touches upon frequently in his essays. Indeed, the next essay in the same book returns to this same picture of Christ as cosmic ruler bestowing his authority upon his earthly vicars – the same church and emperors which exalted him thus. Again Cupitt finds this conception of Jesus to be fundamentally at odds with the biblical picture of Jesus:

Think back to the gospels of Matthew, Mark and Luke. Here, under a varnish of later ideas and editing, we find a clear and convincing picture of a wandering Jewish teacher. Isn't it odd that the prophet Jesus of Nazareth should end up crowning emperors? He did many surprising things, but surely the very *last* thing we would expect (from the gospels) to find him doing is blessing the rulers of this world – people with whom he had absolutely nothing in common.[7]

Throughout the essay Cupitt develops his analysis of the change wrought upon the person of Jesus by the early church, and his increasing identification with the church's own authority. During the course of the centuries, Christian doctrine about Jesus has 'travelled a long way from Jesus himself'.[8] Cupitt identifies two areas in which the disparity is particularly great. He notes that the famous Christian definitions of faith contain no reference to Jesus' teaching, and he cites a dichotomy between Jesus' use of language about God and the church's use of language about Jesus:

> Jesus evoked the sense of God in a subtle, oblique way by his use of language, whereas in a good deal of Christian teaching he has become an absolute manifestation of God in this world.[9]

In response to this, Cupitt argues for a return to the Jesus of history, not in the service of any kind of reductionism – though his arguments are clearly prone to such criticism – but rather in order to recover something vital and dynamic in the person and preaching of the original Jesus which he feels has been lost in the transformation of this Jesus into the Christ of faith with its complex mythology of a Greek-style Saviour-God. It is Cupitt's contention that this is at once true to scripture and true to Jesus' own way of teaching and preaching about God, and therefore to his own self-understanding in relation to God.

Nearly two years later Cupitt made a third excursion into this same field in his essay *Myth Understood*. This represents a broadening of his attack upon the traditional dogmatic statements of belief about Jesus. Such statements are not susceptible of proof, so it is hard to say with confidence that they are true; they are untrue to Jesus' own understanding of his own person and work; they are untrue to the New Testament witness to Jesus; and they are central not to a 'purely religious' Christianity, but only to a developed church which has become burdened with the need to perpetuate itself as an authoritarian institution and with the need to lend support to the maintenance of a particular political and social status quo.

As in the earlier essays, Cupitt is here concerned to recover the religious essence of Christianity and disentangle it from the accretions of time and society and politics. The danger with any long-standing religion as it gains such accretions is that:

> People come to suppose that the essence of religion is doctrine and to think that its chief task is to underpin cultural values, even where the faith was originally quite unconcerned with any such thing. So the time comes when the purely religious as a category is no longer understood, and it is necessary to go back to the roots to rediscover it.[10]

A Christianity like this is diametrically opposed to what Cupitt believes is the core of Jesus' original message about God:

> Christendom made Christianity the most highly ideological of all religions, and inculcated dogmatic habits of thinking which still block the revival of the primitive faith. Dogma sets God behind a screen, declares the screen sacrosanct, and fiercely protects it. But Jesus' message is precisely a call to live without that screen.[11]

Thus in the service of faithfulness to Jesus' own teaching, it is, ironically, the church's teaching about Jesus which most needs revision. If Jesus is to be allowed to speak of God effectively, then the church's doctrine of Jesus' own co-equal divinity must be discarded to make way for Jesus the eschatological prophet of God. The Jesus of history and the Christ of faith are mutually incompatible, and one or other of them must go. Faithfulness to Jesus himself and to his original message demands that it be the latter.

So in these three essays, written in fairly rapid succession, we see Cupitt confronting one of the major doctrinal strongholds of Christianity. More sustained attention – although along much the same lines – is given to this issue in *Jesus and the Gospel of God*, published in 1979. Here the New Testament evidence for the divinity of Jesus is examined rather more closely, and the conclusion drawn that while the New Testament writers accord Jesus an exalted place as Lord, Christ and Son of God, yet none of them teaches the 'later standard doctrine that Jesus is a distinct divine person co-equal, co-essential and co-eternal with the Father. It exalts Jesus as high as is possible without compromising monotheism.'[12] Once again, Cupitt's purpose in asserting this is not destructive but constructive. Certainly he has been led to challenge one of the central tenets of orthodox Christianity, but he has done so in the service of fidelity to Jesus' own message. It is his concern for the validity and contemporary relevance of this message which has drawn him into conflict with the dogmatically defined Christ of faith. Indeed, as he remarks at the end of this section of the book:

> . . . the more seriously we take his message the more impatient we shall become with many of the classical doctrines about him.[13]

Cupitt's 'impatience' with the 'classical doctrines' of christology has grown rather than diminished with the years, and having led him to a 'historical realist view of Jesus',[14] led him later to abandon it, albeit 'very reluctantly' as his dissatisfactions with other aspects of Christianity forced him to leave behind any kind of realist interpretation of faith. A wide variety of conflicts with traditional Christianity produced his later radicalism, but his christological dissatisfactions provide an early example of the nature of his objections to orthodoxy which first impelled him away from it.

Christology is by no means the only area in which Cupitt – even in his earlier years – has challenged the theological status quo. Ethics and morality have been a major object of Cupitt's criticism for many years now, both with regard to the Christian approach to ethics and the 'moral law' in general, and also with regard to the internal ethics of the Christian faith and story itself.

In an early essay entitled *The Ethics of this World and the Ethics of the World to Come*, Cupitt highlights what he considers to be the major problem with almost all considerations of Christian ethics to date. The problem hinges on the fact that Christianity has always tried to uphold at one and the same time the presence in the world of a natural moral law such as St Paul posits in Romans 1, and also the supernatural validation and reinforcement of this law by the supremely good and just will of God. As Cupitt points out, if this is the case, and there is indeed a natural moral law, then it is difficult to see any special relevance which the deity could possibly have in morality. If the natural moral law is in principle autonomous and discoverable by the human race, and if this moral law is simply reinforced by divine command, then one is hard put to it to avoid the kind of position which Cupitt characterizes as 'moral deism'.

To this dilemma Cupitt responds by suggesting a shift of perspective. The shortcoming of invoking God to validate natural moral law – apart from a slide into moral deism – is that it freezes morality: there is no possibility of moral progress. This, Cupitt rightly suggests, is absurd. Any religion, if it is to be worthy of the name, and worthy of people's allegiance to it, must challenge and call forward to a new and better way of living. Thus:

> ... the only morally acceptable way of connecting religion with morality is to regard God not as validating and fixing our present moral ideals and standards, but as inspiring continual dissatisfaction with them and criticism of them.[15]

Such a shift of perspective Cupitt characterizes as being a shift from an ethics of creation to an ethics of redemption in which we are challenged by the presence of an absolute ideal, an ideal which confronts us through an 'eschatological demand' for purity.

For Christianity, this eschatological demand is best represented in the preaching of Jesus, and in his portrayal of this preaching Cupitt is consistent in his understanding (referred to above) of Jesus as the eschatological prophet of God. One of the features of the presentation of the eschatological demand is that it does not – precisely because it cannot in this world – specify exactly what the new world and its values are. Instead, what Jesus does is to:

> ... take the traditional Jewish moral and religious values – values such as justice, mercy, covenant-brotherhood, forgiveness, piety, prudence, compassion for the unfortunate and the outcast and so on – and tell stories about them. In the stories these traditional virtues and values are forced to such superhuman heights as to produce a disclosure of the divine perfection. The absolute moral

ideal, of a human social order which perfectly embodies the divine perfection, is thus shown as infinitely surpassing merely human standards of forgiveness, justice and the like.[16]

In suggesting this movement away from divine validation of an autonomous moral law to a divine criticism of *all* human moral activity, Cupitt is, at this stage in his career, still remaining within the framework of orthodoxy. He is still content to invoke the transcendent – indeed even the divine – but within this framework he is creatively reworking the tradition in a way which gives evidence of his willingness to go beyond the received norms at such points as it may seem necessary so to do.

More far-reaching in its ultimate ramifications, is Cupitt's dissatisfaction not with the Christian approach to ethics, but with the ethics of Christianity itself. At the heart of Christianity is a story, the story of God's dealings with the world, and of man's creation, fall and redemption. And the events and actions of this story have a moral significance and import which is often repugnant. Cupitt quotes Coleridge's apprehension of this major flaw in the Christian story as he singles out those doctrines which alienate us by their moral distastefulness:

Such are the Doctrines of Arbitrary Election and Reprobation; the Sentence to everlasting Torment by an eternal and necessitating degree; vicarious Atonement, and the necessity of the Abasement, Agony and ignominious Death of a most holy and meritorious Person, to appease the wrath of God.[17]

Of these various elements in the story, Cupitt singles out two for particular attention: the doctrines of original sin and of the atonement. Each of these doctrines has an inbuilt tendency to present God in a morally dubious light. The character of God is in constant danger of appearing to be not only imperfect, but also rather less perfect than that of his own creatures whose own moral sensibilities revolt against his apparently harsh and unjust ordering of his creation. Before we have sinned ourselves we are guilty through the sin of another, and an innocent victim must be punished in order to alter this state of affairs through some kind of divine self-appeasement of wrath.

Cupitt sees the problem as being inherent in the insistence of Christianity on an objective story whose events are held to have metaphysical effects. Any such story, he claims, is likely to be open to severe moral criticism. And the problem increases the more the story is developed and dogmatized – in other words the more the events of the story are explained in terms of their metaphysical effects. Indeed:

> . . . it is the most highly developed dogmatic theologies which represent God in the most repellent light. And it will not do to say, 'It's only symbolism', if the symbolism is in fact morally repellent. It is all very well to say that we can now only *think* God through imperfect symbols: but how can it be our duty to be *guided in the moral life* by morally-repellent symbols.[18]

The moral problems are the 'inevitable result of trying to tell an anthropomorphic story'.[19] As soon as God is pictured as being in any way analogous to a human person, and as soon as the story is made an objective one, then immediately God becomes embroiled in a series of morally underhand dealings with mankind which destroy the very story of redemption by a wise and loving creator which that story sets out to tell.

The only way which Cupitt can find to respond to this problem is to question the presence in Christianity of such a story at all:

> So I conclude that the traditional expression of Christianity in the form of a drama or cosmic redemption myth was probably a mistake. For it seems that no such story can be satisfactorily told.[20]

It is not the purpose of this part of the discussion to examine in any detail the soundness of Cupitt's objections to orthodoxy, but merely to outline them coherently. However, it may, in passing, be questioned whether Cupitt's depiction of the Christian story is the only, or indeed the correct one. A cogent case might be made, for example, to the effect that what the story does is not to *alter* any metaphysical state of affairs, such as the relationship between man and God, by any kind of bargaining or appeasement, but simply to show forth the inherently sinful disposition of every human being, and to give vivid expression to the depth of love which God has *always* had for that frail humanity. Perhaps if anything is changed by the story it is not God, or our relationship with God, but simply, having been shown that love, our ability to respond to it and to its author.

Leaving aside the question of the strengths and weaknesses of Cupitt's approach though, the particularly interesting feature of this criticism of orthodoxy on moral grounds is the way in which it has brought Cupitt – perhaps for the first time – to question the validity of a thoroughly 'realist' and 'objective' understanding of faith. In this it is a fascinating precursor of his later views, although at this stage he is content with a question mark against objectivity and does not fully develop the implications of his new position.

Cupitt's final criticism of orthodoxy on moral grounds is also one which contributes to his later thinking, and which lends weight to his objections to what he perceives as the repressiveness in much of traditional Christianity. We have noted already his insistence that any religious understanding of ethics must be one which stimulates, challenges and promotes moral growth. It is precisely at this point, he says, that Christian ethics fails most dismally. Its failure is that of being largely negative in tone, consisting more of 'don'ts' than of 'do's'. Traditional Christian morality is – or was:

> . . . a matter of doing your best to avoid attracting God's displeasure, by reducing your sins to a minimum. It was a matter of working to rule, and keeping your head down and your nose clean.[21]

It is in his later works that Cupitt voices this criticism most fully, but it is clearly another shoot on the same stem as his previous criticisms of Christianity on moral grounds. Again it may be asked whether his portrayal of the Christian tradition is a fair one, or whether he is actually constructing a theological Aunt Sally from selected pieces of that tradition simply in order to be able to knock it down again, but his increasing concern with the supposed moral shortcomings of Christianity is indicative of his dissatisfaction with the religious and moral traditions which he has inherited. The moral negativity of Christianity in particular is closely bound up with its perceived dogmatism and authoritarianism to which Cupitt also objects in the strongest terms, and his analysis of this and response to it will be examined later on. For the present it is sufficient to note that Cupitt has, over the years, formulated a coherent body of inter-related objections to the received understanding and interpretation of faith.

The third specific aspect of Christian doctrine and practice to which Cupitt takes exception from a fairly early stage is that of the ascetic and mystical approach to spirituality. This is another area in which his antipathy to the tradition has increased with the years, though his resistance to it stems from a relatively early date in his career. Ladder mysticism and St Augustine's *ordo amoris* were early victims of this dislike:

> To the scale of being there corresponds a scale of loving, Augustine's *ordo amoris*. On the lower rungs the soul loves God through creatures, but on the highest rungs the soul loves God for himself alone. The intensity with which a thing should be loved must correspond with its dignity in the scale of being. This detestable doctrine, with which Christian mysticism has almost always been entangled, projects upon the universe the same spirit as that which leads snobs to esteem dukes higher than dustmen.[22]

This and other aspects of Christian asceticism, such as the self-imposition of suffering to subdue the flesh, are seen as being morally disgusting and therefore as casting doubt upon the moral integrity of the whole of Christianity. As such they should be excised from Christian practice, and Christianity would be the purer and the better without them. In such a biased and prejudging fashion does Cupitt dispose of the vast numbers of mystics and ascetics who have graced the church since its earliest days! Of latter years his attitude has become even more extreme, seeing the life of the ascetic as being immoral, and seeing the monastic ideal itself as being 'a hospice for those who were terminally sick of life, and a standing denial of the Christian Gospel'.[23]

Although they are all present in his work from an early stage, these three objections to specific facets of Christian doctrine and practice – christology, morality and asceticism – are, in their relationship with one another, a clear indication of the depth of Cupitt's opposition to much of received Christianity which is subjected to a more varied and widespread criticism in his later works. Already by the early to mid-1970s he had expressed significant reservations with regard to the central figure of Christianity – Jesus – and to the two poles of Christian response to Jesus – life and worship, morality and spirituality. From this starting point it is a relatively short step to the development of a sustained criticism of the framework of Christianity; initially its doctrinal and institutional structures, and later on its very essence and claims in terms of objectivity and truth.

## II

The second stage in Cupitt's critical odyssey is his critique of the doctrinal and institutional structures of the church, a critique which is centred on the backwardness and repressiveness of much of this facet of Christianity. As stated earlier, both this and the third stage to some degree overlap with the first, and the three stages do not therefore form an exact linear development through time. They do succeed one another in emphasis, however, even if not necessarily in genesis, and one can thus reasonably speak of a progression from one stage to another. This second major group of objections to orthodoxy has its roots principally in the work of the late 1970s, and finds its fullest and most powerful expression from the publication of *Taking Leave of God* (in 1980) onwards.

One of the principal strands in this development is Cupitt's acute mistrust of the fixity of dogma. Just as with his doubts as to the possibility of constructing a coherent christology along traditional lines, Cupitt is by no means alone in this. Theologians have long been aware of the dangers of dogma because of its proneness to abuse:

Dogma and theology exist for the sake of the Christian message and not vice versa. When this relationship has been reversed and dogma is confused with the actual message, the danger which threatened the Faith has turned into the devastating evil of intellectualism. Here the wall of defence has killed the life which it was there to protect, or at least has almost stifled it; here the wood which was intended to support the tree has used up all the vital sap . . . This disaster is not due to dogma, the formulated Creed of the Christian Church; for without dogma the world invades the Church or lays it waste. The disaster is due to the fact that dogma . . . has itself been deified. When dogma has ceased to be a witness pointing to something behind and above itself, then it is fossilized into a concrete 'word' or fetish.[24]

Cupitt's mistrust goes further than this though. Whereas Brunner feels dogma to be right in itself and only dangerous in so far as it may be abused, Cupitt maintains that there is an inherent and mortally damaging weakness in dogma itself. For Cupitt, it can, does, and indeed must 'fossilize' – to use Brunner's word – of its own accord, and therefore leads to an anti-intellectual, uncritical and ultimately idolatrous world of faith.

As in so many other areas, Cupitt is careful to base his arguments upon an appeal to scripture – or more correctly upon our understanding of scripture. This understanding has changed over the centuries, and now that we 'understand biblical criticism and the human, historically conditioned character of religious ideas, our viewpoint must change'.[25] The traditional fixed doctrines of the church, even its most central ones such as the incarnation or the Holy Trinity, are not susceptible of proof from scripture as we now understand it, and they must therefore be discarded in favour of what Cupitt calls a new kind of 'critical faith'. Once again it is important to point out, in defence of Cupitt against his critics, that even in advocating a change of outlook as radical as this, he is not being wilfully reductionist or destructive. His purpose is not to destroy anything, but rather to 'rediscover' and 're-affirm' what he sees as 'three ancient and vital themes' which have been lost or obscured through centuries of developed dogma: 'the pure prophetic faith that God is one and God is Spirit, the message of Jesus, and the eschatological faith of the first Christians'.[26]

He is willing to acknowledge that his critical faith is a harder and a harsher one than a more traditional dogmatic faith, but it is truer to the reality which it claims to worship. Indeed it is its falseness to God which Cupitt stigmatizes as being one of the chief shortcomings of a faith which depends upon the strict maintenance of fixed dogmatic formulations. In doing this Christianity attempts to define and give bounds and form to the concept of God, and is therefore untrue to the nature of God himself. Dogma, Cupitt argues, is a means of giving a shape to God and protecting us from him by confining him within the bounds of a definition: 'It is like the bandages and clothes wrapped around the Invisible Man in order to make him visible and so less threatening.'[27] Thus it may be alarming to destroy this dogmatic screen between us and God – we lose the protection provided by known definitions and boundaries – but only so will we open ourselves to the awesome and mysterious reality of God who has, as Cupitt rightly comments, 'no shape'.

Ultimately, however, the shortcomings of a dogmatic faith are even more serious than this, and lead finally and inexorably to idolatry. This is simply because as soon as one defines God the possibility arises that a being might be defined who surpasses this first 'God' and would therefore himself be the true God, leaving the 'God' who has previously been defined trailing in his wake as a mere idol. To be true to God, faith in him must be always provisional and changing rather than fixed; always open to a new understanding of the transcendent rather than attempting to confine it within known channels and forms:

> The God of dogmatic and metaphysical belief is an idol people cling to: the true God is always ahead and is apprehended practically and ascetically by a continuing act of renunciation by which one moves forward.[28]

His position is interestingly akin to that of a philosopher with whom he has much in common, and who indeed frequently cites him in her work – Iris Murdoch. In her latest philosophical work, *Metaphysics as a Guide to Morals*, she takes his argument a stage further and writes of the dilemma facing the theist:

> We yearn for the transcendent, for God, for something divine and good and pure, but in picturing the transcendent we transform it

into idols which we then realize to be contingent particulars, just things among others here below. If we destroy these idols in order to reach something untainted and pure, what we really need, the thing itself, we render the Divine ineffable, and as such in peril of being judged non-existent. Then the sense of the Divine vanishes in the attempt to preserve it.[29]

Cupitt's case – echoed by Murdoch – is, as ever, a compelling one, and one can readily appreciate his mistrust of dogma when one considers the history of the church, in which abuse of dogma seems so often to have been the rule rather than the exception. Yet one may well ask whether Cupitt's argument is *necessarily* correct. He has pinpointed one of the sad facts about how dogma has frequently been used in practice, but one can question whether it must always be like this. Is Cupitt's position a logical and theological necessity or simply a response to the goads of the regrettable, but not inevitable, doctrinal failings of the church? In passing, two alternatives may be suggested: firstly that doctrine and dogma do not, when used correctly, attempt to restrict or confine God as Cupitt suggests. Analogy, for example, may be an imperfect theological method, but qualities predicated of God by analogy are not, and never have been, intended to be understood as being identical with, or even particularly close approximations to, those same qualities when predicated of a human being. The relationship is that of a model to the reality which it represents. Models, such as scientific ones, are never intended to be an exact representation, but merely an aid to understanding better the reality behind them. So too with our 'definitions' of God. They are not exact representations, but merely a tool for grasping at least something of the mystery which lies behind them. The second alternative, as we shall argue in Part 2 of this study, is simply that there is, as Janet Martin Soskice has suggested, a distinction to be drawn between 'referring' to God and 'defining' him.[30] Cupitt assumes that whenever we refer to God we also define him, but a cogent case may be argued that even in dogma this is not necessarily so. Whatever the force of these alternatives may be, Cupitt's own insistence on the undesirability of fixity in dogma and his dislike of its repressiveness bear oblique witness to his growing interest in the *via negativa*, a development which has a significant place in his thinking and to which we will return at a later stage.

Cupitt's mistrust of the fixity of dogma surfaced increasingly during the early 1980s, but with the publication of *Only Human* in 1985 it underwent a further change as he challenged not merely the shortcomings of its inflexibility, but its actual status as a theological concept. His criticism draws on the distinction between the supposed truth of dogmas and their status as 'rules'. Initially they are promulgated as 'truths', but if their truth is challenged then they are defended merely as 'rules'.[31] If and when this happens, Cupitt argues, the life has gone out of them. They have been effectively eviscerated, and all that is left is an empty and lifeless husk which not only is not worth defending, but must be abandoned in the interests of that same 'truth' which the dogma was originally designed to serve. Clinging to outmoded dogma has about it an 'all or nothing mentality; it suggests that unless you accept scriptures, creeds and the rest dogmatically, you must reject them altogether'.[32] And this, Cupitt says, is 'absurd'. His criticism is not unjust. All too often Christians back thesmelves, almost wilfully, into a dogmatic corner, and failing to fight their way out by argument, can only belabour their opponents with the dogma itself without reference to its truth or lack of it. Cupitt's response to the problem is not itself invulnerable to criticism, as suggested above, but his diagnosis of a doctrinal malaise in the church is uncomfortably accurate.

His objections to dogma have a particular significance in Cupitt's development. It is no accident that having found their first sustained expression in *Jesus and the Gospel of God* in 1979, Cupitt's next book should have been *Taking Leave of God* in 1980. The connection with the *via negativa* has already been mentioned, and it is clearly only a small step from applying this to the doctrines and definitions of Christianity in the manner outlined above, to applying it to the reality of God himself. From an insistence that, strictly speaking, nothing can be said or predicated of God, it is only going one step further to suggest that there is nothing or nobody there of which (or whom) anything could be said. Thus there is a logical, if not actually a *necessary* development in Cupitt's thought from his doctrinal criticisms of Christianity to his later objections to realism *per se*.

This growing dissatisfaction with the doctrinal foundations of

Christianity is symptomatic of a much wider suspicion of what Cupitt perceives as the restrictiveness of orthodoxy generally. The two major counts on which Cupitt bases his criticism have long and honourable pedigrees behind them. Several nineteenth and early twentieth-century thinkers had voiced them at least in part before him, and Cupitt readily admits their influence (particularly that of Feuerbach and Nietzsche) on his own development. The two counts on which religion is restrictive and repressive are first, that it holds the human race in a situation of slavery by imposing upon it a degraded view of itself which is contrasted with the divine perfection; and secondly that it is locked within itself and unable to escape – or to allow others to escape – the confines of its own pre-conceived vision of the world. Early in *The Essence of Christianity*, Feuerbach voices the first of these criticisms: 'To enrich God, man must become poor; that God may be all, man must be nothing,'[33] and once this mind-set is inculcated, man's fate is sealed. He is locked into this relationship and this vision of the world which is reinforced at all points and given a divine seal of approval. Thus the second criticism becomes justified:

> Faith makes man partial and narrow; it deprives him of the freedom and ability to estimate duly what is different from himself. Faith is imprisoned within itself.[34]

These criticisms are echoed by Cupitt, as are Nietzsche's criticisms of Christianity's 'slave morality',[35] but he adds a new dimension to them by speaking – as his predecessors did not – from within the fold of the church. Furthermore, he develops Feuerbach's criticisms by extending them to the repressive and power-oriented structure not merely of the faith, but of the church as well.

Once again, the roots of Cupitt's critical position extend a long way back into his early career. Initially he gave vent to a fairly gentle dissatisfaction with the imagery of 'domination and submission' in *Crisis of Moral Authority*. He echoes Feuerbach's and Nietzsche's criticism that to exalt the divine is to debase the human:

> In essence, the more seriously the imagery of lordship and servanthood be taken the more it diminishes the believer's moral stature. If the believer, in his enthusiasm, declares that of himself

he is depraved, that he cannot tell right from wrong, that he can do no good thing, that God must enlighten his conscience, fortify his will, direct his path, inspire and assist all his acts – then such language, the more literally it be taken, the more it offends against our post-Kantian sense of ourselves as responsible moral agents.[36]

Writing from a later standpoint he commented that one of the aims of the book was to suggest a means by which a 'genuinely liberal theology' might 'be able to renounce physical and, still more important, psychological terrorism'.[37] In this aim he was justifiably reacting to the worst excesses of Christian history and ecclesiastical repression. The grievance is a genuine one – although it will later be argued that Cupitt's case is somewhat one-sided – and its expression gathers force and frequency in the years from *Taking Leave of God* onwards.

The theme of the restrictiveness and repressiveness of orthodoxy is so woven into the texture of Cupitt's work from *Taking Leave of God* onwards, that there is no merit in undertaking an exhaustive analysis of its many forms and expressions. More significant is the fact that, as with so many of his criticisms of orthodoxy, it undergoes a development during the course of time. This development makes Cupitt's attacks at once harsher, and also directed increasingly towards what he perceives as the necessary – and debased – heart of organized institutional and doctrinal religion.

The development begins in *Taking Leave of God*. In this work he builds on his earlier rather scattered expressions of unease with Christianity's weapon of 'psychological terrorism', and on his varied criticisms of specific doctrinal positions of the kind discussed above. Such doctrinal positions are defended precisely by means of that psychological terrorism, with the result that Christianity comes to be both authoritarian and anti-intellectual. The hierarchy of the church guards the 'deposit of faith' and pronounces it unchangeable. By this means, '. . . all speculative and revisionist religious thought are satisfactorily precluded'.[38] The consequence of this is that:

The only theology there can be is that psittacine recitation of the deposit of faith which in the church press is described approvingly as 'clear teaching'. Any actual thought is heresy.[39]

Whether this is an entirely fair assessement of the situation, especially within Cupitt's own ecclesiastical family of Anglicanism, is open to question, but it does provide a logical foundation for the next step in his argument. This is the assertion that religion does not merely *happen* to repress people, but is what it is *precisely* for that purpose. He portrays a caricature – but a sadly recognizable one – of the conservative view of religion as, 'a dyke against sin, a bridle to restrain human perversity', and adds that it 'cannot be faulted for the severity of its pessimism'.[40] Religion is there to control a debased and depraved human nature, and it is employed to control it not only spiritually and personally, but socially as well. Religion becomes a tool of social control and thereby reinforces its own heteronomy. The overbearing objectivity of religion establishes the control, and once established, the control is self-perpetuating by the simple expedient of proclaiming as a religious truth, which must be accepted, the objectivity upon which it itself feeds and grows. Cupitt's presentation of these ideas is succinct and hard-hitting:

> Objectification is politics, for we project the divine outwards precisely in order to make religion an efficient control system. Divinity can then only be approached through the proper channels, and by the time it gets down to the man in the pew society ensures that it is very highly diluted.[41]

The result is exactly what was intended: that we settle 'for what objectified religion offers – resignation, tranquillity and acceptance of one's allowed place in the scheme of things'.[42]

Such is the effect of religion upon those who are on the inside of the system. The corollary of this, however, is that in order to remain secure in its own existence such a system needs to define an 'outside'. In order to be sure who is 'in', you must first be sure who is 'out'. A heteronomous objectified religion of the kind Cupitt has delineated, and castigated in *Taking Leave of God*, has lost the immediacy of salvation, and therefore needs 'the reflexive conviction of my own righteousness that I can derive from casting out heretics, apostates, infidels and every other sort of sinner'.[43] In a character-istically elegant phrase Cupitt comments: 'Philadelphia comes to be built on a solid foundation of xenophobia.'[44] The internal repressiveness of Christianity has been successfully imposed upon the outside world also.

By the time that he wrote *The Long-Legged Fly* in 1987, Cupitt had become clearer about the effects of this repression, internal and external, not merely on individuals but on the nature of Christianity itself. He had long seen Jesus as a radical and indeed revolutionary figure, as was evident in the discussion of his christology, and he draws the conclusion that Christianity has effectively suppressed Jesus and the radical demands of the message which he preached. He finds a model for this in the 'iconography of late Christendom' in which:

> ... the Crucified rests against the knees of the Father. His human body is unexpectedly small, and is almost nailed to the Father in submission, for above all it had been the Father's job to keep order. He saw to it that the work of Christ and the Spirit was confined to the approved channels, kept religion firmly caged up within orthodoxy, and above all impressed upon us a deep conviction of our own impotence, ignorance and worthlessness.[45]

Humanity is kept in its place, both spiritually and socially, by a church which has a vested interest in maintaining the status quo, and the radical and revolutionary heart of Jesus' message is excised by the very church which bears his name and claims his authority.

The final stage in this aspect of Cupitt's critique of traditional Christianity is his suggestion that power-seeking and repression are so much a part of the essence of organized Christianity that the only way to exorcise the one is to dismantle the other, or as he expresses it:

> The fact is that if modern humanitarian Christianity is ever to become established and to assert itself consistently then it must sooner or later purge itself of cosmic feudalism.[46]

Thus he is led, as the practical outworking of his ongoing critique, to expound his vision of a much more loosely structured and un-doctrinal church, a church which is 'structurally democratic, credally minimalist and consistently libertarian'.[47] Only a church such as this will be free from the restrictiveness, exclusiveness and power-seeking of traditional organized Christianity, and only so will it be true to the nature of its radical, humble and anti-authoritarian founder. Cupitt is governed, both in his critique and his conclusions, by his conviction that Christianity must re-emerge from Christendom and become what it might have been, but never actually was. True Christianity is only now becoming a possibility.

All these frustrating failings of traditional Christianity – the fixity of dogma, the repressiveness of institutional Christianity – find expression in Cupitt's denunciation of the 'backwardness' of the church and of its formulations of faith. In its present form and way of thinking both faith and church are, in T. S. Eliot's words, 'Wrapt in the old miasmal mist',[48] and are more-or-less totally unconnected with the mainstream of modern life. This perception is reflected even in such documents as the usually conservative Doctrine Commission's *We Believe in God*,[49] and the otherwise rather pedestrian *Children in the Way* report.[50] For Cupitt it is out of touch not simply because it is out of date, but because as a result of this religion no longer 'works'. In a society which puts a premium on autonomy and self-determination:

> . . . conservative religion of the sort that sets God authoritatively over the believer nowadays sounds as if it is spiritually backward and not fully conscious of itself. It has become an anachronism; it is spiritually behind the times. Objectifying religion is now false religion, for it no longer saves'.[51]

From a different angle, but with a similarly damning conclusion, he also argues that in a largely anthropocentric world which has yet managed to marginalize man in cosmic terms, a metaphysical and eudaemonistic religion is apt to seem little but 'illusion and a flight from reality'.[52]

### III

Such, increasingly, has been Cupitt's vision of Christianity and of the church, and having proceeded from particular doctrinal issues to a full-scale critique of the shortcomings of doctrinal religion with all of its perceived rigidity and backwardness, it is in keeping with his quest that he should have been drawn into questioning and then rejecting the supposed objectivity of Christianity. In terms of time, this grew up alongside rather than necessarily later than his criticisms of the doctrine and institutions of Christianity, but it is nevertheless reasonable still to speak of a progression from one to the other, since there is a logical, if not a strictly temporal sequence involved.

At a very early stage in his career we can see Cupitt beginning to feel distinctly unconvinced by any too literal understanding of the supposed events of the Christian story, such as miracles, and in particular the resurrection; and his unease with any kind of 'cosmic redemption myth' has already been alluded to.

At this point in time he would not have wished to deny the 'truth' of the resurrection belief that, 'Jesus of Nazareth is risen from the dead and lives as Christ and Lord of the human race';[53] indeed he carefully eschews discussion of its truth or lack of it. All he is concerned to establish is the nature of the grounds for this belief. Were the first disciples brought to this belief by objective facts such as an empty tomb and Jesus talking and eating among them again, or were there other factors at work which might militate against such a straightforwardly 'realist' approach to the resurrection? In pursuance of his argument Cupitt identifies three classes of theories of the resurrection: event theories of the kind alluded to above; theological theories which relate the resurrection to the disciples' sudden grasp of who Jesus was and through this knowledge led them to the belief that he *must* be risen; and what he calls 'psi-theories' which fall into the class of para-normal visions of a para-normal object of much the same kind as out-of-the-body experiences and the seeing of ghosts and UFOs. Of these, the 'psi-theories' are readily dismissed as being, 'in the end hopelessly incoherent'.[54] The 'event theories' are harder to dismiss, but Cupitt clearly feels dissatisfied with the uneasy balance between this world and another world which such a theory demands. Any event theory is asking too much of itself:

It is supposed to be describable in this-wordly terms so that ordinary canons of historical evidence can be applied to it and its occurrence can be rendered historically probable: and it is also supposed to verify Christological beliefs. It is supposed to be both open to ordinary sense-perception and to be an eschatological vision.[55]

The problem with this is that the resurrection then invokes a circular argument in its defence:

> ... the hypothesis of a resurrection-world has been made up in the hope of making the Resurrection-Event intelligible, and the Event thus made intelligible is supposed to return the compliment and verify the hypothesis.[56]

And this, to Cupitt's rigorous though sometimes one-sided way of thinking, will not do. By contrast, the third kind of theory – a theological theory – is more tenable. This begins from the assumption that 'Christological statements are framed by applying theological notions to matters of historical fact.'[57] Thus the various beliefs about Jesus as Messiah, Lord and Son of God and so on would have interacted with the known events of his life and preaching to produce the expectation that he would – indeed must – rise from death. For Christ to be *perceived* as risen, there must first be good theological grounds for believing him to be risen. Thus:

> So far from the Easter Event creating the Easter faith as is commonly said, it was rather the Easter faith which made the Easter Event possible.[58]

In all of this Cupitt remains fairly comfortably within the fold of liberal orthodoxy. His position is one which is echoed, with more specific reference to our contemporary grounds for belief, in, for example, some of the early works of D. Z. Phillips, for whom, in the mid-1970s at least, belief in God is not primarily – or even at all – a philosophical question, but one which rests on the experience of faith and worship rather than on more 'objective' grounds.[59] As with Cupitt, the subjective experience precedes rather than follows from any more objective content which may be imparted to it.

Neither Cupitt nor Phillips is saying anything which others have not said before them, and as far as Cupitt is concerned, he is not questioning the reality of the resurrection, merely the modes of perception and understanding which surround it. Yet in his avowed agnosticism, indeed scepticism, towards the circumstances demanded by an event theory of the resurrection, he is clearly already moving away from a purely objective and realist approach to at least some of the fundamental tenets of Christianity. Once the objectivity of the supposed acts of God is deemed to be 'logically superfluous',[60] it is quite conceivable that God himself should suffer the same fate.

Cupitt has never been too intellectually proud to acknowledge the various influences upon him over the years, and given his avowed interest in the ideas of, among others, Feuerbach, Freud and Durkheim,[61] and also of Nietzsche, it is no surprise that one of the most far-reaching influences at work in his turning away from realism is his increasing acceptance of the various forms of projection theory advanced by the first three of these men.

It is perhaps appropriate to indicate here why I have chosen to trace this particular influence in detail, rather than the equally substantial, although rather different influence of Nietzsche. Nietzsche's influence on Cupitt is, while significant, of a somewhat piecemeal nature: that is, he is cited frequently in support of various aspects of Cupitt's outlook, but never in such a way as to follow through a particular logical argument from beginning to end. This is itself, one suspects, a reflection of the nature of the bulk of Nietzsche's work, with its preference for a more apostrophic and aphoristic style rather than for a consistent and rigorously connected argument. In this more fragmentary fashion, Cupitt acknowledges a debt to Nietzsche on three counts especially: as a critic of Christianity for its repressive and 'slave-morality' oriented outlook; as a prophet announcing the end of objectivity – the 'death of God' and its consequences; and as a visionary of the 'Yes' beyond the nihil. In these three ways Nietzsche provided Cupitt with, as it were, a framework of anti-realism within which to explore the particular and more detailed arguments of other thinkers such as the three mentioned above. I have acknowledged Cupitt's use of Nietzsche's thought in a variety of instances, and especially in its general quasi-apocalyptic rôle as the harbinger of the end of objectivity and the dawning of nihility, and within the outlines of this framework of thought it then becomes important to consider the specific arguments, often drawn from other thinkers, which Cupitt uses to flesh out Nietzsche's prophetic rhetoric. Thus, in this instance, the development of projection theory gives concrete form to Nietzsche's nihilism by providing an argument which reduces our cosmic security to the status of an illusion.

In the development of this theory, the contribution of Feuerbach, Freud and Durkheim is somewhat different, as is their influence on Cupitt, but the common and underlying essence of this class of theories is nowhere expressed more succinctly, or indeed more enjoyably, than in Rupert Brooke's short poem, 'Heaven':

Fish, (fly-replete, in depth of June,
Dawdling away their wat'ry noon)
Ponder deep wisdom, dark or clear,
Each secret fishy hope or fear.
Fish say, they have their Stream and Pond;
But is there anything Beyond?
This life cannot be All, they swear,
For how unpleasant, if it were!
One may not doubt that, somehow, Good
Shall come of Water and of Mud;
And, sure, the reverent eye must see
A Purpose in Liquidity.
We darkly know, by Faith we cry,
The future is not Wholly Dry.
Mud unto mud! – Death eddies near –
Not here the appointed End, not here!
But somewhere, beyond Space and Time,
Is wetter water, slimier slime!
And there (they trust) there swimmeth One
Who swam ere rivers were begun,
Immense, of fishy form and mind,
Squamous, omnipotent, and kind;
And under that Almighty Fin,
The littlest fish may enter in.

Oh! never fly conceals a hook,
Fish say, in the Eternal Brook,
But more than mundane weeds are there,
And mud, celestially fair;
Fat caterpillars drift around,
And Paradisal grubs are found;
Unfading moths, immortal flies,
And the worm that never dies.
And in that Heaven of all their wish,
There shall be no more land, say fish.[62]

Of the three men mentioned above, Feuerbach is rightly held to be the father of the family of projection theories, and indeed his outworking of it is particularly thorough in that his most famous work, *The Essence of Christianity*, is constructed precisely around this perception of Christianity as projection. Mention has already been made of Feuerbach in the context of the tendency of religion to exalt God at the expense of man, and this is a direct consequence of projection. Man has projected on to God all that is best in himself with the result that, 'the personality of God is the personality of man freed from all the conditions and limitations of nature'.[63] The consequences of this projection are aptly characterized by Lloyd Geering:

> The God who originated as the projection of all that is best and truest in the human condition . . . came in the theist's imagination to be set over against man, as the antithesis of his actual self. As the concept of God embraced more and more of what man aspires to be (but is not), the more man found himself to be the polar opposite of his God. God is infinite, man is finite: God is perfect, man is imperfect: God is immortal, man is mortal: God is almighty, man is weak and powerless: God is the sum of all the positive realities, man embraces all the negations.[64]

Feuerbach's response to this was to assert man's need to free himself from this bondage of slavery to what is no more than an illusion, and to assert the autonomy of man now set up in the place of God:

... faith in God is therefore the faith of man in the infinitude and truth of his own nature; the Divine Being is the subjective human being in his absolute freedom and unlimitedness.[65]

The dramatic reversal of man's position which Feuerbach advocates is nowhere better expressed than in the words with which he ends the first part of *The Essence of Christianity*: 'The beginning, middle and end of religion is MAN.'[66]

Freud's attitude to man and his understanding of the mechanics of projection are rather different from Feuerbach's, but the effect is remarkably similar in placing man firmly in control of his own destiny and denying that there is any reality outside of himself. Feuerbach exults in what he considers to be the new freedom of the human race, full of quasi-divine possibilities and potential. By contrast, Freud's assessment of man's position when deprived of religion is rather more stark and sombre; alone in an indifferent universe man must simply make the best of a life which no longer contains the childish props and protections of religion. Without religion men will, Freud admits:

> ... find themselves in a difficult situation. They will have to admit to themselves the full extent of their helplessness and their insignificance in the machinery of the universe; they can no longer be the centre of creation, no longer the object of tender care on the part of a beneficent Providence. They will be in the same position as a child who has left the parental home where he was so warm and comfortable.[67]

The process may be uncomfortable, but it is necessary, for there is no value and no possibility for growth while man remains within the cosy but illusory world of religion. In essence, the mechanics of the projection which has produced this cosy illusion are simple, and Freud's assessment of it does not change substantially in more than thirty years. In 1901 he stated bluntly that:

> I believe that a large part of the mythological view of the world, which extends a long way into most modern religions is *nothing but psychology projected into the external world*.[68]

Religion was simply the projection of the childhood wish for a perfect loving father and a safe environment on to a cosmic backcloth. In 1933 he wrote in very similar terms:

> Religion is an attempt to master the sensory world in which we are situated by means of the wishful world which we have developed within us as a result of biological and psychological necessities.[69]

The effect of dismantling the apparatus of projection is to turn the individual away from the world in which he would childishly like to live and return him to the real world in which he does *in fact* live. Far from helping us to cope with this world, religion simply divorces us from it, and our path to psychological health and maturity demands that we abandon the childish delights of the one and learn to live with the real demands of the adult world.

Both Feuerbach and Freud approach the religious dimension from a predominantly personal angle, and any social effects arise only as a result of the individual being correctly oriented within his environment and therefore towards other people. By contrast, the sociologist Emile Durkheim was instrumental in developing a critique of religion as a form of social projection. His critique is not directed specifically at Christianity in the same way as Feuerbach's and, to a large extent, Freud's had been, but rather at the concept and phenomenon of religion itself. The remarks which he makes concerning primitive religions would therefore apply more-or-less directly to any other more developed religion also. The basic principle underlying his critique of religion is laid down in his discussion of totemism when he says of the relationship between the totem and the society around it:

> It [the totem] is its flag; it is the sign by which each clan distinguishes itself from the others, the visible mark of its personality, a mark borne by everything which is a part of the clan . . . So if it is at once the symbol of the god and of the society, is that not because the god and the society are only one? How could the emblem of the group have been able to become the figure of this quasi-divinity, if the group and the divinity were two distinct realities? The god of the clan, the totemic principle can

therefore be nothing else than the clan itself, personified and represented to the imagination under the visible form of the animal or vegetable which serves as totem.[70]

Any religion can be analysed in this kind of way. The values and ideals of a religion are the divinized aspirations and ideals of a society, and they are focussed in a deity who is a projection of all that that society holds most sacred.

Of these three proponents of projection theory, it is Durkheim who has – in recent years at least – influenced Cupitt most overtly. That this is so is symptomatic of Cupitt's increasingly community-oriented stance as he has developed his thoughts on the rôle of language in the shaping of society and through it – and therefore secondarily – the individual. A relatively early instance of Durkheim's influence on Cupitt, and one which is therefore not bound up with this later discussion of language, appears in *The World to Come*, published in 1982:

> The reason why the personal God is so highly specific, the reason why (in the old language) he is covenanted to a particular community, is that he is actually created by the apparatus of a particular religion, and his vivid reality to the believer manifests the almost boundless power of a society to evoke and to shape the inner experience of the individual. So I have to be aware that my personal God is the expression and the vehicle of the faith of my religious community. There is a Jewish God, a Muslim God, a Russian God, and so on.[71]

In this assessment of the social nature of religion – in which society indeed actually *creates* God – it is not hard to see a source of further ammunition for Cupitt's campaign against the social repressiveness of religion referred to earlier. Again he is admirably consistent in his criticism of Christianity, and the various aspects of it are related in a manner which is far more than merely accidental.

Between them Feuerbach, Freud and Durkheim provide Cupitt with two vital strands of his own argument. Firstly they provide a theory which, in various forms, challenges the supposed 'objectivity' and 'realism' of traditional Christianity, whilst also being able to account for its tenacity in the fight for survival; and secondly, by their implications, they lend support to Cupitt's opposition to Christianity on the grounds of its repressive nature both personally and in terms of society.

Of the three, however, it was Freud who offered Cupitt a vision of the necessity of escaping from the world of projection and living in the 'real' world. Freud exposed what he saw as the complete worthlessness of a world which was no more than an illusion, and the imperative need to abandon it in order to live a life which had even the possibility of being worth living:

> . . . surely infantilism is destined to be surmounted. Men cannot remain children for ever; they must in the end go out into 'hostile life'. We may call this '*education to reality*'.[72]

Freud's critique of religion is heavily value laden, and Cupitt is careful not to reflect Freud's rather personal and emotive scheme of value judgments, but the conclusions he reaches are broadly similar. The old view, widely held even among theological liberals, is that 'at a deep level the cosmos is personal' and that therefore 'in the long run all shall be well'.[73] Such a view is not, in Cupitt's opinion, readily tenable any longer. Too much has changed in our understanding of ourselves and our world to allow us to take refuge any longer in what would now be a conscious piece of self-deception. What has happened is that:

> . . . the liberal ideology is mythical and has collapsed. The notion of historical progress is mythical, and the notion that the cosmos is friendly to us is mythical. We do not have purely objective, culturally-neutral knowledge of how things are cosmically. Once you have got into the habit of noticing the way *all* peoples naïvely first project their own values and cultural conceptions upon the cosmos, and then claim that the cosmos backs them up, you can no longer do it for yourself. You see only too clearly that every claim to cosmic backing is just ideological.[74]

Thus, in its various forms, the projection theory provides Cupitt with a useful tool for elucidating his own objections to orthodoxy. It connects up admirably with his strictures on the authoritarianism and repressiveness of Christianity, and it enables his critique of Christianity to enter a new phase by offering a foundation for a sustained attack on the claims of Christianity to 'realism' and 'objectivity'.

In this attack, Cupitt is, as we shall see in Part 2, often guilty of working from premises which he has neglected to prove, or indeed often even to underpin in any way. His easy, fluent and persuasive style carries one forward, and one is occasionally in danger of finding oneself convinced by his arguments without ever having been able to pin down quite what those arguments were!

For the most part then, with the partial exception of the 'survey' material in *The Sea of Faith*, Cupitt takes for granted the collapse of objectivity in religion without necessarily explaining how this supposed collapse has come about. It is, to the post-modern mind at least, self-evident that it has collapsed, and as a result he is able to proceed by means of generalizations of a kind which render any approach other than his own not only obsolete but ludicrous.

Cupitt's approach *is* subject to severe criticism on these grounds, but to dismiss it in this way is by no means fair to Cupitt in that it criticizes him for not doing something which he has never had any intention of doing. He may indeed be guilty of arguing from ill-supported premises, but the reason for this is simply that he is not especially concerned to support them. His purpose is not to construct a laborious and rigorously logical argument to prove that realism in religion is no longer tenable in the current intellectual climate. This he is content to take largely on trust, and allow the groundwork of others – including the projection theory – to support his own particular contribution to the argument. Instead, what he is concerned to do is not so much to construct a theoretical case from the 'bottom up' as it were, but to pinpoint what he considers to be the major practical failings of an objective approach to religion. Reference to these failings is so diverse and so much woven into the texture of Cupitt's work that there is little merit in attempting to isolate and comment upon every last discussion of them. Instead it is more pertinent to identify three major areas in which 'objectivity' and 'realism' are found to be deficient. These areas are, briefly: the attitude of realism to this world and to the present; its adequacy, or lack of it, in purely religious terms; and the question of whether or not it can be said to be ultimately 'meaningful'. To these areas we now turn in more detail.

## IV

It has been noted on several occasions that Cupitt maintains a remarkable degree of internal consistency in his criticisms of Christianity. All the various threads are woven together at least implicitly if not always explicitly, and he is rarely guilty of self-contradiction. Thus it is no surprise to find that his most recent thoughts, which hinge on the primacy of language and the all-encompassing immediacy of the present, should have emerged as a logical development of his earlier attention to the problem of the perceived dichotomy between realism and the conferral of value upon the 'here and now'.

The effect of realism, Cupitt claims, is to devalue the here and now. This he sees as inevitable. After all, if there is – objectively – a world in which all values are perfectly realized and in which eternal meaning and truth truly reside, then there is not much one can find to say in favour of an imperfect world in which human beings grope around in the semi-darkness clinging to whatever fragments of meaning they happen to stumble upon. The function of realism is to 'induce us to see ourselves as being relatively small, weak, ignorant and dependent'.[75] The attention of people is distracted from the present and they are drawn to a 'yearning for the Beyond'.[76] In doing this they are stripping the present world of any intrinsic value. It becomes a secondary thing which receives whatever value it may have indirectly and derivatively by reflection, rather as the moon has no light of its own but merely reflects the light of the sun. Such a stripping away of value is damaging not only to our understanding of ourselves and our world, but also to the religious life itself. It loses vigour and creativity and becomes purely reactive:

One had *first* to look to the Beyond. The religious life waited in suspense until the Beyond had *first* commanded it, legitimated it and conferred value upon it – and only then could it begin in good conscience.[77]

So realism is damaging to our sense of ourselves and of the value of our world and our life within it, and it is damaging also to the religious life itself. It is, furthermore, damaging to the moral life also. Again the argument is that our own moral sense and moral strength are weakened by the need to appeal first to an objective reality beyond ourselves upon which we depend. We need, says Cupitt:

> . . . to forget the platonic idea that there's an order of higher truths out there that we have got to grasp theoretically before we can act aright. That claim reduces the moral life to the level of something like being a good soldier: you learn the ropes, you learn what is required of you and then you do it. So long as we remain in the grip of the primitive notion that the human being is in the world as a servant is in a household, no truly human morality can be framed. Our life becomes merely a routine job with a tatty list of ready-made rules.[78]

Far from living in dependence upon an overbearing objective 'world out there' we need to return to *this* world, and learn to create value and truth from within it: only so will we come to any kind of maturity and stature as responsible spiritual and moral agents.

The consequence of such a necessity to return to this world is quite simply that 'the old sort of God must go'.[79] And he must go because '. . . he did everything, he had finished all the creative work already and he wouldn't let human beings truly invent any values or accomplish anything on their own'.[80] Again the emphasis is on the tendency of realism to stunt rather than to promote human spiritual and moral growth. If the human race is to aspire to this growth – as Christianity declares that it should – then the traditional framework of Christianity itself must be dismantled in order to offer to man the autonomy and responsibility which is claimed as a precondition of such growth. Here again it may be questioned whether Cupitt's analysis of the effects of objectivity is entirely unbiased; whether complete autonomy is the ultimate good which Cupitt claims it is; and indeed whether Cupitt's own 'internal religious requirement' which takes the place of an objective God is any less constraining than the God whom it replaces. However, his strictures on objectivity on the grounds that it devalues the human and the present and makes for a stagnant spirituality and morality do also have an honourable pedigree among the critics of Christianity.

As so often with Cupitt, it is perhaps Feuerbach whose influence is most apparent. Lloyd Geering aptly characterizes the implications of Feuerbach's discussion of how the concept of God arose and the manner in which it then effectively cornered the market in moral perfection:

> As God represents actual man projected into perfected form, so heaven represents the actual world projected into perfection. The potential which originally this world was seen to possess was posited in another world and becomes eternally divorced from this world by the same gulf as that which separates God from man. There is no way, thereafter, in which this world can ever realize its full potential. It remains lost forever and man's salvation consists in his being delivered by divine grace from this world and translated into another world.[81]

In such a situation it is no wonder that, as the only possible way of escape from his doomed world, man is drawn towards what Cupitt calls 'yearning for the Beyond'. In complete contrast to this, the perspective which Cupitt is arguing for is much more like that envisaged by Troeltsch:

> If the absolute authority has fallen which, in its absoluteness, made the antithesis of the divine and human equally absolute, if in man an autonomous principle is recognized as the source of truth and moral conduct, then all conceptions of the world which were especially designed to maintain that gulf between the human and the divine, fall along with it. With it falls the doctrine of the absolute corruption of mankind through original sin, and the transference of the ends of life to the heavenly world in which there will be deliverance from this corruption. In consequence, all the factors of this present life acquire an enhanced value and a higher impressiveness, and the ends of life fall more and more

within the realm of the present world with its ideal of transformation.[82]

In such a world as this human beings gain, or perhaps regain, their
dignity and stature as free and creative agents, and the world
becomes a place in which the meaning and value of the present are
enhanced, and our human life within it is set free from 'yearning for
the Beyond' and directed towards the task of creating value and
meaning in the here and now. It is in precisely this kind of a world
that the modern consciousness finds itself, argues Cupitt, and it is
therefore quite simply time that religion woke up and took notice of
this fact. Modern consciousness has burst the bonds of its
dependence upon the beyond and is establishing a new autonomy. It
is becoming more responsible for itself. And a part of this autonomy
is located in a changed understanding of the spiritual life itself. If the
religious life is to remain in touch with the rest of life, then we must
no longer depend upon the 'Beyond' to validate and rule our spiritual
pilgrimage. On the contrary:

> We must choose our own religious values because they are
> intrinsically precious, rather than because any external being
> commands us to adopt them and threatens us with sanctions[83]

and a return to an 'objective' religious outlook is ruled out by this
same principle of autonomy which suggests that any such return
would be 'morally dubious'[84] in that it would be a denial of our
potential for freedom and creativity in religion, and a return to
precisely that subservience in religion whose passing Cupitt at once
celebrates and builds upon. Whether in fact autonomy and objectivity are as mutually exclusive as Cupitt would have us believe is
open to question, but his insistence upon the value of this world in
religious terms is nonetheless a salutary reminder of an oft-
neglected theological realm and also a significant factor in his own
irritation with the shortcomings of traditional Christian theology and
spirituality.

Cupitt's criticisms of traditional 'realist' Christianity on the
grounds of its attitude towards the here and now, and its denial of
autonomy to the human individual are certainly important, but they

do not strike at the heart of realism in the same way as his second group of objections to it. This is based on the inadequacy of realism in religious terms. Christianity claims to be, and is, a religion, and yet, argues Cupitt, the irony is that in its traditional form it is not what he calls 'religiously adequate'. His criticism of Christianity on these grounds is particularly telling in that he bases it upon the fundamental question: what is the nature and function of any religion? If Christianity fails to measure up to this test, if it fails to achieve the purpose of religion, then clearly our understanding of it will need to be radically transformed before it can begin to function effectively as a meaningful religion. So to the question of 'What is true religion?' Cupitt returns the decisive – and eminently reason-able – answer that it is 'religion through which salvation can be had'.[85] This in turn raises the question 'What is salvation?' and to this Cupitt's answer is more contentious. Its adequacy will be examined later, but for the present it may stand unchallenged. Salvation is, he says, 'a state of the self', and as such 'it has to be appropriated subjectively and existentially'.[86] Naturally enough, in terms of Cupitt's argument this turns out to be a remarkably convenient answer, as it immediately calls into question the need for, and indeed even the possibility of, an objective religious realm. Religion is neatly relocated in the practical rather than in the supernatural or metaphysical realm, although this is itself another example of rhetorical polarization in the service of his argument.

However, once religion is thus defined as being a purely practical undertaking which lives purely in the present world (and again the internal consistency of Cupitt's arguments should be noted *vis-à-vis* the comments above) and once salvation is defined as being an existential and subjective 'state of the self', then it is clear that theological realism is redundant and indeed destructive of the very salvation which is the essence of religion. The business of religion, and with it faith, becomes, 'a disciplined, practical striving to attain a life-ideal that emerges from within our own natures'.[87]

As has already been indicated, if the religious world is truly of this kind, then theological realism, and with it an objective God, is at best unnecessary and at worst destructive of true religion. That an objective God is not only unnecessary but also undesirable, even from a religious point of view, is a case which Cupitt puts very clearly indeed; and an objective God is undesirable precisely because he is, strange though it may sound, religiously inadequate in that he cannot fulfil the function of religion which is to produce salvation:

> If I could have theoretical knowledge of God as a distinct object other than myself, including knowledge of what it is that God wills, and if these facts about God and God's will were in themselves sufficient to impose religious obligation upon me, then faith would be through-and-through heteronomous. I would be subject to an almighty will ruling me from without. How can such a heteronomous faith ever be the means whereby I become autonomous and fully-liberated spirit? It is impossible. This appears to be a conclusive religious argument against the objective existence of God. An objective God cannot save.[88]

Clearly this argument is closely linked to Cupitt's arguments with regard to the backwardness and repressiveness of traditional Christianity, but here he goes further than this and defines objectivity as the source of heteronomy and his more voluntarist approach as the means of fostering man's autonomy, and thereby of facilitating his salvation, according to Cupitt's own understanding of that term.

There is then in Cupitt's thought a dichotomy between an objective God who cannot save and is therefore religiously inadequate, and a non-realist approach to faith which while apparently reductionist is, in fact, more religiously adequate and will lead to salvation. Throughout his work Cupitt is adept at anchoring rather abstruse and esoteric arguments by means of an apt illustration, and in *The Sea of Faith* he characterizes these two positions as being summed up in the persons of Descartes and Pascal. In them is made manifest the dilemma which faces the modern religious consciousness. Following an extended discussion of them and of their different approaches to religion Cupitt comments:

> In the contrast . . . between Pascal and Descartes we see a striking early example of a puzzle that crops up repeatedly in later years: the claims of theological realism and of religious seriousness now pull in opposite directions. Either you can claim to have an

objective God, like Descartes, or you can have an authentic Christian faith, like Pascal. It is one or the other: take your pick.[89]

The final, and perhaps the ultimate failing of an objective God, in religious terms, is not even, however, that he is religiously inadequate. It is that he is an idol, and therefore potentially destructive of the true nature of religion. To seek him is to seek a chimera, and in the process to forsake the true religious quest and to forfeit the only genuine salvation which religion offers – that of autonomy, freedom and moral and spiritual stature.[90] As a result of this criticism and of the other criticisms on religious grounds which we have outlined, Cupitt's objections to and struggles against theological realism are seen to be central to his conviction of the need for a radically new understanding of Christianity in which the 'rational and moral' replaces that which he sees as its current roots in 'idolatry and superstition'.[91]

The final group of arguments against realism *per se* which we have chosen to examine are those which criticize it on the grounds of its explanatory power and intelligibility. The two things are closely related, for Christianity claims to explain a good deal about the way in which the cosmos works, and if it can be shown to have failed to provide such an explanation, then the basic intelligibility of its categories and concepts is called into question, simply because we then have no means of verifying its claims, or even of testing them out against reality.

As with several of his other objections to orthodoxy, this group finds its first sustained expression in *Taking Leave of God*, a book which is primarily devoted to refuting the traditional realist claims of Christianity.

Cupitt's argument has its starting point in a detailed examination of several of the traditional proofs of God's existence. In varying ways these appeal either to the existence of the creation itself or to the supposedly benevolent ordering of it in order to establish the existence of God. The arguments are inconclusive on both counts, says Cupitt. The creation cannot be shown to be contingent and dependent upon an outside cause for its existence, and neither can its by no means universally benevolent ordering be shown to be the result of the will of a good, wise and loving creator. Indeed, appealing to God tells us nothing of the reasons why the cosmos should be ordered as it is; and conversely, appealing to the cosmos tells us nothing about the nature of God. The arguments fail to shed light either on the creation or on its putative creator.

The plight of realism becomes even worse when not only intellect, but faith also fails to provide us with any information about God. This is because faith, as defined by Cupitt, is 'a virtue, not a means by which we gain esoteric information about occult entities',[92] and as a result is not 'theoretically cognitive' and provides no 'reliable information about a world-transcending God at all'.[93] If this is so, then the language of faith, which speaks of such a God in terms which purport to be claiming some real knowledge, is in danger of falling into unintelligibility. This slide is given added momentum in Cupitt's eyes by the effects on our understanding of ourselves and our world which have been produced by the (largely) French philosophers of language headed by such figures as Derrida and Foucault. Their influence upon Cupitt's thinking will be examined in more detail at a later stage, but here it is sufficient to note that they have been instrumental in providing a framework which has enabled him in recent years to develop a philosophy of religion founded upon the primacy of language and upon the inability of human thought or activity to escape from its confines. There is, as he very frequently puts it, 'quite simply, no outside'.

In a world where this is taken to be true, immediately all statements which purport to refer to an entity beyond this present language-dominated and governed world are by definition unintelligible – they are attempting to establish a referent beyond language, and this has already been defined as impossible. One might be forgiven for suggesting that Cupitt's interpretation of post-structuralist philosophy has an enviable and at times too convenient ability to define itself in such a way as to render it invulnerable to criticism, and also that it looks suspiciously like another attempt to establish some of the positions held by the now discredited school of logical positivism during the earlier years of this century. It is, for many people, except its own practitioners, in danger of looking like a ragamuffin dressed up as a prince.

Allowing the position for the present, however, the consequence is that living inside history and inside language, 'a God out there and values out there, if they existed, would be utterly useless and unintelligible to us'.[94] Once the notion of an objective God has been thus disposed of, the remaining pretensions of Christianity to realism tumble with him. There is no longer any place for talk of God's activity or providence or will, and we can no longer speak coherently or intelligibly of any kind of relationship with God or of any purpose or hope extending beyond this life into another. One is returned inexorably to this world and to the grip of history and language which thus becomes even stronger and more all-pervasive. So Cupitt argues for the meaninglessness of such concepts as the resurrection and a life after death[95] and the possibility of Christ indwelling the believer.[96] In living with these and other similar concepts for so long, the Christian faith was, as we saw earlier, turned away from this world towards another supposedly better one: it was 'radically anti-human and anti-life'[97] and only now with the disappearance of this world of illusion which has been condemned to the realm of the unintelligible, and therefore the useless, can Christianity find its true identity as a religion *of and for* this world:

> For over seventeen centuries Christianity was transmitted in a time-capsule, in a state of suspended animation. Now we can thaw it out and bring it to life.[98]

This concern with rediscovering Christianity and bringing it to life underlies all of Cupitt's three groups of objections to realism here discussed. If traditional realism produces the pernicious effects which Cupitt claims it does then it is small wonder that he is committed to opposing it. Contra realism – and not infrequently *contra mundum*! – Cupitt seeks to restore value to the here and now, and to find a religious approach to life which is at once meaningful to the modern, or even the post-modern, mind, and also adequate in purely religious terms. The last – and of latter years the most significant – strand in Cupitt's objections to orthodoxy has already been briefly alluded to above. This hinges on his understanding of the function and the boundaries of language. The issue of language, and what can and cannot be said, has long been one which has fascinated Cupitt, and over the years it has come to be increasingly bound up with, to the extent of providing the foundation for, his particular objections to realism.

Initially Cupitt's interest in the language of religion was focussed on the question of what it is and is not possible to say about God. Thus in *Christ and the Hiddenness of God* the whole of the first part of the book is concerned with this issue. In examining it, Cupitt highlights a familiar problem of theologians, namely the dilemma posed by the grosser anthropomorphisms of God-talk on the one hand, and the sometimes rather vague and empty phrases of intellectual theology on the other hand. Cupitt – again echoed interestingly by Iris Murdoch in the passage quoted previously on pages 34f. – defines the problem thus:

If theology's basic concepts ever become clear and specific, it is falling into idolatry; if they are refined away, theology falls into vacuity. A vivid personal faith and a pure spiritual faith are at odds with each other. Is there any *via media* between anthropomorphism and agnosticism at all?[99]

In *Christ and the Hiddenness of God* Cupitt uses the person of Jesus, and the allusive and oblique way in which he speaks of God as a means of solving the problem, but only a very few years later he finds it necessary to shift his ground to a more all-encompassing (and in some ways traditional) answer to it. The shift becomes necessary when he perceives a secondary problem of specific and positive talk about God, namely that not only does it threaten to fall into anthropomorphism and ultimately therefore into idolatry, but also it reinforces the tendency of religion to reduce man to a state of heteronomy. The more God is absolutized, the more we are presented with the possibility of living under the dominion of a cosmic tyrant who will allow nothing, and least of all religion, to change and develop. There are clear links here with several of Cupitt's other objections to orthodoxy, and his solution to the problem is based upon the grounds to several of these objections: that is, the need for freedom in the religious life. And the only way to develop and to maintain this freedom is to embrace the *via negativa* which relativizes all positive statements about God by acknowledging that God is beyond *all* our representations of him, and that ultimately we can only say what he is *not* rather than what he *is*:

> No system of doctrines, rituals and moral principles whatever can be absolute: God himself, God as pure transcendent Spirit, is always more than God in symbolic representation. So the *negative way* in religion leads the believer to transcend even the most 'orthodox' and authoritative symbolic apparatus.[100]

At this point in his career, and for the next few years, Cupitt holds broadly to this position. It allows him, as we have seen, to make room for a measure of agnosticism about the dogmatic content of Christianity without necessarily leaving behind a substantially orthodox framework of thought, as when he is dealing with such issues as christology or the nature of the resurrection event. It has also been noted, however, that whilst the *via negativa* is undoubtedly an approach to theology which has a long and honourable pedigree within the Christian tradition, it also contains within itself the potential for a slide into a more thoroughgoingly negative approach to theology. It is one thing to assert that ultimately nothing can rightly be said about or predicated of God, but quite another, although it is only a short step away, to maintain that there is actually no being there of whom anything could be said anyway. And it is this step which Cupitt takes somewhere between the publication of *Jesus and the Gospel of God* in 1979 and *Taking Leave of God* in 1980. Between the two books Cupitt's fundamental attitude to religion undergoes a radical transformation. At the end of *Jesus and the Gospel of God* he could still speak of the possibility of 'salvation by a final encounter with God',[101] and has as his intention the 'purification' of our conception of God rather than its dismantling. For all the insistence upon the primacy of the negative way, God is still – though largely indefinable – a real entity experienced as transcendent and set over against the believer. By complete contrast he speaks of God in the opening pages of *Taking Leave of God* as, 'a unifying symbol that eloquently personifies and represents to us everything that spirituality requires of us'.[102] God, he says, 'is the religious concern, reified'.[103] At this stage in his career, Cupitt's acute awareness of the limitations of language, feeding, and in turn feeding upon his growing sense of the oppressive and tyrannical nature of theological realism, has led him to cross the divide from the *via negativa* to a fully non-realist position. His objections to realism have finally overcome his avowed reluctance to abandon it.

Following this fundamental shift of perspective, Cupitt's fascination with language necessarily took a new turn which required several years to develop clearly and which has only found its full expression in his most recent books. Thus latterly he has been developing, as was noted earlier, his thoughts on the primacy of language and its position as the framework of our entire affective and cognitive life. In many respects this development was inevitable. It would have been unlikely in the extreme that Cupitt could have lost his long-standing interest in the problems of language, and given its continuing place in his affections, the change in his approach to it is entirely consistent. Having been led, partly by language-related issues, to the abandonment of realism, there was clearly no longer any future in addressing the problem of what can and cannot be said of God. Once you have established that there is no objective God of whom you can say anything, the problem simply disappears. From this point onwards, therefore, the nature of language rather than the nature of God becomes the prime factor in Cupitt's approach. Where previously the nature of God dictated what could and could not be said of him, now the nature of language dictates what can and cannot meaningfully be said of anything, God included. Thus language itself becomes a means of reinforcing the anti-realist approach to religion, to the development of which its own short-comings in speaking of God had contributed. It is a curious inversion of roles, but nonetheless a consistent one.

More detailed attention will be given to this aspect of Cupitt's thought at a later stage, but for the present the outlines of his position, and the reasons why he sees the nature of language as an unanswerable objection to the realist traditions of orthodoxy, can be delineated by a brief glance at one of his latest works, *Creation out of Nothing*. In the Preface to this book he sets out his basic premises on the nature and supremacy of language and its relationship to the idea of God. The chief theme of the book is, quite simply, 'the production of reality by language'.[104] The reality produced by language extends even to God, for, 'like us, God is made only of words', since 'God's own thought and his Word of self-revelation are also just the language in which they are expressed'.[105] If this is indeed the case, and if Cupitt is correct that language determines and indeed produces reality, then realism in theology is plainly a lost cause. The language which we use to talk of God has, ironically, become his undoing, and to the wide variety of objections to orthodoxy which we have examined there is now added the overruling one that realism is not only outmoded, repressive, world-denying, religiously inadequate and meaningless, but logically and linguistically impossible as well. Whether one agrees with Cupitt is, of course, another matter, but if one allows his arguments, then the case against realism is compelling indeed. Once the impossibility of realism is established, there is little more to be said, except perhaps to add the time-honoured conclusion of philosophers and logicians – *QED*.

During the course of this examination of Cupitt's career we have noted the varied (but internally remarkably coherent and consistent) body of objections which he has constructed with regard to orthodoxy and traditional modes of Christian thought, and which have led him increasingly to abandon such ways of thinking. At this point our attention must turn to the path which Cupitt has himself taken away from orthodoxy in response to these objections, and to the theological and spiritual framework which he has constructed in its place. There will, inevitably, be some small degree of overlap between this and the preceding discussion, but if we would understand Cupitt then it is imperative that we should attempt to grasp and to assess the new kind of faith which emerges from the ashes of the old, once the old has been melted down in the self-professedly refining and purifying fires of Cupitt's criticism.

# 3

# Departure from Orthodoxy

## I

In the previous two chapters, something of the immense fertility of Don Cupitt's mind has become evident. Throughout his career he has been an extraordinarily creative theologian, very much in the manner of the artist-theologian whom he increasingly takes as a model.[1] Furthermore he has always tended to write at great speed, and as a result his books and articles do not follow a rigidly logical path in what might be called the manner of more 'Germanic' theologians. One suspects that Cupitt has usually written simply on the basis of what has interested him at any given time, rather than because he is following any long-term *a priori* theological schema. Consequently his work is liberally sprinkled with theological blind alleys, one-off excursions into areas of interest which have never been followed up.

Clearly it would be possible, in assessing his career, to follow any or all of these excursions and comment on them exhaustively. To do this would, however, add little – except tedium – to one's understanding of Cupitt's development. In discussing his objections to orthodoxy it was remarked that he builds up – digressions notwithstanding – a coherent body of such objections, and the same coherence is discernible in the path of his departure from orthodoxy, provided only that one ignores the distractions of the digressions along the way. Cupitt's path may not unfairly be likened to that of a tacking sailing vessel – the basic direction always remains clear, even if it involves a good deal of to-ing and fro-ing in order to get there. Thus in this discussion attention will be focussed on what is, I believe, a very clear and internally logical movement away from orthodoxy which results over the years in the formulation of two new positions, depending upon, respectively, the end of metaphysics, and the primacy of language.

From his earliest years as a theologian, then, Cupitt has been preoccupied with the problem of what can and cannot be said of God. His dissatisfaction with what he perceives as the 'grosser anthropomorphisms' of Christian language was alluded to in both of the previous chapters, and, as was noted, he analyses in some detail the language which Jesus used to speak of God and takes its allusiveness and obliqueness as a model for our own talk of God.

In view of this preoccupation with the limits of talk about God, it is hardly surprising that Cupitt should have developed an early interest in the concept of the *via negativa*. In common with other intellectual disciplines, theology is a thing of fashion, and this theological method, stemming largely from Proclus and Pseudo-Dionysius, had fallen on hard times during the previous one hundred years or so. It had received a battering from, amongst others, Dean Inge, because of its tendency towards 'apatheia', and others had turned against it because of what they saw as an inbuilt critically destructive attitude towards finite existence. For Cupitt, however, the *via negativa* was a key factor in the development of the first of his major movements away from orthodoxy, and the strength of his attachment to it as a theological method may be explained partly by the mere fact of its freshness after a period of substantial redundancy, and partly by the degree to which it was compatible with another major preoccupation of Cupitt's – his search for spiritual autonomy and freedom.

Cupitt's lifelong interest in the negative way has been touched on frequently already, and what is important at this stage is not so much to trace its every appearance in his writings, but to ascertain by what process it led him to a fundamental shift in his theological position.

Thus we have noted already the five stages of religious experience depicted in *The Leap of Reason* which culminate in a constant movement from affirmation to negation and back again, and we have seen his earlier essay in this direction in *Christ and the Hiddenness of God*. In this context, however, a passage from the original preface to this book is instructive. He writes:

I agree . . . that theology, to be true to religion, must continually strive for objectivity, but I agree also . . . that it is in principle (not just in fact) not completely attainable. That is, I try to show the restless iconoclastic character of belief in God, which continually strives after intelligible content, and yet must by its own inner dialectic always negate any proposed specific content. We think God through human imagery, and yet deny its adequacy: we must so think, and we must so deny.[2]

At this early stage, Cupitt's primary reason for the adoption of the *via negativa* is admirably orthodox – to avoid the dangers of anthropomorphism and incipient idolatry. He is concerned to safeguard the ancient purity of monotheism, even if, in order to do so, his method must be, at times, a disturbingly and radically iconoclastic one.

As he presents it here, the *via negativa* is pursued not merely for its own sake, and not in the service of any hidden polemic against traditional thinking. Indeed, he is using a traditional method as a means of rediscovering the ultimate transcendence and therefore the 'hiddenness' of God in the face of some of the 'cosier' aberrations of nineteenth and twentieth-century theology. The *via negativa* is being employed to safeguard the freedom of God from human representations of him. God, in his infinite transcendence of us is free Spirit, and cannot be tamed or chained down in thought or language or image.

Paired, as it is, with Cupitt's attempts at (qualified) affirmation in speaking of God, the *via negativa* is employed with a finely balanced restraint in his earliest works, and indeed Cupitt shows himself to be acutely aware of the need for this balance if negativity is not to topple over into nothingness. In its classical form the *via negativa* forbids not only statements as to what God is, or is like, but even denies that it is possible to formulate any such statement in a meaningful way. Thus it is a method which will not allow us to say, 'God is not this, not this, but that', but always insists that the form is, 'God is not this, not this, and *not* that'.

As a method it has, as Cupitt perceives, much to commend it in terms of keeping before us the awesome mystery and transcendence of God, and thereby setting our relationship with God in an appropriate perspective; but it is a method which requires the *via positiva* as its opposite pole and counterbalance. By itself it is dangerously unbalanced for the simple reason that alone it 'cannot make clear whether or not there is anything left for God to be. It does not distinguish theism from atheism'.[3] And this, Cupitt acknowledges, will not do: '. . . at least one affirmative statement about God is necessary to save theology from emptiness'.[4] In realizing and acknowledging the dangers attendant upon the use of the negative way in isolation, Cupitt has avoided these dangers in his own work for the time being at least. For the future, what is instructive, though, is that as his use of the *via negativa* develops later on, Cupitt himself becomes unable to 'distinguish theism from atheism'. At a later stage in his career Cupitt will willingly embrace the path he has overtly eschewed at this earlier period.

Throughout the 1970s, however, his use of the *via negativa* remained consistently oriented towards safeguarding the transcendence of God. Such developments as did occur were formulated only gradually and manifest themselves rather as changes of emphasis rather than as fundamental changes of outlook, at least until *Taking Leave of God* in 1980. Two changes of emphasis in particular are significant for the future.

The first of these is the gradual withering away of Cupitt's attempts to speak positively of God. During the 1970s the negative approach becomes increasingly dominant with the result that by 1979 he could write:

> It is all too easy for human beings to believe; what really requires courage is to learn to disbelieve. God is known by unknowing, believed in by disbelieving all that is not God, and nearest when strangest.[5]

Unlike his earlier work there is no attempt to balance a statement like this, and the thrust of the whole book is precisely that God is *not like* anything which can be imagined or spoken of him; but rather that he and his kingdom can only be approached by a radical overturning of all our human thoughts and ways. We can indeed only say with any confidence that God is not like anything we may imagine him to resemble.

Cupitt's insistence that this is our only possible approach to God – through the way of un-knowing – opens the way for the second change of emphasis in his use of the *via negativa*. Originally what had been safeguarded was the freedom of God, but alongside this there develops a growing concern for our freedom too, also safeguarded by the *via negativa*. The freer and more transcendent God becomes, the less we are enslaved to an anthropomorphic deity of our own devising, and the more our own spirit becomes free also, no longer bound to immutable dogmatic formulations of faith before which all rational thought and intellectual enquiry must humbly submit. So Cupitt can resolve the apparent paradox raised in *Jesus and the Gospel of God* of the need for a 'critical faith'. The paradox rests on the definitions of criticism as 'free and sceptical enquiry' and faith as 'humble, dogmatic and credulous', and Cupitt resolves it by invoking the results of the use of the negative way in theology:

> . . . the resolution of the paradox is that critical faith is immediate, pure, spiritual and free precisely in its insistence on the trans-cendence of God, and its recognition of the merely human character of all our representations of God.[6]

This echoes a series of remarks which Cupitt made in an essay written several years earlier entitled 'The Meaning of Belief in God'. In the course of the essay he discusses religion under its dual aspects of order and freedom. Order is imparted by the use of symbols, creeds and the like, which provide a common bond of loyalty and a common perception of God; this is the function of the affirmative way in religion. Conversely, the negative way is the source of freedom in the religious life as we recognize that:

> No system of doctrines, rituals and moral principles whatever can be absolute: God himself, God as pure transcendent Spirit, is always more than God in symbolic representation.[7]

Thus a connection is made not only between the negative way and the freedom of the believer, but also between the negative way and the limitations – indeed the need for their transcendence – of systems of doctrines, symbols and so on. Pursued to its conclusion, the negative way is pre-eminently a way of freedom:

> Aspiring after a God who is free, transcendent Spirit, the believer becomes free spirit himself. Religion itself teaches this, and every believer must discover it, at least in death.[8]

In view of this it is hardly surprising to read in an autobiographical aside in the introduction to this volume of essays that Cupitt has long '. . . equated anthropomorphism with bondage to idols, and the negative way with spiritual freedom'.[9]

Similar references to the *via negativa* are scattered throughout Cupitt's earlier work, and in their increasing frequency and their growing insistence on the link between the *via negativa* and spiritual freedom in particular, one can sense a gradual building up of pressure which must sooner or later manifest itself in a fundamental change of outlook on Cupitt's part. This change took place with the publication of *Taking Leave of God* in 1980. Until this work the implications of Cupitt's negative way theology had remained largely unspoken, and their direction emerges clearly only with hindsight. In *Taking Leave of God*, however, the various aspects of this theology, previously apparently unrelated, are gathered up and developed further, and immediately their consequences become clear. It would appear that a new perspective, founded largely on this bringing together of his disparate thoughts on the *via negativa*, took shape in Cupitt's mind at this time. In retrospect one can see that the various pieces of the jigsaw were there at least in embryo for several years prior to 1980, but it is as though in *Taking Leave of God* the fragments of a mosaic suddenly piece themselves together and arrange themselves into a coherent pattern. The ideas of freedom, autonomy, divine transcendence, the limitations of doctrine, and the restrictions of objectivity have all been there for some time, but in *Taking Leave of God* they are fused, through the medium of the negative way, into a theological schema which represents a major development in Cupitt's thought and consequently in his position with regard to orthodoxy. Before *Taking Leave of God*, all but the most conservative would have seen him as 'orthodox', if somewhat radical at times; after it he became perhaps the Church of England's 'arch-heretic', and was branded, to use the title of Scott Cowdell's book, as an 'atheist priest'.

What, then, took place in this book? It was, I believe, a fusion of his previous ideas about the *via negativa* – now worked out more fully and in a more organized fashion – with a new realization of the implications of that negative way if followed to its own logical conclusion. Underpinning the new developments in his thought there was a complex of ideas with which he had long been familiar, but which he now examined in greater detail and assembled in a more structured and less random fashion.

In this piecing together of his ideas, the most basic of all the functions of the *via negativa* – to counter an over-anthropomorphic approach to God – is not forgotten, although Cupitt does provide it with a deft twist in the tail which makes it all the more amenable to the ideas with which he wishes to associate it. Thus he says that prior to the seventeenth and eighteenth centuries, '. . . the old tradition of the negative way and the emphasis on the practical character of religious knowledge helped to check crude realism'.[10] The twist in the tail consists in two separate pieces of clever argument. First, Cupitt brings the term 'realism' into the discussion, and, of course, this is a term which is open to a wide variety of interpretations. At one level it is commensurate with the iconoclastic properties of the *via negativa*, and Cupitt can be read as saying only that God must not be reduced to our conceptions of him. For 'realism' read 'anthropomorphism'. On another level, however, 'realism' is a loaded theological term with a very specific set of associations attached to it, and it is of course these which Cupitt will develop in the course of his argument. The traditional proponents of the *via negativa* would not have felt entirely at home with this interpretation of 'realism', but by using the fluctuating meanings adhering to the one word, Cupitt has, by clever sleight of hand, brought the eminently traditional and respectable concept of the *via negativa* around to a position which is now consistent with his increasingly 'anti-realist' (according to the second definition of 'realism') approach.

Nor indeed is this all that Cupitt achieves in the one sentence. He also succeeds in linking the *via negativa* with the practical and regulative aspects of the Christian faith. This is a traditional (although not a universal) emphasis – that God cannot be known in himself, but only in his effects and demands upon us – but it is a particularly useful association from Cupitt's point of view as he proceeds to develop his ideas of God as the 'guiding ideal' of the religious life. He then expands upon the relationship of the *via negativa* to the idea that God can be known only in his effects. Again Cupitt is careful to scour the tradition for any possible sources of support, and he succeeds in yoking together two such disparate characters as John A. T. Robinson and Thomas Aquinas. Both concur in the primacy of the *via negativa*, and both argue that God can only be known in his effects. To be fair, Cupitt does acknowledge that

> It is true that Thomas Aquinas, for example, was much more willing than Robinson to try to project the metaphysical existence of God as a distinct world-transcending being[11]

but this is presented as a minor difference of emphasis which does not substantially affect the primary likeness which binds them together, namely the pre-eminence of the *via negativa*. (Whether in fact the *via negativa* is as prominent as this in Aquinas is open to question. He may equally well be interpreted – as he is by Richard Swinburne – as the great re-discoverer of the *via positiva* after the largely negative emphasis of the sixth to eleventh centuries.[12]) Allowing Cupitt's analysis for the present, however, it happens that the theological method by which Cupitt reaches his conclusions is provided with a cloak of the most perfect traditionalism and respectability, whilst the conclusions themselves, which touch on the existence or non-existence of God are relegated, strategically at least, to a second-order status.

The main purpose in the forging of this unlikely alliance between Robinson and Aquinas, however, is simply to reinforce Cupitt's contention that there is a significant strand in traditional thinking which would place 'religion' before 'theology'. The link between Robinson and Aquinas is that both would have agreed that

> . . . we have no knowledge of God as he is in himself, for we know God only as he enters into our experience. Talk about God is talk

about human experiences, understood as dealings with God or as being effects of God.[13]

By arguing for the traditional roots behind Robinson's perceived modernity and radicalism Cupitt can open the way for the claim that his own thinking, though very different in its conclusions, is faithful in its premisses and its spirit to the deepest concerns of religion. He is willing to jettison much of traditional theology in order to uphold the vitality of the religious tradition.

Having established this connection between the *via negativa* and the pre-eminently 'practical' and 'religious' rather than theological and metaphysical nature of our relationship with God, Cupitt can then continue to build upon it. The next step is to fuse these ideas with his developing thinking on the freedom and spiritual autonomy which is the fruit of the *via negativa*. The connection is essentially a simple one: the negative way culminates in the unknowability of God, and as a consequence:

> Religious language then perforce becomes expressive, not descriptive, and the relation to God has to be enacted in spirituality because it can in no way be articulated in knowledge. A high and orthodox emphasis on the divine transcendence forces me in the end to a non-cognitive or (as people say) 'subjectivist' philosophy of religion.[14]

In other words, as through the *via negativa* God becomes objectively unknowable, he ceases to be an overbearing external force which constrains us from without, and becomes an internalized spiritual value or good, with the result that we are freed to grow towards that good rather than commanded to submit to the dictatorial will of a being who is perceived as being 'over against' us. Cupitt captures the essence of this liberating inward movement in characteristically crisp phrases: 'The "higher" God is the more inward God is, and the less we know of him the more he makes us grow spiritually.'[15]

Before proceeding any further with this attempt to account for the first major shift in Cupitt's position, it is as well to note that the progression which I have attempted to establish in Cupitt's thought is in keeping with the occasional hints which he has given regarding his own development. There is always a danger in the reconstruction of someone's thought that one will bring one's own preconceptions and prejudices to bear and produce an account of what one would have liked them to have thought, rather than of what they have *actually* thought. This is especially so when the reconstruction involves the effort to follow and bring into sharper focus particular threads and areas of thought which may – as in Cupitt's case – have been developed piecemeal (although logically enough), rather than in a more overtly systematic way. That Cupitt's use of the *via negativa* is at the heart of his journey from his early career to the position outlined in *Taking Leave of God* is confirmed, or at least given credence, by some of Cupitt's own remarks in the introductory chapter of *Taking Leave of God* in which he recounts the outline of his pilgrimage thus far:

> . . . over the years I have tried to combine belief in God with spiritual freedom by pressing the themes of the 'negative theology' and the divine transcendence ever harder. Eventually I was saying that God does not determine and cannot be thought of as determining the spiritual life from outside, for God is altogether unspecifiable. God had to become objectively thinner and thinner in order to allow subjective religiousness to expand. It is only one step further to the objectively atheous position here propounded.[16]

Thus fortified with Cupitt's own 'imprimatur', we can proceed to examine what is specifically new in the position espoused in *Taking Leave of God*.

Thus far this discussion has been confined to a group of ideas which Cupitt held for a number of years prior to 1980, among them the primacy of the negative way, the need for religious freedom, and the utter transcendence of God. During these earlier years there was no systematic development of these ideas and little overt discussion of the relationship between them. In *Taking Leave of God*, however, what was previously implicit becomes explicit and, as we have seen, a more coherent body of thought centred on the negative way emerges.

The major development in *Taking Leave of God*, therefore, was not so much a new thought or idea on Cupitt's part, but rather a realization of the implications of what he had thought for some time. Once the various strands came together their combined direction and implications became evident and Cupitt was led inexorably to follow these implications, to take the 'one step further' and to reach the 'objectively atheous position' to which he refers. This comes about through the recognition that God is not only unknowable in objective terms, but also that his objectivity itself is not religiously significant. No longer for Cupitt does religion depend upon the objectivity of God. The *via negativa* had always insisted that we can only know God in practical terms – through his effects upon us – and that 'God' was at least as much a regulative as a descriptive term, and Cupitt has simply pushed this emphasis to its extreme, but logical, conclusion. Provided that we acknowledge the regulative ideal enshrined in the word 'God' then it does not matter that we cannot know what stands behind it, or indeed whether *anything* stands behind it at all.

The result of all this is, briefly, the end of religious metaphysics. Cupitt remarks of the negative way that it was, 'at its best an attempt to inhibit the development of a metaphysical theology and to safeguard the primacy of religion',[17] and now in his own extreme application of it, the negative way has succeeded not only in inhibiting, but in forbidding the possibility of a metaphysical theology. What God is or might be in himself, and indeed the prior question of whether he exists at all, has no relevance to the religious life which is concerned only with the individual's voluntary acceptance of the 'religious requirement' which is symbolized by the word 'God'. Thus the question of God's existence, non-existence, or supposed modes of existence are, in religious terms, non-questions:

> There cannot be any religious interest in any supposed extra-religious reality of God, and I have argued all along that the religious requirement's authority is autonomous and does not depend upon any external imponent.[18]

Certainly Cupitt would argue for the end of metaphysics on a variety of other grounds connected with a late twentieth-century perception of 'reality' (not least the contribution of Nietzsche to the decentering of consciousness and the abolition of fixed or eternal values), as well as by invoking the *via negativa*, but the central place of the *via negativa* in this argument stems from the fact that through it Cupitt claims to establish that metaphysics and objectivity are not only not available to us any more, but are also not even necessary to authentic religion. Implicit within religion itself is the same destruction of metaphysics which is demanded by factors external to religion. Thus Cupitt can argue consistently against the charge of reductionism. His non-objective vision of religion is not merely a concession to outside pressures, but rather it is a position which, he maintains, is consistent with, and dictated by, the highest aspirations of religion itself. Voluntarist and non-objective religion is therefore no loss, but a gain, as religion becomes more 'purely religious' and less metaphysical. Religion, at last, becomes true to its own internal demands.


## II


The consequence of this 'end of metaphysics' in doctrinal terms is obvious, and this provides the second major new development in *Taking Leave of God*. Prior to 1980, Cupitt had certainly been critical of orthodoxy and had often sat somewhat loose to it in the interests of his own spiritual development, but he had never entirely dissociated himself from it or rejected the doctrinal content of faith *per se*. Individual doctrines and dogmas had been criticized for their spiritual or intellectual shortcomings, but the *idea* of a doctrinal and credal faith had never been seriously challenged in itself. Now, with the 'end of metaphysics' came a new dimension to Cupitt's radicalism – a conviction that doctrinal unorthodoxy was not only permissible but positively virtuous and entirely necessary. This was logically invitable. Once you have dispensed with metaphysics, with an objectively 'real' God, and with the notion that there are objectively 'real' eternal verities, then doctrine becomes devalued immediately. If there is no 'real' God about whom one can form beliefs, then such beliefs cease to be right or wrong, or even possible. Doctrine, as previously understood, becomes not only redundant but logically incoherent. Thus, by Cupitt's own admission, his voluntarist approach to religion is 'doctrinally very unorthodox'.[19] Traditional interpretations of the nature of God, the work of Christ, atonement and salvation are left behind, as are traditional understandings of such Christian activities as prayer and sacraments. Again, however, Cupitt would argue – reflecting the increasing frequency of references to Nietzsche in his work from this point onwards – that this is not loss, but gain. Religion is set free from dogmatism and rigid intellectualism which 'reduces religion to infantile dependence upon paternal authority telling us what to think and what to do',[20] and is enabled to become, as Cupitt would see it, more purely spiritual, more concerned with the 'specifically religious' dimension of life, and less concerned with a slavish toeing-the-line of obedience to, and right belief in, a transcendent despot.

Such a doctrinal relaxation represents a gain not only in terms of the internal workings of Christianity, but also in its relationships with other faiths. Christianity is no longer exclusive in its claims, and no longer feels obliged to defend the uniqueness of its relationship to God by exposing and denigrating the supposed shortcomings of other faiths. The way is opened to a new pluralism in religion in which Christianity becomes one religion among many, and freedom and openness become the guiding principles of the relationship between religions just as they do within Christianity itself:

> We already have such pluralism in art and in morality, and we accept that it is in those domains a good thing. Now is the time to accept that the same principles hold in the case of religion. The age of religious chauvinism and totalitarianism is over: let the age of religious free expression begin.[21]

This 'age of religious free expression' depends, as does the whole of Cupitt's position in *Taking Leave of God*, on a redefinition of what we mean by the word 'God'. We have seen something of this already in our examination of Cupitt's approach to metaphysics and his new-found freedom from the fetters of traditional doctrine. However, his retention of the concept of 'God' when all else might seem to be being abandoned, is extremely significant. It is, in large measure, his retention of 'God' – albeit under new management –

which enables him to maintain a claim to the label 'Christian'. One can think of a number of other modern intellectuals of a broadly humanist outlook for whom, as for Iris Murdoch, 'God' has become 'good', and who have therefore consciously and deliberately re-nounced all formal connection with Christianity. In contrast to such figures, Cupitt is not willing to let this happen, and 'God' remains. What does Cupitt understand by 'God' at this stage in his development, and what is his place in Cupitt's spiritual world?

Clearly, as we have seen already, God is no longer an objective being. It no longer makes any sense to speak of him as existing or acting as traditional religious language has done. So without metaphysics, what is God? Cupitt's answer is that God is an internalized concept. He is a bundle of values and ideals which express and symbolize our highest aspirations:

> God is the mythical embodiment of all that one is concerned with in the spiritual life. He is the religious demand and ideal, the pearl of great price and the enshriner of values.[22]

And, Cupitt adds: 'He is needed – but as a myth.'[23]

These are telling and revealing sentences. It is worth considering at least briefly why Cupitt needs God, and why, most particularly, he needs him as a myth. At a very basic level, Cupitt needs God – or at least the idea of him – to lend credence to his claim to be developing a distinctively Christian religious standpoint. It is only by retaining some of the traditional outward signs of Christianity that Cupitt can plausibly state that

> We have sought to describe . . . a modern and fully-autonomous spirituality, which may claim to be the legitimate successor of earlier Christian spiritualities.[24]

Secondly, and springing from this, Cupitt needs God in order to be able to maintain any semblance of continuity with traditional Christian language and practices. Again, God is necessary for Cupitt to be able to claim to 'speak of God and to pray to God'.[25]

Thirdly, God is necessary in order to provide a focus for, and to give shape to, our highest values and aspirations. That human beings do have such values and aspirations is indubitable, but being largely conceptual they are apt also to appear rather formless. God therefore performs the useful function of focussing these ideals in the perfection of a divinity to which we can all aspire. He provides, as it were, a 'non-objective objective correlative' – if such a thing makes any logical sense! – for our values and ideals.

There are, however, severe problems with God as thus under-stood, which are no less damaging to this concept of God than Cupitt's criticisms are to a more traditional idea of God. Thus if the traditional picture is vitiated by its being open to the charge of wish-fulfilment on a cosmic scale, then this alternative understanding of God would appear to be little more than a rather feeble pretence designed to provide a focus in an intrinsically focus-less universe. In arguing for a God such as this, Cupitt is in danger of 'saying the thing which is not',[26] and it might be more in keeping with the otherwise rigorous honesty of Cupitt's mind to admit that this particular emperor is not so much naked as non-existent. As it is, Cupitt's use of God reminds one more of a suit of clothes with no emperor inside them!

Such criticisms apart, however, Cupitt continues to need to speak of God for all the reasons which we have outlined. Equally clearly, it is just as important to Cupitt that God is confined to the realm of myth rather than that of objective reality. It is only as myth that God can make room for the degree of spiritual autonomy which Cupitt demands. We have noted previously his objections to the over-bearing and domineering nature of God as traditionally understood, and the only way in which God can answer these objections is by retiring obligingly to the world of myth.

In doing this God fulfils a second function. He not only makes room for spiritual freedom, but also answers what Cupitt calls the human 'need' for myth. He discusses the human need for story, and correctly observes that the religious life – and with it religious truth – 'must be expressed in story form',[27] and adds the significant rider that, 'religious stories are myths'.[28] As so often, one can see Cupitt's point, but one suspects a piece of deft sleight-of-hand on Cupitt's part. He is well aware, as are all theological writers, that like such terms as 'realism', 'myth' is a theologically loaded word and carries with it differing value-judgments depending upon one's fundamental religious outlook. As a technical term for a religious story it is unexceptionable, but in the context of Cupitt's argument in *Taking Leave of God* it is clear that the term has been freighted with all of Cupitt's own religious presuppositions, and that for him the realms of 'myth' and 'reality' do not touch except in a symbolic fashion. Given this outlook, the phrase 'religious stories are myths' says rather more than it would do if myth were used in its strictly technical sense. Technically what Cupitt says is true, and yet one must enter the caveat that when 'myth' is understood in Cupitt's sense then the phrase 'religious stories are myths' stands as a prime example of the false conversion of a non-convertible proposition. Certainly all myths may be stories, but that does not necessarily mean that all stories are myths in Cupitt's loaded sense of the term.

If we allow this development, however, we see that by the end of *Taking Leave of God*, God has become for Cupitt part of a myth – useful but fictional – and has been transformed from an objective being into a symbolic focus of the human religious and moral quest. This shift of emphasis from God's existence to his 'function' is something which Cupitt develops extensively during the succeeding few years, and which is related both to his demand for spiritual autonomy and to the relaxation of the dogmatic framework of Christianity which he advocates. It is important for the future, although not immediately, to note that by this stage God has become also a word rather than primarily a being, that is, his definition in linguistic terms rather than his existence determines what he can properly be said to 'be'.

Although there are by no means infrequent hints of this linguistic development of Cupitt's thought, nonetheless in the years immediately following *Taking Leave of God* Cupitt was largely content to expand upon the position developed in that book, and it was some time before he followed the implications of viewing God as a linguistic rather than an ontological entity. In *Only Human*, therefore, he concerns himself extensively with examining the function of God in his brave new theological world.

In doing this, Cupitt is quick to acknowledge a problem in this regard, namely that it may not be altogether easy to perceive the function of God in a religious world in which we are required to 'give up ontology':

> What job does the word do now? Is it just an expletive, is it used merely to add emphasis, or does it do something distinctive in shaping our practice?[29]

In other words, in a world which we have built, and upon which we impose our pattern of laws, values, rules and perceptions, what place is there for God, and what sense does it still make to speak of him? Once the objective framework of his existence and his creation and redemption of the world have been swept away, what role, if any, can he meaningfully be said to fulfil in the affairs of the human spirit?

Cupitt's answer to this is that God, as concept and symbol, remains important. He is simply transmuted from being into meaning:

> The objects of faith, such as God, are seen as guiding spiritual ideals that we live by, and not as beings. The very idea of an ontology is, in truth, one of the first things that critical thinking obliges us to give up. The world is not made of beings but of meanings, and religious meanings are purely practical.[30]

Defined in this way, God functions as an ideal, a focus of aspiration, a symbol of what humanity is striving to become. God is, in Cupitt's explicit definition in *The Sea of Faith*: '. . . the sum of our values, representing to us their ideal unity, their claims upon us and their creative power'.[31]

As God's function changes in this way, so too does doctrine. It becomes, like God himself, regulative not descriptive: it sets before us a picture, a set of values or a mode of being, and offers not an ontological and metaphysical account of reality, but a mythical, affective one which draws us towards the ideal by vision or story rather than by demanding our allegiance to itself as 'fact'. Thus armed with his new understanding of God, Cupitt can re-write, for example, the doctrine of creation:

... the truth is simply that God's creation of the world is a religious idea; that is, it is a mythic, archetypal, exemplary and inspiring model for our creating of our world ... The creation-myth in effect says, 'You can do it; here's how'; and the god functions as a guiding standard or norm.[32]

The same method of re-interpretation would equally well hold good for the other major doctrines of Christianity: they are all myths which function as the guiding ideals of the religious life. Clearly such a programme of doctrinal re-interpretation sits very comfortably alongside Cupitt's long-term preoccupation with the achievement of spiritual autonomy. Doctrines are no longer constricting external demands for allegiance, but internalized ideals expressed in mythical form which attract affectively rather than coerce intellectually or morally.

The major consequence of this is that spirituality replaces dogma as the primary characteristic of Christianity, and that Christianity is seen as being '... primarily a way, a path rather than a system of doctrines'.[33] In fairness it should be said that Christianity has – at least in its more enlightened moments – frequently seen itself in this light from its earliest days, and that therefore Cupitt's statement of this understanding of Christianity is not substantially new or original. What makes his position so thought-provoking is not so much its newness, but rather the implications which flow from this under-standing of Christianity as spirituality when it is combined with his post-metaphysical perception of the spiritual life.

The primary implication of such a position is that the onus is on us as far as the creation of any kind of spiritual or religious value is concerned. In a traditional approach, values can be seen as originating in God, and we participate in them by reflection or aspiration. The values are 'there' independently of us, and all we are required to do is to choose our response to them. Value, in traditional Christianity, is a 'given' of the religious life. Not so in Cupitt's religious world. It is a world emptied of all the reassurances of traditional Christianity, and emptied too of all intrinsic value. The world simply *is*, and we simply *are*, and neither has any meaning or value attached to it merely by virtue of its existence. If there is to be value in such a world, and in our human lives, then it is up to us to create it:

Put at its simplest, the task is to learn to practise religion just for its own sake, disinterestedly, and to become a creator rather than a passive recipient of religious meaning and value.[34]

This is the prime religious task of humanity, and its importance cannot be overestimated: 'A world in which people have become active creators of religious value is what I mean by the Kingdom of God.'[35]

Closely related to this task of the creation of value is the second implication of Cupitt's position, which is the nature of the value which is to be created. In his scale of values Cupitt puts a premium on freedom, which is at once a pre-condition of the creation of other values and itself a prime value. The end of metaphysics frees Christianity from spiritual oppression at the hands of both God, and, in his name, the church, and whatever spirituality emerges is therefore necessarily one in which autonomy is seen as a virtue. Indeed, Cupitt defines his task as being 'to argue that a certain spirituality and form of life are possible, desirable and liberating'.[36] By itself, however, this freedom, however intrinsically valuable, is not enough. It is, once realized, curiously content-less, and the question remains, 'Freedom to *what?*' Freedom remains the key, however, since Cupitt's answer is to look beyond *my* freedom and suggest that the highest value which human beings can create is that out of my own freedom I should seek *yours* also:

> ... the test of the presence of divine love in us must be how generously and disinterestedly we will the *other's* freedom with our own.[37]

So our spiritual life hinges on a paradox: that our freedom individually to create value and become most fully ourselves is dependent upon our willing that same freedom and self-realization for others, which may involve, of course, the voluntary limiting of our own freedom in the service of the higher good. There is a curious echo here, in humanist terms, of the paradox of our relationship with God expressed in terms of the Prayer Book collect, '... whose service is perfect freedom'. The principle remains the same; it is merely the object of the sentence which has changed, and our freedom is now most fully expressed in the service, not of God, but of our neighbour. Thus:

> Faith will become a free decision to follow the Christian path to holiness because it is recognized that the highest form of creative self-realization is, paradoxically, that of which selflessness makes us capable, and because it is seen that the practice of disinterested love is the highest basis for society and the best response to our mortality'.[38]

These related ideals of freedom, creativity and selflessness are among the fundamental values of Cupitt's spiritual world, and doctrine is retained only in so far as it functions 'to show us in condensed and symbolic form what this practical reality of religion is, and to guide us along its path'.[39]

Such an exaltation of spirituality over doctrine may be radical, and certainly entails a far from traditional or orthodox understanding of the nature of the spiritual life, but it is nonetheless entirely consistent with the general trend of Cupitt's thought. It is, in both *The World to Come* and *Only Human*, a logical extension of the position which Cupitt first outlined in *Taking Leave of God*. This high degree of consistency owes its existence, in large measure, to the fact that the thread which still continues to link all of Cupitt's thought together is the classical method of theology, the *via negativa*. We have discussed at some length the influence of this theological method on his thinking in the years leading up to *Taking Leave of God*, and it remains a vital factor in Cupitt's depiction of the spirituality of the 'age of religious free expression'. To do without doctrine, and to eschew the false certainties of a past age is, for Cupitt, an extension of the 'way of unknowing'[40] of the mediaeval mystics, and his spirituality of freedom is only possible in a faith which permanently struggles against the 'idolatry and superstition'[41] engendered by a theological realism which is centred around an anthropomorphic deity. Freedom and creativity of Cupitt's variety are only possible when everything else has been stripped away. The task of spirituality is to go on saying 'No' to every false consolation until the nihil is faced, for only then beyond this can the human spirit begin to say 'Yes' to *its own* freedom and creative power.

Cupitt's achievement, then, through these three closely related books, *Taking Leave of God, The World to Come* and *Only Human* is to have created a dogma-less, 'immetaphysical' (to coin a neater term than the more usual, though clumsy un-metaphysical) Christianity which is rooted in a spirituality of freedom and creativity, and to have done so largely by means of a radical but consistent use of one of the oldest methods of theology, the negative way. Pursued to its conclusions the negative way leads to the 'nihil' and Cupitt's spirituality flourishes on the farther side of it. Both God and doctrine are retained only in so far as they serve to inspire as an ideal and to act as a 'guiding norm' for the religious life; and both are interpreted in terms of function not ontology, and are consequently of a regulative rather than a descriptive nature. Cupitt would not deny the value of a religious approach to life, nor indeed the human need for a religious outlook. His basic contention, though, is that this is a freely-chosen response to the demand of an 'internal religious requirement' rather than a response to any extra-human metaphysical reality which makes demands upon us from outside. Human beings do seek a religious outlook and dimension to life, and Cupitt's Christianity offers a perspective which combines human autonomy with the security of a place in an established religious tradition. In an uncertain world, Cupitt's attraction lies in his ability to sustain and develop a vision of a religious life which offers both the security of community and continuity, and the freedom of creativity and individualism.

## III

Cupitt's development of an undogmatic, immetaphysical Christianity with its emphasis on spirituality and the practical nature of religion, represents the first major shift in his position, and it was substantially complete by the time he published *Only Human* in 1985.

It might be thought that one such far-reaching revision would be enough for most people, and that Cupitt might be content at this stage to rest awhile and merely enjoy the practice of his new 'Hyperborean faith'. The reality, however, is otherwise. We have already alluded to Cupitt's career as a spiritual journey or pilgrimage, and like all good pilgrims Cupitt is reluctant to remain too long in one place. No sooner has he arrived than he is already planning the next stage of his journey. And once again it is a tribute to Cupitt's integrity that this should be so; for just as his first major shift in *Taking Leave of God* was in large measure a working out of the necessary implications of his previous thought, so too the seeds of the second major shift in his position have already been planted in the process of completing the first. To have 'ceased from exploration' after *Only Human* would have been a denial of the restless, questioning spirit which had led him thus far, for alongside the consolidation and expansion of the position reached in *Taking Leave of God*, his next two books already begin to witness to a new strand in his thought which was inexorably to lead him onward once more.

The starting point for this next stage in Cupitt's development, then, is the simple but fundamental assertion that religion – in common with everything else which goes to make up our world – is a 'human construction'.[42] That is to say that we have made it, and that it is therefore necessarily located only inside the realm of the purely human. There is, and can be, no religious escape from this realm, since even the religion which has sometimes purported to be such an escape is as purely human as that from which it seeks to escape. There is, as Cupitt succinctly and frequently puts it, 'simply no outside'.

If this is the case, then traditional metaphysical, objective religion is clearly meaningless, since it puts forward the claim to have a referent outside itself, which we have already defined as being a logical impossibility. In this new perspective, therefore, religion must undergo a profound metamorphosis if it is to survive. As we have noted, Cupitt never denies a human religious need, but the question must be addressed: How is this need to be met, and what will the function of religion be in a world which is outside-less? What will be the factors and parameters which will determine the nature and function of religion? And it is in the answering of these questions that Cupitt takes the first steps on the next stage of his spiritual pilgrimage.

The two factors which, more than any others, determine the boundaries of the human realm of thought and action are history and language. Central to Cupitt's argument is the assertion that these constitute the human realm in its entirety, and that there is, 'no escape from history and language'.[43] At this stage in his career, Cupitt is not denying the possibility – or indeed necessarily the sense of – a realm beyond history and language, but merely saying that we can have no cognitive connection with it,[44] and that whatever there may be beyond our experience, it is impossible for us to speak meaningfully of it.[45] Later on he will go further in radicalizing his interpretation of the 'outsidelessness' of history and particularly of language, but for the present it is sufficient for him to say that for all practical purposes, religion included, these are all we have to work with and within.

The consequence of this is that both meaning and knowledge become public rather than private property. As participants in a world of language they lie on the surface of our communication with other people rather than belonging to a realm apart from the ordinary everyday human world and therefore beyond language:

> All meanings and all knowledge are established socially, in the public world. The belief that there can be inner, ineffable private knowledge of publicly-significant truths is nonsense: you cannot claim both public truth and private validation for the same belief.[46]

In such a world the function of religion changes drastically. Like everything else it is couched in, and bounded by the linguistic and historical framework of human life, and now that this is realized even within religion itself, it cannot coherently claim to offer any access to any other world. Its acceptance of the critical, self-conscious spirit of the age has turned it back in upon itself – back into this world. What then becomes of its 'truths' of salvation and sanctification, and its restless moral criticism of the here and now and its striving for a better order? Does religion lose its message along with its metaphysics, its redemption along with its realism?

Cupitt's answer, in varying modes of expression, is 'Not necessarily'. The stories, myths and ideals of a religion remain powerful even on a purely human level. Religion may not be able to lead us to an extra-human world, but it can lead us towards the good of a better human one. The dualism of the world below and heaven above may have been lost, but religion can still function with a dualism which contrasts 'the present age with an age to come'.[47] That Cupitt should have entitled a book *The World to Come* is a pointer to the importance of this new dualism, and in it he deftly delineates the character and function of religion in the making of a new world:

> No longer able to look up to a real supernatural world above, it instead projects the better world and the better self that it seeks forwards, as goals of ethical striving. The better world is not a world above but a world to come. Religious objects will thus be seen not as metaphysical beings above us, but as ideals or postulates which supply us with goals to inspire action and principles to guide it. It used to be thought that religious belief expresses a kind of picturesque metaphysics, but instead it must now be seen as offering a path to spiritual perfection to the individual and to the community . . . The demythologizing of the ancient religions and the breakdown of the old foundation of the moral order is leading us to a time when we will have to choose the new world, because no other possibility remains to us.[48]

We may be unable to escape this world, even with the help of religion, but we are still able to transform it – or at least to strive for transformation and have the ideal before us – and religion functions primarily as an aid to transformation in providing both ethical goals and ideals and, through its story of redemption, the hope that this secular and humanist redemption is an achievable goal which is worthy of our striving. Such is the place of religion in a human world bounded by the constraints of history and language.

The seeds of a new emphasis here are not so much to be found in the central idea of a religion which has no objective referents – no metaphysics – for, as we have seen, Cupitt had already reached this position in *Taking Leave of God*, and is merely developing and expanding this central thesis in *The World to Come*. Rather, the new element – the one which will become determinative for Cupitt's next major shift – is that of the primacy and inescapability of history and especially of language. He has begun to ask the question: 'If there is no longer an objective God who determines the nature of religion, then what is it that must determine and shape our response to life and with it our religious outlook?' And the answer is, increasingly, language; and this realization will in turn affect Cupitt's understanding of religion during the succeeding few years. The idea of *The World to Come* is an interim one in that it sets religion in the framework of language and sets out a possible future for religion in such a world, but it fails as yet to make any real integral and reciprocal connection between the two. Language and its inescapability is a constraint upon religion, but not yet a significant factor in determining its identity. In *The World to Come* language only shows religion its limitations by confining it to this world and the hope of its betterment; it does not yet contribute to determining the nature of religion from within, or help religion to understand how language can assist a purely human religion to achieve its salvific ends. It is these aspects concerned with the essential and inherent relationship between language and religion which will prove determinative for Cupitt during the succeeding years.

The centrality of language to this phase of Cupitt's development is made manifest in the Introduction to his next book, *Only Human*. In this Introduction the figure of Derrida is mentioned for the first (and by no means the last) time, and the notion of the inescapability of language is restated, and its implications stated, in a more uncompromising fashion than previously. Thus even as recently as *The World to Come* Cupitt had maintained the possibility of an 'Ineffable' beyond language, even though we could not imagine it, know it, or even speak coherently of it. Now, however, even this is denied, and there is no longer even the barest possibility of an 'outside':

> Once we have become fully conscious of our languages and other forms of symbolic communication as sign-systems through which everything thinkable or knowable is mediated, then we see that there can be no sense in the idea of transcending language . . . How can there be 'words' not themselves part of language, that we can use to state the relation of language to 'reality', or whatever it is that we naïvely imagine to stand beyond language? And when we grasp this we become dizzy, for we see for the first time that the human realm is now absolutely alone. There is no sense in the idea that there could be any guidelines or reference-points external to it that might help us to get it into perspective. That is why it is so hard to say what the human situation is: there is no

longer anything else with which to compare and contrast it. As in a late Beckett play, the world is just voices, talk, meanings, symbols.[49]

So, as he will insist on many occasions, humanity, language and communication is all there is: 'It is all social, and nothing but social.'[50] The implications of the inescapability of language are stated starkly enough indeed, but the gap still remains: language exercises a constraint upon the religious life, creating the conditions in which it must be lived, rather than becoming also a factor within the religious life itself which is able to determine its positive response to those conditions. Thus having delineated his new world in *Only Human*, Cupitt, asking the question, 'What religious response can we make?' can only answer:

> ... there is absolutely no alternative now but to identify this human world of ours with the religiously satisfactory world, to love it and to strive to realize ethical and spiritual values in the here and now.[51]

Having posed the question for religion, language has as yet no part to play in formulating the answer. It is to the fusion of religion and language in this way that Cupitt next addresses himself, and which constitutes the essence of the second major shift in his position.

IV

For such a fusion of religion and language to take place, there is one fundamental pre-condition which must be met. Language has to become not merely functionally but ontologically primary in our understanding of ourselves and our world. That is, language has to move from merely exercising an *a priori* external constraint – however great – upon our perceptions, aspirations and ideals, to being internally constitutive of them: being, in other words, constitutive of their meaning and message. If language in this way 'creates' the world, rather than merely restricts what can and cannot be said of it, then language will be able in turn to become a creative factor in our response to that world at a religious as well as at a merely functional level.

This change in the status of language takes place in Cupitt's work from *The Long-Legged Fly* onwards. In this new group of books he acknowledges not only, as he has done before, the inescapability of language and its all-inclusiveness, but also its position as, in a very real sense, the 'creator' of the human realm. It thus acquires a new status as being ontologically prior to all else within that realm. This perception of language is at the heart of Cupitt's thinking from now on, and the thought of each new book consistently takes it as a starting point. Thus, in the Introduction to *The New Christian Ethics* he can write:

> In all modern philosophies of language, the sign and structures, it is generally accepted that the world is just the human world, that this human world of ours is a communications network, and that it is constituted within and by language,[52]

an understanding which is put even more succinctly in *The Long-Legged Fly*, in which he tells us that '. . . we are *constituted* by the world of signs in which we are immersed'.[53]

It is this new assessment of language as constituting both ourselves and our world which enables Cupitt to close the gap between religion and language which we noted earlier. Language, when it has become this powerful and all-embracing, effectively fills the space vacated by God, who has ceased to be a being, and become, with a certain pleasing and apposite irony, simply a word!

Just as God, conceived of as a being, used to determine the nature of religion, now language is able to do so. Language, in Cupitt's new understanding of it, is now powerful enough not only to set the conditions for religion, but also to contribute to religion's response to those conditions. Religion ceases to be externally constrained by language, and becomes instead simply a part of the whole world of language, with the result that language itself creates a new potential within religion and opens up new religious possibilities. Thus the gap between religion and language is now closed, and religion takes its place alongside all other human activities within the determining realm of language.

This understanding of the relationship between religion and language is central to the further development of Cupitt's thought. By itself, however, it represents a somewhat barren statement of 'the way things are' – or at least, are perceived to be. Such a statement of 'how things are' is essential to the task of investigating and establishing what may be the nature of religion in a language-dominated world, but although it places religion firmly within the world of language, it does not by itself address the question of how religion is itself moulded and shaped by its place within that world. To discern the shape and contours of the religious life in a world constituted by language is Cupitt's main concern in the years following *The Long-Legged Fly*.

What, then, are the implications for the religious life of the ontological primacy of language? Perhaps the most obvious such implication springs from the 'horizontalness' of language; the fact that language refers everything back to itself and has – in modern linguistic theory – no possibility of reference to anything outside itself. Language refers only horizontally, to more language, and not vertically to a world beyond language, and thus language itself constitutes the boundaries of the real: 'The surface play of phenomena – words, signs, meanings, appearances – *is* reality'.[54] The only world available to humanity, and therefore to religion, is this world, the world which we create in and through language; and this, Cupitt maintains, actually opens up new and creative religious possibilities, since because it is through language that we 'create' our world, it is also through language that we can 're-create' it and invest it with new values. Traditional religious language is ostensibly vertical in its meaning, at least in part; but Cupitt argues that:

> . . . after the linguistic revolution the philosophy of signs shows us that the meaning of religious language is – and always was – to be understood in terms of its horizontal outworking.[55]

If this is coupled with the contention that our world, and indeed we ourselves, are only imbued with meaning in so far as we impart it ourselves through what Cupitt calls our 'evolving discourse about them',[56] then it can be argued that the horizontalness of religious language imparts the potential for a new and creative valuation of human life and endeavour. The values and qualities imputed to God can now be predicated of human life, in its potential even if not in its actuality: the striving of the human spirit for oneness with God can now be interpreted as a striving for a new oneness of humanity, and the self-offering of the believer to God can now be seen as the self-offering of the individual in the service of the community. Thus the horizontalness of language challenges us afresh to impart new values to this life, to cherish it as being all we have, and to strive to refine existing values and create new ones within it. The paradigm for this creation of value and the radical revaluation of human life is to be found in the life of Jesus. Read horizontally, as it were, the life of Jesus is seen as one dedicated to self-giving on behalf of others, and to the radical transformation of values through his attitudes to the poor, the sick, the sinners and the outcasts:

> By daring to give religious value not merely to the poor and outcast but even to the wicked, he began the critique of value. Thereby he opened up a programme of religious action that will never be completed, for it requires a perpetual scrutiny of received evaluations and an effort to create ever new ones.[57]

This critique of existing values and the creation of new ones is at the heart of the religious life, and it is fuelled and given impetus precisely by the horizontalness of language which turns religious language back to this world and focusses its aspirations on the here and now rather than on a world above, or even, in contrast to the Cupitt of only a few years previously, a world to come.

A second consequence of the primacy of language flows as a direct corollary of this horizontalness and the turning of religious vision and striving back to this world. It is that according to this vision Christianity is now at last able to become what it has always been striving to become, a religion of incarnation and salvation; and human beings are able similarly to fulfil their potential, a fulfilment previously denied them by the restrictive slave-mentality of traditional Christianity with its hierarchy of power culminating in an objective and all-powerful God.

Previously, Christianity has been beset by a fatal paradox. On the one hand it claimed to be a religion of incarnation, of God becoming man, of the divine becoming one with humankind; and yet, on the other hand, it maintained an absolute disjunction between God and man, such that even the God-man Jesus was always pictured in an attitude of subservience to his all-powerful Father.

The realization that religious language, like all other language, must be interpreted horizontally, has resolved this paradox. If 'God' is merely a metaphor for the ideal of human striving, then God has at last become fully humanized, fully incarnated, and the vast gulf between the divine and the human has been bridged. Christianity has achieved its 'fundamental task' of 'uniting the divine and the human and has thereby mediated salvation'.[58] This salvation consists in the ability of human beings to 'see life as it is', that is, as this-worldly, horizontal and purely contingent, and say 'Yes to it'.[59] Humanity is at once redeemed from its alienation from God and from its alienation from the world. Previously humanity lived in a state of uncomfortable suspension between the two. Now, language with its entirely horizontal perspective has returned us to this world and enabled us to see it and accept it for what it is. Language has become the instrument both of incarnation, and, consequently, of salvation.

Just as the second implication of the primacy of language – human salvation and autonomous responsibility – flows from the first, which was the potential for the creation of value, so too this new found autonomy and responsibility for meaning and value provide the impetus for the third major effect of language upon religion: its consequences for ethics and aesthetics. In the new language-dominated religious world these two are intimately connected, aesthetic activity being at once a good in itself, and a vehicle for the creation of other and more strictly ethical goods.

Even prior to any such connection with aesthetics, however, the world of language is charged with a new ethical potential. Cupitt argues that the traditional religious world dealt with 'immortal souls' and eternal and unchangeable verities, and that this world view is largely inimical to the possibility of change or of real ethical striving involving a revaluation of the world. For traditional religion, the good (defined as those who believe) are saved, the wicked are condemned, and there is no means of re-evaluating that which has been decreed from all eternity. Clearly Cupitt can be accused here, as so often, of caricaturing traditional Christianity, but still one feels the justice of his criticisms when one considers the moral self-righteousness of so much of Christian history which has condemned rather than attempted to save the lost, and the social self-satisfaction of comfortable Christianity which has willingly acquiesced in, and indeed supported, a theology of 'The rich man in his castle/The poor man at his gate', without attempting to change a set of values which reinforces its own smugness.

By contrast to this fixed unchanging world of immortal souls and eternal decrees, the shifting, changing human world of language can actually be seen as a world with more potential for ethical striving and deep-rooted change. Language is the means by which we interpret and describe the world, and our descriptions are the bearers of our values: they at once express the values we hold, *and* at the same time reinforce them. And our language influences the way we act. There is no absolute distinction to be drawn between words and deeds. Thus, just as it may be the bearer and reinforcer of current attitudes and values, so too language may also be the means through which these attitudes and values can be radically changed, and through which, thereby, we actually come to act in a different and more ethical fashion. In the course of outlining how an authentic Christianity is all about a radical ethical revaluation of the human world, Cupitt describes the process with characteristic brevity:

> We change reality by redescribing it. How? – Because description always involves metaphors and evaluations. When we redescribe reality we change the metaphors under which it is viewed, and therefore we change the relative values of things. This revaluation then influences the way we act.[60]

Thus language, in its inherent potential for change, as well as in its horizontalness, contributes directly to the possibility of a new – or at least renewed – ethical urgency in Christianity.

The function of language in producing a religious life which is ethically creative is readily extendable to the concept that such a life is, in turn, itself an aesthetic creation. Just as language is the medium of the aesthetic creativity of literature, for example, so too the ever-changing language-in-action of ethical and religious striving can be the medium for the creation of the aesthetically pleasing life. My life can be viewed as the ongoing, ever-changing and never completed production of a work of art, which is open to be judged, as art may be, not only by its 'beauty' but also by its utility, by the values which it shows forth, and by the benefit or good which others derive from it.

Our ability to see life in this way – and indeed the necessity of doing so – derives from the autonomy and horizontal nature of our lives in which, through language, we are the creators and arbiters of value and meaning. Again we are, in Cupitt's view, committed to giving up fixed essences and 'thinking in terms of a compulsory, permanent, extra-mental Truth of things', and to admitting that there is only 'our own ever-changing historical production'.[61] Our commitment to this has, of necessity, to be rather like that of an artist to his work – total, whilst yet recognizing the contingency of all that we are and do. Thus:

> ... the religion I make up for myself, my personal Christian-life-project, can be evaluated aesthetically ... like a work of literature, my Christian-life-project can be contextualized within the tradition to which it belongs, and against that background it can be judged aesthetically.[62]

The religious life, therefore, is one which is 'grateful to art',[63] and within which the life of the religious community as well as that of the individuals within it can be seen as one which is largely, though not exclusively, devoted to an aesthetic and creative understanding of itself.[64] 'Religion as art' is the culmination of Cupitt's endeavour to close the gap between religion and language. Language is no longer merely determinative for religion, no longer merely the framework which sets out the terms of a religious response to life and dictates the limits of the possible. Between religion and language a two-way process of osmosis has taken place. Religion is constituted within the world of language, and our understanding of language is trans-formed to render it no longer a constraint upon, but rather a positively enriching factor *within* our religious response to life. Language, in all its horizontalness, plasticity and shifting uncertainty at once goads and inspires the human spirit to a new religious awareness – of transience, of freedom, of responsibility both ethical and aesthetic. The creative potential ascribed to the divine has been radically humanized, and in the now overtly horizontal world of language humanity is able to achieve an autonomy and dignity – indeed a 'salvation' – which vertical understandings of religious language had, often covertly, conspired to deny it.

This fusion of religion and language represents the conclusion of the second major shift in Cupitt's position, and with it the movement of thought which began in *The World to Come* and *Only Human* is substantially completed. The position here outlined forms a consistent development of the position delineated earlier as characteristic of *Taking Leave of God*. The first major shift, represented in this book, was simply towards an immetaphysical and undogmatic religion concerned solely with this world, and in which the old objective entities such as God functioned solely as practical guiding ideals and norms for the religious life. In his second shift Cupitt goes an important step further, and religion is not only rooted firmly in this world, but it is also intrinsically bound up with the way this world is, and the way in which it comes to be what it is: that is, primarily a linguistic world in which communication across the flux of change is all there is for us. Language has become not merely determinative for, but constitutive of religion.

There is, however, one other effect of language to add to those discussed above, which introduces a curious, because unnoticed irony into Cupitt's discussion. In the position outlined in *Taking Leave of God*, God as the objective focus of religion had disappeared, and religion simply had to face the void, return to this world, and get along without him as best it might. In Cupitt's later work, however, language replaces God as the prime ontological reality. It sets the terms of our existence and provides (through creativity) the means to cope with it. There is thus a sense in which language now stands where God did, in that it lays down the rules and also provides the means of response – which, if one felt mischievous, one might argue was quite a good definition of divine grace!!

Such an echo of traditionalism aside, however, Cupitt has, in his later work, developed an understanding of religion which, though it is rooted in his own earlier work, is substantially new. In *The Long-*

*Legged Fly* and *The New Christian Ethics* he argues for a voluntarist, creative, aesthetic and linguistically oriented approach to faith, and in *Radicals and the Future of the Church* he examines in some detail the implications of this understanding of religion both for individuals and for the corporate life of the church as a community of faith. In these three books he has produced an important contribution to the church's never-ending task of self-criticism of, and reflection on, both its theology and practice.

V

Cupitt's most recent thinking does not fundamentally alter his position in any major respect: it simply fills out the picture somewhat by following his new lines of thought to their logical conclusions, although it will be seen that Cupitt himself seems to admit that this in itself opens up new potential for further developments in the future.

In his most recent three books, *Creation out of Nothing, What is a Story?* and *The Time Being*, the realm of language – and with it aesthetics – moves towards being subsumed in the wider and more overarching concept of 'story'. Admittedly Cupitt had expressed interest in narrative, and especially in the narrative shape of human life, in many earlier works, but here, in his most recent thinking, the importance of story is greatly enhanced. Language remains important as providing the building blocks of story, but Cupitt increasingly recognizes that we communicate not so much through language *per se*, but through language which is built and crafted into story. Story rather than language becomes the prime medium of human communication. Such a development is consistent with Cupitt's earlier thinking, in that it fuses the twin axes of language and history, the importance of which, as the major parameters of human life and religion, was what initially drew Cupitt to move onward from the position reached in *Taking Leave of God*. Put at its simplest, if you employ language in the service of history, or put a history into language, then you have a narrative, a story. This primacy of story even over language in terms of human communication is already implicit in *Creation out of Nothing*, in which it is language which creates the 'story' of creation, but it is made explicit in *What is a Story?*:

> We can now descry the sense in which a human being is entirely culturally-formed, and made of stories all the way through. We can gain access to our brains and our biological feelings only through language. But in language our feelings are already represented as ordered into 'melodies' – meaningful sequences, or sentence-shapes. And the sentence-form is already narrative and expressive. So a human being can live only within an order of meanings; that is, a human being is always already busy constructing life as a story.[65]

For the most part, this new appreciation of the place of story at the heart of human life does not materially alter Cupitt's horizontal and voluntarist and aesthetically creative approach to religion – indeed at many points it emphasizes the aesthetic aspects of the religious life by reinforcing the connection between life and art. There is, however, as was noted above, one implication flowing from the primacy of story which opens up a further possibility of future development, especially when one is dealing with a mind as committed to pilgrimage as Cupitt's – although in what direction this will lead him presumably only Cupitt can tell!

Cupitt has long held that language is outsideless and that therefore there is no place in religion for the idea of the transcendent – such a concept is quite literally unthinkable. We cannot, through language, think about a concept which is supposed to lie beyond language. With the increased emphasis on story, however, the scenario changes slightly, in that story opens up possibilities which language *per se* cannot. A story *can* point us outside itself – it can posit the existence of, and point us towards another realm. It can tell us of other times and other places, and it can even presume to speak of the transcendent and point us towards that, at least in imagination. Admittedly we shall never get there, never grasp the transcendent, because of the paradox that even while it is speaking of the transcendent, a story is still using language which, Cupitt has already established, cannot be escaped from. He expresses the paradox deftly:

... what we are trying to escape to is supposed to be a non-narrative realm of timeless, changeless silence and emptiness – but stories of escape are still stories. You can't narrate yourself out of the world of narrative. Wherever you narrate yourself to is thereby incorporated within the world of stories.[66]

In spite of this, however, there is still room once more, through the medium of story, for the idea of the transcendent, albeit only as a myth. And as a myth it now becomes important once again in Cupitt's thought. It is important because through it we are inspired and given a vision – however fleeting – which enables us to return to the 'real' world and live and act in it with more love, conviction, vitality and commitment. Our glimpse of such a vision and return to the world of everyday is 'a dual movement of the spirit that we need to keep on making'.[67] Indeed, Cupitt goes further than this, and calls the quest for the transcendent a '*felix culpa*, a happy fault, a life-enhancing mistake that we need to keep on making'.[68] Religion needs this yearning after the transcendent in order fully to be able to love this world and to love humanity. Again there is a delightful irony in the fact that religion needs the inspiration of a fiction in order to turn with any zeal or commitment to the world of everyday. It will be extremely interesting to see what use Cupitt will make of this re-introduced and newly important 'myth of transcendence' in the future.

Finally, there is a similar irony in Cupitt's closing statement of his position in *What is a Story?*, for once again, while he does not depart from his central thesis of the outsideless, fragmentary, fictitious and purely communicative two-dimensional nature of our world, there is nonetheless an acknowledgment that the mere statement that our world is such a world is, in a partial sense at least, self-refuting. For to say that 'such-and-such is the case' demands a more comprehensive, omniscient and all-embracing vision than the world as thus defined allows to be possible. Thus Cupitt is consistent in his vision of the world:

... we will accept that our life is no more than a bundle of stories, mostly half-finished. Our makebelief will be a fictioned belief that, nevertheless, our life still matters, fragmentary and fictitious though it is. We'll have to produce from nowhere, and just by spinning stories, the conviction that our life is worth living.[69]

Yet at the same time he acknowledges that this is itself a statement about our life which is of the same status – epistemologically speaking – as any other foundational statement about life, including the kind of religious master-narrative which he himself has so long denied and resisted. As he says:

> ... now we can perhaps finally admit that we have after all presented a new master-narrative. It could not be avoided. We found we had lost all the old master-narratives and were now continuously improvising, retelling, embroidering, making it up as we go along. But in relating all this we found that not to have a master-narrative is also still to have one.[70]

Such a statement, coupled with the renewed importance of the transcendent – even as a myth or a fiction – opens up rich possibilities for the future. One cannot predict what Cupitt may say or think next, but one may simply note that it is interesting that out of all Cupitt's wrestling with the shortcomings of orthodox religion, and his persistent forging of new positions consonant with the mainstream of modern thought in a variety of disciplines, he has in his most recent work outlined a perception of both life and religion as primarily constituted by, and understood through story – an idea which might well leave the authors of most of the Old Testament feeling surprisingly and strangely at home in the late twentieth century!

In spite of these by now rather unnerving echoes of former days produced by the internal ironies and paradoxes of Cupitt's position, it remains true that whatever its future development, Cupitt's current standpoint is a long way from any orthodox, traditional understanding of Christianity. It is, however, within its own terms, a remarkably 'systematic' and coherent view of religion. Religion is yoked to story and language as it was once yoked to God, and a potential framework for the religious life has been created. It remains now to ask two related questions. Firstly, is Cupitt's sustained exposée of the shortcomings of orthodoxy as damning and damaging as he believes, such that we *must* abandon objectivity, metaphysics and a 'personal' God? And secondly, are his alternatives to such a view of Christianity as satisfying and adequate, both intellectually and religiously, as he maintains?

# Part Two

# Realism and Anti-Realism

# 4

# The Case against Realism

Cupitt's radicalism has been greeted for the most part, as was noted in the Introduction, either by silence or by direct refutation. Neither of these responses does justice either to the quality and persuasiveness of Cupitt's thought and writing, or to the seriousness of the task with which he is engaged. This task is nothing less than the rescue of religion from the clutches of obsolescence, ineffectiveness and inadequacy, and the church can hardly deny the need for such a rescue, even if it is unhappy about the means by which Cupitt proposes to effect it.

For Cupitt, in his increasingly outspoken way, diagnoses and attempts to prescribe a remedy for a very real malaise in the life of the church; and all too frequently those of his critics who have rejected the prescribed therapy have rejected the diagnosis also. But it is far from certain that this diagnosis is as inaccurate as either Cupitt's critics or the church at large would like to believe. Cupitt is an academic, but his books and articles are not intended to remain within the confines of the study and the library, or merely to provide the material for endless seminars. He writes for a purpose, and in the consciousness of a real church 'out there' whose concerns he is addressing. That church, he argues, is passing through a critical period in its history; a period which demands of it some radical changes in both thought and practice if it is not to suffer the fate of the dinosaurs and perish in a climate to which it has failed to adapt.

Cupitt is not alone in portraying a church in crisis, and one does not have to look very far to acknowledge the force of this judgment. Throughout the majority of the Western world at least, the church has been pushed increasingly towards the sidelines and become a marginal factor in society. Overall attendance figures, although they seem to have 'bottomed out' recently, have fallen consistently for many years, and the attitude of those outside the church is characterized either by indifference or by ridicule. At best the church is just another 'club', and at worst it is an anachronism which manages to be at once pernicious *and* irrelevant to the business of twentieth-century living.

With such an attitude abroad, it is hardly surprising that there is a lack of confidence and a sense that all is not well within the church also. There are a variety of divisions on matters both of morality and church order, and a widespread sense that the church is increasingly losing touch with reality, both in terms of its structures and organization, and in its teaching and practice.[1] The world of the church is becoming ever more escapist; a fact which may be viewed with relief or exasperation according to temperament. The church offers either a blessed escape back into the lost certainties of childhood, or the spectacle of potential and resources squandered in the effort to prop up these same illusory certainties. If the church is laughably irrelevant when seen from the outside, it is culpably so when judged from within.[2]

The ultimate irony of the church's marginal and ineffective position – an irony which graphically underlines the church's own degree of responsibility for its troubles – is that it should have happened at a time when interest in 'religion' *per se* is on the increase. The church – to use an economic parallel – is not a casualty of a general depression in its market area. Religious book publishing and interest in religious movements of all kinds is booming, especially among the more fundamentalist sects whose authoritarian outlook and assertions of moral and spiritual certainties and absolutes appear to have a strong attraction for many people in an otherwise uncertain and rapidly changing age. The organized church, indeed, stands out as an unique casualty in such a climate. That this should be so lends credence to Cupitt's diagnosis of a fundamental malaise within the church, and also to his insistence on the importance of the 'purely religious'. One can sympathize with his feeling that the organized institutional and doctrinal face of the church should be earmarked for sacrifice in the interests of religion.

More specifically, Cupitt identifies a number of areas in which the malaise is at its most destructive. These are, briefly, the moral failings of Christianity, both in doctrinal and personal terms; its disparaging attitude towards the here and now; its backwardness and repressiveness; and its use of over-anthropomorphic imagery with an inbuilt tendency to degenerate into idolatry.

These four areas (all of which have been examined in some detail in the previous chapters) by no means exhaust Cupitt's catalogue of the failings of traditional Christianity. To them could be added the charges of unfaithfulness to scripture and to the person of Jesus, a consistent abuse of power, both spiritual and material, and many more. They are relevant not because Cupitt is unfailingly accurate in his analysis and presentation of the church's failings, but because collectively they indicate that his conviction of a fundamental malaise in the church is founded on something more solid than merely personal prejudice or a gratuitous desire to shock the establishment. On the contrary, his criticisms are painful precisely because they are, for the most part, well-founded. Many of the failings which he identifies are visibly present in the life of the church, and represent a serious threat to its continuing health in both the practical and the theological realms. Already the church is regarded by many people as coming into the same category as Linus' security blanket, providing a haven, however illusory, in the midst of shifting and uncertain reality, and there is a very real element in the church which would welcome a return to an ultra-doctrinaire fundamentalism, a fundamentalism which would bring new vigour to the obscurantism which, as Cupitt observes, has been the church's consistent response to intellectual progress.

Thus the criticisms which Cupitt makes of orthodoxy, and the questions which he raises regarding its ability successfully to overcome them, need to be faced and addressed realistically. His portrait of the church, while not a flattering one, is too close a likeness for the church to be able to ignore it or dismiss it. If the cogency of his criticism is once admitted then, for Cupitt, the central and pressing question becomes that of the viability of traditional realism in Christianity. It is this insistence on a 'realist' under-standing of faith which is responsible for many of the most serious failings which Cupitt has delineated, and as a result there looms the very real question: Is a realist interpretation of Christianity able any longer to do justice to our understanding of ourselves and our world, and to meet the religious and spiritual needs of the late twentieth century?

## II

Cupitt's answer is unequivocal. Realism must go, for it is precisely the insistence of Christianity on realism which has created the problems which the church faces. It is realism which is responsible for the moral dubiety of the Christian story, and for the moral inertia which it creates in the believer, and it is realism too which is responsible for the backward, repressive, grossly anthropomorphic and world-denying aspects of Christianity. It is responsible for these problems, and it is also incapable of solving them for two basic reasons: firstly, it does not sufficiently recognize or allow for certain values which, Cupitt says, are constitutive of true religion; and secondly it fails to take account of the fundamental nature of the human realm as linguistic and relativistic.

First, then, there are – as we have seen in the previous chapters – certain values which, Cupitt maintains, are essential to the living of a responsible, moral and mature human life. Of these, the most basic and vital is that of freedom. Freedom is, Cupitt observes, a necessary pre-condition of goodness,[3] and therefore also of moral growth and maturity, and such freedom is, he claims, not available within a realist understanding of religion. Realism is inimical both to 'pure' spirituality, untainted either by fear of punishment or hope of reward, and to genuine moral striving and progress in virtue pursued for its own sake. The presence of a 'real' God in religion fosters the development of a self-seeking spirituality, and a passive morality, neither of which is compatible with the kind of freedom which Cupitt has posited as the fundamental religious value.

This complex of values, centred on an autonomy which *demands* the rejection of realism is one of Cupitt's two major weapons in his assault on orthodoxy. The other is relativism coupled with linguistic theory, which, by a clever theological pincer-movement, completes the demolition of realism by the simple process of ruling it out as being neither enlightening nor even intelligible. In a world in which all human knowledge and experience – including religious knowledge and experience – are perceived as culturally conditioned and historically relative, the idea of any fixed objective religious realm begins to look increasingly improbable, and certainly the possibility of gaining access to, or understanding of such a realm (even if it were to exist) becomes a logically incoherent notion.

Even by itself this argument was compelling enough to lead Cupitt as far as the rejection of realism, but its force is vastly increased if Cupitt's use of the insights of recent philosophy (especially French) into the nature of human language and knowledge are taken fully into account. This linguistic philosophy, pioneered by such figures as Derrida, Lacan and Foucault, is important as far as Cupitt is concerned precisely in its insistence on the inescapability of language and its self-referential character from which this inescapability derives. Thus language always refers to more language:

> Look up a word in a dictionary. There you find that its origin, its history and its various uses and meanings are all explained in terms of other words. Some of these may be unfamiliar to you, so you go on to look them up as well – and soon you find yourself browsing, wandering back and forth through the book indefinitely. One word leads to another, and so on forever . . . The dictionary's world is self-contained.[4]

This is a fundamental challenge to traditional philosophy, and therefore to theology. The traditional starting point for philosophy has been 'Being' or 'Matter' or some such concrete entity. Now, it is argued, the 'true universal stuff, in which and of which everything else is constructed, is the sign and communication',[5] and this carries with it, as Cupitt deftly illustrates with his example of two people looking up at the night sky and seeing two entirely different things, the surprising and threatening corollary that:

> . . . there is no objectivity and nothing is *there* until the spectator has interpreted what she has seen in terms of a theory and has expressed herself in language. So objectivity enters only with language . . . Objectivity is given in and with language; it is not, as

realists suppose, something external to language around which language wraps itself.[6]

Language then is the prime reality. It does not, as was almost universally previously supposed, mirror some objective external reality, but rather it is the medium through which that reality is created. Without it there is only an undifferentiated and meaningless flux, and this only takes shape and meaningful form when it is interpreted and communicated through the agency of language. Communication then, elusive and ever changing, is the appropriately evanescent medium of our transient existence, rather than any more apparently stable entity such as matter or being, and clearly this will, if it is once accepted, have potentially radical implications for one's assessment of the validity of realism in religion.

This is by no means the first language-based attack upon religious realism, and indeed, in its questioning of the traditional understanding of the relationship between language and 'reality', modern linguistic philosophy has been compared by some critics to various species of empiricism and most particularly to logical positivism in a new dress. Thus Scott Cowdell can speak of Cupitt's 'quasi-positivistic limiting of the range of admissible evidence for theological reflection'.[7] More pertinently, David L. Edwards recognizes both a resemblance and a distinction. He remarks that: 'As a revolt against the tendency to classify everything in a pattern imposed by religion, metaphysics, Marxism or existentialism ... [French deconstructionism] may be regarded as the Parisian equivalent of English empiricism',[8] but he qualifies this with the vital observation that '... whereas the empiricists have tended to assume that things are real, the deconstructionists come nearer to the "idealists" in their rejection of that common sense'.[9] The qualification is important, for whatever the superficial resemblances may be, it is precisely in its points of difference from logical positivism that modern linguistic philosophy derives its strength and proves hardest to overturn.

The viability of logical positivism depended to a marked extent on the acceptance of the verification principle. This principle has many times been shown to be unworkable, not least by Keith Ward,[10] and it was largely its collapse as an underlying principle of the system which led Sir Alfred Ayer to make his celebrated remark in an interview with Brian Magee that the most important defect of logical positivism was that, 'nearly all of it was false'.[11] In contrast, deconstruction, at least as it is interpreted by Cupitt, does not depend on any such principle for its intellectual underpinning. Rather, it takes its stand on certain *a priori* axioms about the nature of language itself, and its relationship not to reality, but primarily to knowledge, and therefore to what is knowable and communicable. Thus we can only *know* what we are able to articulate in language; there is no thought or knowledge outside of language. As a result it is, by definition, impossible for us to step outside language and conceive, in any meaningful way, of any realm beyond it. The question of the existence of any such realm is thus neatly sidestepped – whether it may exist or not is immaterial (though it probably cannot), but what is certain is that we are completely incapable of conceiving of it or relating to it in any meaningful way. Any other realm than this present language-dominated one therefore becomes at once irrelevant to us and logically and linguistically nonsensical. It is simply a non-concept.

Cupitt's use of deconstructionist ideas therefore differs substantially from logical positivism in its understanding of the relationship between language and reality. Logical positivism took as its basis the empirical world, and language only made sense in so far as it referred to it and could be *shown* to do so. Reality came first and language second. Deconstruction turns this relationship upside-down. Language is now the starting point and 'reality' only makes sense in so far as it refers to language and can be shown to do so. 'Reality' is what can be conceived linguistically. Language now comes first and reality second. Deconstruction, as a result, is much harder to falsify than logical positivism ever was. Positivism could be falsified by disrupting the supposed relationship between reality and language, showing it to be misguided. Deconstruction starts from the principle that we are encapsulated within language, and cannot think or know anything outside it, and there is therefore no escape route by which it can readily be falsified. As Cupitt remarks with an almost indecent glee: '. . . if you don't like my idea of the ubiquity of language, would you please for the sake of consistency step forward and state your objection in some medium *other* than language?"[12] Rather like a rolled up armadillo, there is no obvious point of entry to the linguistic circle: the fact that we cannot criticize the ubiquity of language in a medium other than language merely reinforces its ubiquity! In a way that logical positivism was never able to be, deconstruction is well-equipped to challenge theological realism and also realism *per se* – for what is 'real' is simply whatever is expressed in language. From this perspective language is logically and ontologically prior to reality and what we call 'reality' is created through language. Cupitt's position is therefore antipathetic to every manifestation of realism in philosophy and science as well as in theology.

Between them then, the complex of values centred on freedom, and the modern understanding of relativism and language present a weighty and cumulative challenge to realism in all its forms and especially in religion. It is accused of being inimical to the modern quest for autonomy, and inadequate in its pre-critical understanding of man's knowledge of himself and his world. The justice of these charges, and the potential of realism to respond to them, will be examined in the following chapters; but given the weight which Cupitt attaches to them, and the cogency with which they are related in his thought, it is small wonder that in his search for religious fulfilment he should have sought an alternative path to that of realism.

## III

Clearly, any understanding of religion which is not 'realist' must, by definition, be 'un-realist' or 'anti-realist', and this would be true of all of Cupitt's thinking since *Taking Leave of God*. However, as was remarked in the previous chapters, Cupitt is not a thinker who stands still for long, and one may therefore, as he himself does, attach a wide variety of labels to his various positions since then. These labels have included 'voluntarism', 'fictionalism', 'constructive theology', and, in his most recent books, 'expressionism'. Each of these positions builds on the earlier ones, and therefore it is sufficient here to concentrate on the more recent aspects of Cupitt's thought and to acknowledge the presence of the earlier positions underlying the later ones.

Cupitt argues forcefully for the ability of an 'expressionist' understanding of religion to succeed where realism fails. It is, he maintains, more satisfying, more intellectually honest, and more life-enhancing than realism, both at a theological and at a practical level.

At the level of theology and philosophy, expressionism takes account of modern – and indeed of 'post-modern' – thinking in a way which realism signally fails to do. The key elements of expressionism were delineated in the previous chapter and need no recapitulation here. What is important here is Cupitt's claim that this approach to religion is eminently compatible with, and appropriate to the modern world. It meets the requirements of autonomy and creativity in the religious life, and it takes the greatest possible account of the most recent thought in such areas as historicism, relativism and deconstruction. Indeed, it does so to the extent that, as we have seen, language becomes not merely a constraint upon, but rather the fundamental constituent of religion. Religion just is what is said about it, as Cupitt himself might have remarked.

Cupitt argues, with no less conviction than skill, that this is a truer and more satisfying estimate of both man and religion than that which is fostered by realism. It recognizes the thoroughgoing relativism and the linguistic boundaries of the world we live in, and accords to man his rightful place, value and potential. It is therefore not only more intellectually respectable than the outmoded categories of realism, but also more religiously satisfying as it enables man to understand himself and his world, to cope with it, and to respond appropriately to it. His life is no longer schizophrenic, torn between the demands of this world and the next. We are enabled to live a unified life, and, to rescue a term from the clutches of existentialism, an 'authentic' one. Expressionism, it is argued, succeeds most remarkably at precisely those points at which realism fails most abjectly.

## IV

Finally, his attack on realism is especially cogent in that his aim is never purely or gratuitously destructive, but rather it is to preserve religion by freeing it from the shackles of realism. It has already been noted that his outlook is fundamentally 'religious', as is evinced by his consistent concern for the 'purely religious' or the 'purely spiritual', and this bears testimony to the fact that Cupitt recognizes an element in religion which its more purely destructive critics dismiss or ignore altogether. This element is its claim to possess – or at least to offer access to – first, a reliable framework of values and the appropriate criteria for evaluating our moral and ethical life; and secondly, an accurate assessment of human knowledge in general and the criteria for establishing the truth of religious knowledge in particular. Some such claim to a degree of authority in the realms of values and knowledge is an inherent part of the religious outlook.

Many of the critical traditions which Cupitt acknowledges as formative would, in themselves, disparage the claims of religion in one or the other of these areas. In his own intellectual and spiritual pilgrimage, however, Cupitt has evolved a new understanding of these traditions which acknowledges the destructiveness implicit within them, and which yet allows, and indeed affirms, the importance of the religious quest. He does this principally by driving a wedge between religion and realism, and thereby freeing religion to become a part of the temporal, linguistic and post-modern world in a way which it is claimed realism is not capable of doing.

It has always been assumed within Christianity that 'realism' and 'religion' are, if not synonymous, at least complementary. Religion is about the relationship of this world to another one, and with an eternal God 'out there', or at least with a realm defined as transcendent; and religion derives its criteria for assessing values and knowledge primarily from that other world. It is the source of true values and knowledge, and the human task is to apprehend these and apply them both outwardly in the arena of human relationships, and internally in the movement of the spirit towards God. With such an understanding of religion it is hardly surprising that the traditions we have discussed should have been perceived as threatening and inimical to it.

Cupitt, however, denies this age-old equation of religion with realism. He readily acknowledges the destructiveness of modern thought to any realistic system of beliefs, and accepts that as far as traditional objective and metaphysical beliefs are concerned, 'we have little or no reason to think them true', since they 'evidently belong to a bygone age'.[13] What he denies strenuously, though, is that this vitiation of realism invalidates the notion of religion *per se*. One approach to religion may have been ruled out, but Cupitt insists that realism is not the only option open to religion.[14]

Certainly religion loses its claim to absolute values and absolute knowledge once realism is disallowed, but this does not invalidate its claim to have its own unique contribution in these areas. It merely precludes the possibility of external and *a priori* absolutes in religion as in the rest of life. Thus Cupitt avoids undercutting religion as such, even when he is being at his most scathing with regard to realism. The religious quest, and with it our understanding of values and knowledge may need to be modified – indeed to a great extent completely re-thought – but the religious dimension of life retains a fundamental validity.

In the new religious world which Cupitt has created there are certainly severe limitations imposed on our understanding of both values and knowledge as compared with the traditionally grandiose claims to absolute certainty propounded by realist religion. In common with the various critical traditions we have examined, Cupitt espouses a position which entirely undercuts a realist approach. There is no future and no sense in clinging to the old objective ways of thought. We must admit that all is fiction:

> ... a human person is not a timeless metaphysical unity, but an often rather loose-knit collection of roles that we fall into and act out in the many contexts, games and relationships of life. We are the collections of stories that we are acting out, the stories that proliferate and reproduce themselves in us. We are temporal beings, who live in what film makers call 'sequences'. We are not immortal souls, simultaneously self-possessed and self-conscious. We are unavoidably caught up in all the uncertainties of interpretation.[15]

We must admit that human life is, essentially, 'a tissue of fictions'.[16]

Once this is admitted and we are cut off from the traditional anchor of objectivity and a defined place in the pre-conceived and structured universe, there are two major and profound consequences for our understanding of values and knowledge. Firstly, as Cupitt has been saying repeatedly ever since *Taking Leave of God*, there are no values until we create them:

> The end of the old realistic conception of God as an all-powerful and objective spiritual Being independent of us and sovereign over us . . . makes it now possible and even necessary for us to create a Christian ethic, almost as if for the first time. We are no longer like people who find ourselves in a ready-made City, surrounded by structures and values and Powers already fully operative and leaving us with little to do but purify our hearts and keep the rules. The cosmos no longer seems to us like a pre-established household in that old way. On the contrary, it seems to be we ourselves who within our cultural history have gradually evolved both our picture of the world and our values. That is, it is we ourselves who alone make truth, make value, and so have formed the reality that now encompasses us.[17]

And secondly, just as our values are human ones, so too our knowledge is no longer absolute, but is bounded by the limitations of what can be said and thought in a world in which language has replaced metaphysics as the key to understanding it: 'In terms of knowledge, the world becomes a communications network, a dance of signs',[18] or more forcefully:

> Truth is human, socially-produced, historically-developed, plural and changing. We may make some progress by working at the various local uses of 'truth', but big, global capital-T Truth is a myth, and we would do well to give up talking about it, because there is nothing interesting to be said about it. Capital-T Truth is dead.[19]

Realism, and with it absolute values and knowledge, is consigned to the cultural scrap-heap, but Cupitt's attack on realism derives its greatest strength *precisely* from the fact that throughout it he maintains the value of religion *per se*. *Realism* is to be abandoned precisely because *religion* must survive. If the two are yoked together as they have tended to be in the past, they will stand or fall together.

Thus the separation of them which Cupitt establishes is essential as he sees it to the survival of religion in a post-realist and 'expressionist' culture.

So Cupitt argues passsionately that once freed from the shackles of realism, religion is free to make a continuing and no less vital contribution to human life. Our values and knowledge may be human and relative, rather than divine and absolute, and they may be all we have or can have, but limited and partial though they are, they are of the first importance *because* they are all we have, and the essence of religion is the continual making and re-making of our values and the continual re-interpreting and re-evaluation of our knowledge.

In this there is at once a break with tradition and a vital continuity with it. The break comes with the dethronement of realism, and the consequent loss of moral and epistemological absolutes, but the continuity derives from the fact that religion, no longer dragged down by realism, remains actively concerned with the realms of knowledge and value, and there is still the possibility of speaking meaningfully of religious knowledge and religious values. Religion is therefore, Cupitt would argue, re-interpreted but not eviscerated in his transformation of it.

Cupitt's concern for the validity and meaningfulness of the religious life is unremitting. Indeed the importance of religion's contribution to human life increases once it is freed from metaphysical speculation. Religion becomes 'a cluster of spiritual values',[20] and these spiritual values are at the heart of a committed, positive, purposeful and satisfying response to life:

Because of our need now to find ways of making value out of valuelessness, one of the threads of narrativity running through our life will continue to be our personal variations upon the old story of Christ. His promise of the Kingdom of God to the poor is precisely the sort of promise of revaluation to the devalued that we still need to hear . . . His life-story can still encourage us to take up the cause of something or other that is currently unpopular and out of favour, and it still embodies the old values of love and reconciliation. Reimagined, those values can yet become ours, too.[21]

Such an 'expressionist' understanding of religion is appropriate to the fluid, linguistic, social and relativistic world in which we live, and yet it is also, Cupitt maintains, still one which is coherent and potent enough to impart value and meaning to human life. Religion such as this is 'true' in the only sense in which it needs to be true, and in which, in any case, it makes sense to speak of truth:

> When I say that Christianity is true I mean that this particular system of signs and house of meaning is trustworthy and reliable as a medium and a vocabulary in which I can frame my own religious life. Christ the Word is truth, that's all,²²

and more importantly still, this kind of Christianity can – and indeed must – be seen 'as a body of ideals and practices that have the power to give ultimate worth to human life'.²³

Claims to absolute 'objective' knowledge aside, it would be hard to find a more august statement of the aspirations of religion. Religion thus understood is at once more compatible with the modern mind and more religiously satisfying than realism with its outmoded world-view is able to be. It is as though Cupitt has stripped away all the excrescences of past ages, much as one might remove the architectural excesses of the baroque, roccoco and Victorian periods from a classical building, and he would claim that as a result of his work not only does the building still stand, but is simpler, more satisfying, and purer than it was before.


V


In his critique and restructuring of religion, then, Cupitt uses with great freedom and subtlety the critical tools established by his predecessors, and he employs them to great effect at the expense of traditional realism. At the same time, however, he is unwavering in his commitment to the value of religion, and it is precisely this which makes his critique of realism so potent. He cannot be dismissed simply as an 'enemy of religion': of realism, certainly, but not of religion. And he attacks realism *because* he values religion. Were religion to have no value, then it and realism could safely be equally ignored and allowed to stand or fall together. They would, in the modern world, either perish utterly, or remain as arid monuments to a past age of faith – a picturesque and partially inhabited ruin. But Cupitt's concern for religion impels him to drive a wedge between it and realism and to denounce the one in order to maintain the other. In this concern for religion he shows himself to be a deeply serious thinker on the spiritual life and on the future of both church and Christianity, and as such he deserves to be taken seriously by that church and that faith. Stewart Sutherland remarked ten years ago in a review of *The World to Come*, that

> ... theologians and philosophers must be assessed on their questions, as well as on their answers. The point that much of the inevitable tribal ecclesiastical criticism will miss is that all of the questions which Mr Cupitt asks are important, and that a church which fails to take them seriously is suffering from a failure of intellect and nerve.[24]

Cupitt's position may have undergone further development since then, but Sutherland's comment remains valid. Traditional ecclesiastical orthodoxy needs to take Cupitt's questioning and criticism seriously. It may or may not find that it has to argue with his answers and with the expressionist faith which he espouses and commends, but it must come to terms with the questions which he asks and the failings which he highlights. Cupitt is right: faith and church are in danger of being left behind and finding themselves adrift in a world in which they are no longer equipped to survive. Cupitt's analysis is penetrating enough to show the reality of the danger. His concern for religion and the spiritual life makes his critique of realism all the more telling; and the expressionist faith which he has developed represents a serious challenge to outmoded and narrowly traditional ecclesiastical thinking. Faced with his challenge, traditional 'realistic' Christianity has three options: it may ignore both his questions and his answers and risk sharing the fate of the dinosaurs; it may espouse his answers and risk exchanging the prison of realism for the prison of language; or it may heed his questions and see whether, within itself, it has the resources and the courage to find alternative answers coherent enough to be reasonably believed and expressed in the kind of world which Cupitt has shown ours to be. It is this alternative which will most test the strength of the church's 'intellect and nerve', and it is to this third alternative – or at least to the possibility of it – that we shall ultimately turn. First, though, the validity of Cupitt's own theological method and content must be examined in some detail in order to highlight why it is that, for all the acknowledged strength of his challenge to realism, I believe that Cupitt's proposed alternative to it is finally unsatisfactory both intellectually and religiously.

# 5

# Contra Cupitt: Technique and Method

## I

Thus far in this study we have been concerned with outlining Cupitt's development in some detail, and with presenting him as a theologian deserving of serious attention from the church at large. In the previous chapter particularly, the cogency of his challenge to the church was forcefully highlighted. If the church is to remain intellectually and morally credible in the modern world then it must address itself to many of the questions and criticisms which Cupitt raises. This is not to say, however, that Cupitt's views should be allowed to go unchallenged – indeed, it is my contention that they should no more be unchallenged than ignored. As an expression of a post-modern approach to religion, Cupitt's views must be taken into account, but they must also be evaluated. The nature of the church's response to Cupitt must be two-fold. It must first evaluate Cupitt's position in terms of both the method and the content of his arguments and his underlying philosophical assumptions and schema; and secondly it must, as we remarked at the end of the previous chapter, re-assess its own traditions and see whether within them it can discover the resources to provide a credible and coherent alternative to Cupitt's radicalism. This second task will be addressed in the final chapter but our immediate attention must turn to the adequacy of Cupitt's response to the problems he outlines and the questions he raises. Thus in this chapter and the two which follow, we shall examine in turn the shortcomings of Cupitt's theology in terms respectively of its technique and method, its philosophical and theological content and its approach to the increasingly dominant issue of language and reality. The nature of Cupitt's development having already been discussed at length, the issues in these chapters are not necessarily approached in chronological order, but are treated in a more organic way in terms of similarity of subject matter, rather than with regard to the date of their genesis in Cupitt's work. Certainly there is, as has been demonstrated, a logical progression in his thought, but this lends itself as equally to a thematic as to a chronological treatment.

Cupitt, as should have emerged very clearly in the previous chapters, brings a distinctive and unique voice to the discussion of theology. It is therefore appropriate to begin this critique with an assessment of his technique and method of argument, since it is largely this which gives his work its characteristic flavour. He is, as we have argued, a highly readable and compelling thinker and his immediate approachability and engaging style are partly what make his challenge to the church so direct and powerful. His lightness of touch and attractive and persuasive prose conceal, however, a number of major weaknesses and inadequacies. In this study I shall focus specifically on five such weaknesses: a one-sided presentation of arguments; a number of questionable assumptions and premisses; the mis-representation of realism; the mis-representation of the character of traditional Christianity; and a tendency to produce fine rhetoric allied to a tenuous argument. There is inevitably some degree of overlap between these categories, but they nonetheless represent a useful, if broad, classification which will enable the various objections to Cupitt's method to be voiced with some degree of clarity.

Firstly then, he is guilty of one-sidedness in his method of presenting arguments. To a certain extent this may be as inevitable for Cupitt as for any advocate concerned to press his case, but Cupitt is inclined to go too far, and in the interests of rationalism ironically loses his own objectivity.

He does so first and foremost in his general attitude towards and presentation of traditional Christianity. This, as we have already seen, he consistently presents as being backward and repressive. *The Sea of Faith* provides a fine example of his attitude towards it:

> There is a small-town moralism which is prying, envious and vindictive, which is little more than a conspiracy of sadism, and which has in the past all too often succeeded in passing itself off as

Christian. It has been able to do so because when religious beliefs are understood in a realist and objectified way they do indeed become tools of oppression, producing first a religious psychology that is self-punishing and self-mutilating, and then an ethic that is determined to give others as bad a time as we have given ourselves.[1]

And this attitude could be found repeated in almost any of Cupitt's works since 1980.[2]

It is this perception of traditional Christianity which has led Cupitt to abandon so much of it, and which provoked him to dismiss nearly eighteen centuries of Christian history as being almost utterly worthless:

> . . . the truth is that we can today be Christians only at the price of saying that there wasn't any Christianity to speak of before the later eighteenth century, and certainly none of any interest or relevance to us. The earlier religion was a power-structure and a kind of ritualized platonism, otherwordly, radically anti-human and anti-life. There is though one thing to be said in its favour: in the figure of Christ it retained a frozen image of the human, suffering, naked, glorious, which one day would be democratized and dispersed so that we might all come to feel, about each other, like *that*. For over seventeen centuries Christianity was transmitted in a time-capsule, in a state of suspended animation. Now we can thaw it out and bring it to life.[3]

That there is some justice in Cupitt's strictures has already been acknowledged. At times Christianity has undoubtedly been guilty of exactly the kind of repression which Cupitt denounces, and has perpetrated as many moral and physical atrocities as any other ideology or system. But Cupitt is misled by this into identifying these abuses with the essence of Christianity as it has been practised. The very real concrete shortcomings of Christian faith and practice do not vitiate the religious ideal or the content of the gospel preached over the centuries. Cupitt's scornful dismissiveness is fair neither to the scriptural roots of Christianity, nor to the more enlightened believers of every generation. Certainly the potential for repression and repressiveness *is* there, but Cupitt entirely overlooks the equally strong potential for freedom, joy and affirmation of life. Jesus, at least as he is presented to us by the gospel writers, is hardly credible as the begetter of such negativity. Cupitt's portrayal of Christianity is false to a substantial part of the New Testament witness. St John, for example, presents Jesus as saying, 'I came that they may have life, and have it abundantly', and 'These things I have spoken to you that my joy may be in you, and that your joy may be full', and similarly the epistles are frequently concerned with stressing the spiritual freedom which is the consequence of faith.

Throughout the centuries, too, there have been Christians who have affirmed both the freedom of the spirit and celebrated the goodness of human life and the created order.[4] This strand of Christianity may need to be emphasized afresh as part of a balanced approach to spirituality, but its presence in the Christian tradition cannot be summarily dismissed. However serious the lapses into negativity and repression may have been, Christianity has always had freedom and life at its heart.

Closely related to this overwhelmingly negative presentation of the outlines of traditional Christianity is Cupitt's equally partial portrayal of many of its specific doctrinal positions. Examples could be culled from almost all of Cupitt's books, and almost at random two may be drawn from the first of his 'non-realist' works, *Taking Leave of God*: his understanding of providence,[5] and his attitude to life after death,[6] which he describes elsewhere in even more outspoken terms as a 'barmy fantasy'.[7] The idea of providence is presented as operating in one of two possible modes, which might be conveniently labelled 'fundamentalist' and 'deist'. Of these, the first is so absolute and thoroughgoing as to be either spiritually crushing or laughable according to one's standpoint, and the second is so vague and attenuated as to be virtually meaningless; and because providence cannot reasonably be thought of as operating in either of these two ways we cannot believe in providence. Similarly, the issue of life after death is presented as being principally a problem of how 'I' can be said to survive as 'me' in another time and another place – just as I could not remain recognizably 'me' if translated to mediaeval Japan, so equally I cannot believe in a recognizable 'me' beyond the grave. I am a 'period piece' and as such my identity is restricted to the here and now of my place and time in this world. Life after death is therefore a meaningless concept to which I cannot attach any content.

It is not the purpose of this chapter, or indeed of the succeeding ones, to offer a detailed point-by-point refutation of the many issues on which I find Cupitt's arguments weak or inadequate – space alone would not permit such an exhaustive undertaking – but rather to indicate, at least briefly, the shortcomings of his approach and sketch out the possibility of a coherent alternative. Thus in the present instance, Cupitt signally fails to allow for a less extreme understanding of providence than either 'fundamentalism' or 'deism'. He does not acknowledge that providence may be neither deterministic nor vague but may be understood as operating more holistically and organically in relationship both to 'natural law' and human nature and will. Providence need not be an 'all or nothing' affair in which God either pulls every string like a celestial puppet master or does so little as to be reducible to nothing. Indeed we might expect a more complex relationship than this in an incarnational faith in which God is at once beyond and within, other than and one with his creatures. The details of such an understanding cannot be worked out here – that is a volume by itself – but even the possibility of such an understanding is something which Cupitt entirely fails to consider.

In his approach to life after death, too, Cupitt is not open to any other framework than the very limited one which he expresses with the help of his example of the mediaeval Japanese. He likens life after death to existence in another time, and denies that this is meaningfully possible. In this he fails to account for the wider perspective which is opened up by the concept of an 'eternal present'. It may be that we do not have to postulate such a difference as Cupitt would have us believe. It may indeed be impossible for me to conceive of myself in another time, but it may equally be that in a world beyond time and place the problem disappears. A substantial refutation of Cupitt's position would take too long here, but enough has been said to indicate that once again Cupitt's presentation of his argument is both unbalanced and readily controvertible.

With such an outlook, both with regard to the general outlines of Christianity and its specific doctrines, it is hardly surprising that Cupitt's choice and use of illustrations for his arguments should frequently betray this same imbalance. Again one could pick and choose from almost any book, but a particularly noteworthy instance occurs, interestingly, in one of his earlier books, *Christ and the Hiddenness of God*. In discussing the resurrection he is concerned to get away from a physical 'resurrection event' and move towards a more theological understanding of the resurrection. In support of this he invokes St Paul:

> For example, St Paul, explaining the gospel in some hellenistic synagogue, might reason like this: he would argue from the Old Testament about the true character of the expected Messiah and the manner in which God would bring in his kingdom at the end of time. He would try to show that the Messiah must suffer, and he would speak of Jesus, the crucified Messiah, and argue that this man is now made Lord and Christ, the first fruits of a universal harvest. That is, I can imagine him preaching and proving Jesus as crucified and risen Messiah without it being necessary for him to invoke a Resurrection-Event or eyewitness testimony to it. They are, I think, logically superfluous, and were perhaps developed rather in the way the legend of Mary's virginal conception of Jesus was developed, as a picturesque reinforcement.[8]

Whatever one may think of Cupitt's actual argument here, his interpretation of St Paul is dubious in the extreme. Cupitt's thesis may or may not be correct – that is not the issue here – but to call St Paul as a witness merely because he does not speculate on the 'how' of the resurrection is far from sound. Cupitt entirely ignores the fact that St Paul is saturated in the resurrection, and that the reason for his lack of speculation is, almost certainly, that he simply takes a resurrection event as a given. For all Cupitt's persuasiveness, there is little doubt that St Paul, if asked, would have declared himself a firm believer in a much more physical kind of resurrection than Cupitt would have us believe. Whatever the theological merits of Cupitt's position, his use of St Paul to support it is specious and misleading.

Finally, in this context, it is interesting to note that I am by no means alone in taking exception to Cupitt's use of one-sided generalizations in support of his arguments. It is one of the things which has most consistently annoyed his reviewers over the years.

James Mark calls his arguments 'sketchy and idiosyncratic',[9] and Graham Slater says with barely suppressed irritation:

> I felt, as I invariably feel when reading Cupitt, two contradictory emotions: admiration that he can write so well, and astonishment that one who knows so much can indulge consistently in such sweeping and, in my judgment, misleading generalizations.[10]

In terms of theological soundness, Cupitt is inclined to be carried away by his own persuasiveness to the detriment of his judgment.

## II

One of the reasons for the partiality of Cupitt's style of argument is the fact that these arguments often spring from a number of assumptions and premises which are at best unfounded, and at worst downright false, and this forms the second major objection to Cupitt's method.

Thus his critique of traditional objective Christianity as backward and repressive begins from the assumption that objectivity in religion is, and must be, restricting and enslaving.[11] Objective realism is incompatible with autonomy.[12] Two objections may be raised to this. Firstly, it is an *a priori* assumption which he makes little or no effort to substantiate, other than by stating that any relationship with an objectively conceived God must be, either overtly or covertly, one of slavery. His argument is circular. Such a relationship is one of slavery because objectivity and autonomy are mutually exclusive. They are mutually exclusive because a relationship with an objective God is one of slavery. Neither premiss – neither that of their exclusivity and that of the necessarily slave-oriented mentality of objective religion – is seriously examined or logically supported. They are simply stated as apparently self-evident truths.

To the present writer, as to many other Christians, however, they are not self-evident truths, but highly questionable assumptions. They focus exclusively on one strain in Christianity and expand it into representing the whole. Certainly there is a servant/master (rather than slave/master) relationship involved, but this is not the whole story, nor is it surprising or morally reprehensible if one believes at all that the relationship of faith is one which involves a meeting of the finite with the infinite. Alongside this master/servant model there run a number of other understandings of our relationship with God which stress the freely-offered nature of our devotion.[13] Coercion or domination have no place in our relationship with God, and many Christian writers have stressed the nature of that relationship as being one in which we are drawn by love to respond with our own freely offered love. It is therefore highly arguable whether Cupitt's premisses are as self-evidently valid as he supposes.

The second objection is simply that Cupitt proposes to replace God with an 'internal religious requirement'.[14] This, as much as God ever did, makes demands upon us which are searching, judging and heavy; and Scott Cowdell is right to question whether the cause of autonomy is served by Cupitt's change of allegiance:

> We may . . . wonder whether submission to the religious requirement involves any less heteronomy than submission to an external force, just because the 'God pole' is internalized . . . How is it that the 'laundering of God' involved in this process of internalization turns a 'a spiritual ogre' into an acceptable religious image? Keith Ward is not entirely off the mark when he calls Cupitt an apostle of heteronomy after all, '. . . grovelling odiously before stern and unbending duty'. What is internalized is not necessarily less oppressive than what is external.[15]

Cupitt defends himself on the grounds that this subjection to the 'internal religious requirement' is '. . . a judgment upon myself and a way to salvation that I have freely invoked upon myself and for myself',[16] but Cowdell's criticism holds good. An entity does not have to be personal for me to be enslaved by it (it may be, for example, either a 'thing' such as drugs, or a 'value' such as patriotism), and equally if Cupitt can claim freely to choose his 'internal religious requirement' then a more realist believer can claim freely to choose his relationship with, and service of God. Once again Cupitt's assumptions are far from proven.

A similarly unproven set of assumptions underlie Cupitt's approach not merely to what he sees as the spiritually damaging effects of objectivity, but also to the possibility of realism as a coherent religious perspective. He assumes, in essence, that the conditions for objectivity and realism in religion have failed, and that objectivity has therefore simply collapsed. The foundations for this assumption amount to little more than a brief survey of the rise of modern consciousness and a review of the failings of the traditional proofs of God.[17] Thus secure in his position he can go on to say that '. . . we know in our hearts that supernaturalism [as he disparagingly calls realism!] is mythical and pre-scientific . . . that it has become too crude and vague to be viable and that its consolations are imaginary . . . that it is done with',[18] and that as a result:

> The only truly religious God is and has to be a man-made God. Your God has to be, let's be blunt about it, your own personal and temporary improvisation.[19]

Amid the supposed wreckage of objectivity, the way to salvation lies in the internalizing of the concept of God. This internalization is partly a consequence of the end of objectivity and partly a means of reinforcing its demise. The two understandings of God as 'real' or 'internalized' are mutually exclusive.

> Religion is not metaphysics but salvation, and salvation is a state of the self. It has to be appropriated subjectively or existentially. There is no such thing as objective religious truth and there cannot be[20]

or, perhaps even more outspokenly:

> . . . we should not suppose God to be a substance, an independently-existing being who can be spoken of in a descriptive and non-religious way . . . No external object can bring about my inner spiritual liberation. I must will it for myself and obtain it within myself. Only I can free myself.[21]

It is this assumed conflict between internal and external notions of God which leads Cupitt to see figures such as Descartes and Pascal[22] and St Paul[23] in such cut and dried terms, as representing between them, in the case of Descartes and Pascal, and within one individual in the case of St Paul, the conflicting claims of an objectively real external God on the one hand, and a subjective and internal but more authentic God on the other. In the end the choice must be made:

> Either you can claim to have an objective God, like Descartes, or you can have an authentic Christian faith, like Pascal. It is one or the other: take your pick.[24]

Here again Cupitt's assumptions are open to dispute. It is far from clear, on a number of levels, that objectivity and realism are as dead as Cupitt claims. On a purely practical level a realist apprehension of religion is still meaningful to the vast majority of Christians, and not merely to naïve fundamentalists. Admittedly they could be wrong, and Cupitt's voice could be that of a prophet in the wilderness, but their 'reasons' for a realist vision of faith are at least as well-supported as Cupitt's 'reasons' for an unrealist and subjective vision.[25]

There is a growing movement in both philosophy and theology away from the 'subjectivist' and 'materialist' mood of the 1960s and 1970s, and towards a rediscovery of the 'otherness' and 'over-against-ness' of the physical world, and with it of God.[26] Perhaps we do not 'create' as much as Cupitt would have us believe, but rather interpret a world which is an external 'given'; and if the world is perceived like this, then the way is open for God to be perceived thus also. Equally, while it is true that history and language and culture are relativizing influences, they do not rule out the possibility of an absolute beyond them – only the possibility of our perceiving that absolute absolutely, as it were! Our perceptions are all conditional and changing, but they may still coherently be claimed to be perceptions of a reality beyond all our relativities. Even the rise of a modern consciousness aware of itself and of its own temporal and historical nature does not preclude the possibility of an objective realm of the spirit, and nor does it condemn all talk of such a realm to meaninglessness. It merely demands that we acknowledge the inadequacy and provisional nature of all our attempts to conceive or speak of it. Realism, as we shall argue more fully later, is not so easily written off.

In the same way, a realist faith does not preclude the 'internalization' of God, and nor does the ability thus to internalize God destroy his reality as an objective metaphysical being. The two approaches are not, as Cupitt attempts to insist, mutually incompatible, and he is rightly, in my view, taken to task by various critics and reviewers: David L. Edwards for his 'over-simplification' of the position of some eminent modern Christians including Pascal;[27] Maurice Wiles for presenting a 'sharply dichotomous picture' which is 'seriously misleading';[28] and John A. T. Robinson for his consistent 'appealing to false either-ors'.[29]

Given the ultimate inadequacy of Cupitt's position, there is a certain irony to it, in that his desire to internalize God is well-rooted in the Christian spiritual tradition, and he is entirely correct when he draws attention to the Israelite prophets as being among the prime examples of both the wish and the need to experience God within as well as outside us.[30] He points accurately to their insistence on an 'inward covenant, a law written on the heart' as opposed to a purely external system of sacrifices, feasts, and so on; but, vitally, he fails to take account of the fact that (just as in his treatment of St Paul discussed above), the prophets would still themselves have had no hesitation in affirming the existence of God over against them as well as within themselves. Indeed, far from God being simply within them, they are drawn into God who is perceived as being overwhelmingly 'other'.[31] Cupitt is right that God needs to be internalized, but the Israelite prophets are poor allies in his effort to suggest that this dispenses with God's objective reality. Similarly, the whole of the Christian tradition has sought to find and maintain a balance between internal and external conceptions of God. It may indeed be that we need Cupitt's insistence on the internalized aspects of God as a counterbalance to a rather formalist and socially respectable trend in nineteenth and early twentieth-century Christianity, but a completely internalized God is as much in danger of degenerating into a mere reflection of my ego as an overly externalized one is of becoming nothing more than an empty irrelevance.

As so often, Cupitt is not without insight into the requirements of the spiritual life, but the assumptions and premises with which he works, while they succeed in highlighting the problem, succeed also only in producing a solution which is as dangerously unbalanced as the problem he criticizes.


## III


This imbalance in Cupitt's approach, and particularly in the pre-suppositions which he brings to theology, contributes to, and is in turn reinforced by his inability or unwillingness to do any kind of justice to – or even give credence to – the views of his theological opponents, and it is the presence of this blind spot in his thinking which forms my third major objection to his method.

Clearly I am not suggesting that equal importance should be attached to every conceivable variety of theological opinion, but Cupitt is unwilling to make distinctions amongst those who oppose him, and he fails to distinguish between naïve fundamentalism and a more thoughtful and critical – whilst yet still broadly realist – approach to religion. He is, it seems, not open to seeing *any* realist interpretation as having any intellectual or spiritual merit, and this, for a large number of intelligent but more traditional Christians represents both a glaring omission and a gratuitous slight to the measure of their progress in the spiritual life. Maurice Wiles expresses something of this sense of chagrin when he remarks with some asperity: 'A critical realist position is not the naïve impossibility that it is assumed to be.'[32] The truth of Wiles' remark will be taken up more fully in the final chapter. For the present it is sufficient to note the shortcomings of Cupitt's treatment of realism.

Wiles' comment illustrates the fact that a cavalier treatment of realism has been a hallmark of Cupitt's work for some years – indeed, almost from the moment he abandoned it. The only change which the passage of time has wrought is that his strictures have become harsher than ever, and his tendency to mis-represent realism has become more pronounced. Thus in *What is a Story?*, the second of his recent trilogy of 'expressionist' works, he manages, within the space of a few pages, to equate the whole of realist belief with two mind-sets which would be quite foreign to many intelligent realists, and which writers such as Wiles would repudiate quite as forcefully as Cupitt.

In discussing the place of the Bible and of its claim to revelation in Christianity, Cupitt argues that any such claim to revelation in scripture must involve not merely realism but 'ultra-realism' and therefore, by implication at least, fundamentalism:

> From this it follows that people who are committed to a very strong belief in the scriptural revelation of truth are thereby committed also to ultra-realism ... in order to explain how a chain of sentences can both be fully adequate as an expression of God's mind, and also fully adequate as a theological account of how things have gone, are going and will go with humankind in the real world. By 'full adequacy' we mean thoroughgoing literalism, which is the doctrine that sentences can both have exactly the same form and content as the pre-linguistic mental intentions they express, and also can exactly copy the objective course of salvific events out in the trans-linguistic real world of human history. Literal truth is a point-by-point exact match, both of words to thoughts and of words to things.[33]

A few pages later he echoes the substance of this charge, whilst at the same time making the connection with fundamentalism more explicit, and also accusing realists of depending upon a theory of 'linguistic supernaturalism':

> On this theory, 'linguistic supernaturalism', depend the ideas of metaphysical realism, a superhuman realm, God as personal, a natural order, scriptural revelation, the immutability of dogma and much, much more. In short, my error theory is that religion so far has depended upon a common mistake about language, a mistake too big for most people to give up. Their desperate attempt in highly unfavourable conditions to maintain this old mistake, at least in the religious realm, is what the world calls fundamentalism. They are struggling to fix and control language so that it can continue to be God's speech, resist historical change,

compass absolutes and express pure Truth. Revealed religion requires language to be a superhuman and heavenly thing.[34]

The major error here is in the assumption that these sweeping generalizations do actually encompass the whole spectrum of realist belief. Cupitt is wilfully blind to the rich variety of opinion which can be contained within the term 'realist', and he equates one particular – and extremely conservative – standpoint with the totality of realist belief. Admittedly in doing this he makes it extremely difficult for a realist of any kind to criticize him, for as Wiles astutely comments: 'Any question about the existence of God is ruled out of court as unacceptable, on the ground that it is framed in terms of a discredited realist view',[35] but at the same time the more critical realist must cavil at being labelled 'fundamentalist' or being told that he is a prisoner of 'linguistic supernaturalism' or 'super-realism'.

The possibility of a realism which is not reliant upon either a fundamentalist doctrine of inspiration or revelation, or a linguistic supernaturalism or super-realism will be more fully explored in the final chapter. My concern here is, like Maurice Wiles at an earlier point in Cupitt's career, to protest at the way in which he tells realists what they may and may not believe, and the specious manner in which their views are moulded on Cupitt's theological procrustean bed so that they can then be dismissed as having failed to measure up to the *a priori* standards of coherence to which we have already alluded.

## IV

Cupitt's attitude to realism which we have referred to above, leads him, not surprisingly, to caricature the beliefs and thought-world of those who are more traditional in their approach to Christianity. This objection to his method is closely related to those outlined above, but it does represent a distinct and separate failing of his approach in that his zeal for his own understanding of Christianity leads him to make a number of assumptions about what others must believe. These assumptions, it will be seen, are not necessarily accurate.

Thus in *The World to Come* he caricatures the mind-set of the realist believer:

People who live within a single supernaturally-guaranteed framework naturally see no need for irony. For them one view of things is secure. Taking it that their framework is objectively founded, they hold as a matter of faith that it simply must be unfalsifiable and proof against all threats. And so in a sense it is, for *they themselves make it so*. The community has thoughtfully equipped them with 'blocks to falsifiability', devices for explaining away any counter-evidence that may crop up. They seize on these devices gratefully and use them readily to defend the framework against criticism, but they must do it unconsciously so as not to become aware that their cherished 'objectivity' is nothing but a socially-created and socially-maintained illusion. There is unhappily no way in which they can learn how deeply they deceive themselves.[36]

Two aspects of this statement at least are open to criticism. Firstly, Cupitt assumes that all realists do and *must* think in a particular way, and specifically that they must be *certain* of the factual and objective truth of every item of their belief: certain, that is, that there is a one-to-one correspondence between, for example, the language of faith and the God of which it speaks, or between the language of salvation and what will actually happen to us after death. Some realists presumably may think like this. If so, I, as a realist myself, would agree with Cupitt that they are on very shaky ground indeed. But Cupitt does not allow any latitude of belief among his opponents, and assumes that *all* realists are deluding themselves into certainty. Like many of his arguments it is very difficult to counter for the simple reason that he can turn round and say, 'There! I told you! You are still arguing from a realist standpoint, and therefore you are deluding yourself!' However, I intend to show in the final chapter that realists need neither be so certain as Cupitt suggests, nor rely so heavily on a one-to-one correspondence of language and reality as he assumes. This attempt, if successful, also at least partly defuses the problem of delusion, in that it allows for a more 'open-eyed' realism than Cupitt is willing to acknowledge.

The second criticism is simply that not only does Cupitt 'pigeon-hole' his opponents by means of caricature but he also falls himself into the failing of which he accuses them. That is, the difficulty in answering his position, referred to in the previous paragraph, lays Cupitt open to the charge of producing for his own schema exactly the same kind of 'block to falsifiability' which he accuses realists of having erected in order to protect their citadel! As we shall see again later, a relativistic approach such as Cupitt's cannot, without risking self-contradiction, ever become too certain of itself.

This weakness in Cupitt's presentation of the overall 'world-view' of realists extends also to his treatment of specific aspects of the practice of a realist faith. Nowhere is this more true than in his denunciation of traditional Christian ethics. Here again he is guilty of caricature. To begin with he is sceptical about whether there has ever been anything which might reasonably be called *Christian* ethics, in the sense of being creative and life-enhancing, and he places the blame for this fairly and squarely at the door of the objective deity of traditional Christianity:

> While the old God was about, he prevented Christian ethics from becoming truly creative. He alone made history, had all the power and fixed all the values. He alone was in the strongest sense an *agent*, a doer. Christian ethics could not become *Christian* while he was about . . .[37]

The consequence of this is that ethics was reduced to a servile time-serving in which the individual Christian strove to keep his own soul pure and avoid the wrath of this all-powerful God. Positive and creative ethical effort came a very poor second to self-preservation:

> Only your own inner purity matters . . . A Christian should think only of himself, of his sins, and of how he can become pleasing to God. Thus if I give money to a poor man, my action is meritorious insofar as I do it only for the sake of my own relation to God, and not for the poor man's sake. This remained the motive for Christian philanthropic action during its classic period, the fifteenth to seventeenth centuries. Those who founded schools, almshouses and hospitals did so, not principally in order to change

things for others in this world, but in obedience to Christ and in order to improve their own chances of salvation in the next world. So much for Christian ethics.[38]

Clearly Cupitt's understanding of the ethical dimension of the believer's relationship to God is bound up with his quest for autonomy discussed earlier in this chapter and the criticisms of his position expressed there hold good also with regard to ethics: namely that he has an extreme and unbalanced understanding of the relationship between the believer and an objectively real God.

More importantly here though, Cupitt's entire presentation of Christian ethics as traditionally practised is a travesty of the best, at least, of that tradition, and certainly of the Jesus who stands behind that tradition. It may well be that Cupitt's criticisms are justified when looking at certain individuals or even at certain periods in Christian history, but he writes off, as being of no account, the persistent strand in Christian teaching which has exhorted such values as kindness, compassion and love both within the Christian community and to the world at large. Similarly he fails to account for the philanthropic movements which have been largely inspired by this strain within Christianity, such as that for the abolition of slavery, or the persistent efforts of Christians to work among the poor as doctors, nurses, teachers, agriculturalists and so on – work undertaken not to keep their own souls pure but for the sake of the poor themselves, and out of a simple faithful following in the footsteps of the Jesus who went about doing good. Again Cupitt makes the mistake of identifying a defect in some aspect of Christian practice with the totality of the Christian faith. No one would pretend that Christianity has a blameless ethical track-record, but it has neither been so repressive and uncreative nor so self-seeking as Cupitt tries to suggest. Polemic has again triumphed over reason.

Finally, in this systematic mis-representation of realist Christianity Cupitt caricatures the ethos and practice of the church. He presents the church as acting in the interests of a false and damaging, because restricting and externalizing faith, and indeed actually seeking by its worship and structures to perpetuate such an understanding of religion. In the course of a sustained denunciation of the church as it at present exists he characterizes it as having been, 'almost from the very beginning . . . a punitive power-structure with an orthodoxy' whose hierarchy 'have the franchise on . . . [God's] authority, power and truth'.[39] Given that this is how he sees the church's nature, it is hardly surprising that he sees its task as being, '. . . to assist the government on the moral front by turning people into sheep because, as we all know, sheep are emblems of Christian virtue'.[40] Once again the connections with Cupitt's self-confessed obsession with autonomy are not hard to see.

The principal issue here, though, is not whether this quest for autonomy is intrinsically beneficial or otherwise, but whether this quest has not led Cupitt once again to produce a picture which is little more than a travesty of the truth. As so often, there is just enough justice in his strictures to lend credence to his viewpoint – one only has to dip very lightly into, for example, renaissance church history to realize that – but equally, the admitted shortcomings of the church of any age should not be equated with the totality of its nature and self-understanding. It has been argued previously that Christianity has always contained within itself a recognition of the importance of freedom to the spiritual life, and the same holds true for the practice and worship of the church. Certainly there have been attempts at various stages in history to coerce beliefs or enforce conformity to a particular rule or discipline, but alongside this there has run an equally persistent vein of freedom from hierarchical or unthinking doctrinal shackles.[41] There is a balance to be struck between the inevitable structural and organizational needs of any large body such as the church, and the need to respect and foster the freedom and well-being of its individual members. Cupitt may very well be right that all too often the church has erred on the side of structure to the detriment of the individual, but in this instance as in others, he takes the error of practice to be a defect in essence. He is correct in criticizing the church for a far from perfect history (and indeed present!), but he is sadly misguided in assuming this to be the necessary consequence of a realist faith. Cupitt's penchant for caricature, though it makes for attractive reading, only serves to highlight a superficial and prematurely dismissive approach to the creative and regenerative potential which is still available within a realist understanding of the Christian faith.

## V

Thus far in this chapter we have isolated some of the presuppositions and attitudes which Cupitt brings to theology, and seen how these affect – on the whole adversely – his theological method. Finally, in this context of method, it is important to see how fundamentally Cupitt's style of argument is dictated by these same assumptions. With this task achieved we will then be in a position to turn our attention to the actual positive theological content of Cupitt's position.

It has been commented already that Cupitt stands out among theologians as being eminently readable. His books are always enjoyable, and as a result they communicate his ideas with a great deal of persuasiveness. His style is hard to resist, and it can therefore escape the reader's notice that his rhetoric can effectively conceal a less than watertight logic. One can be carried along by Cupitt's command of language, and fail to realize that one's judgment is being seduced into unthinking acquiescence by means which are more aesthetic than theological.

This tendency to persuade by style rather than content is one which has become more noticeable in recent years. It is, no doubt, unintentional, but nonetheless almost inevitable, as Cupitt has become at once more assured and more prolific – an average of a book per year for the last ten years, to say nothing of television and radio work and an academic teaching programme! In the circumstances it is hardly surprising that occasional carelessness in argument should creep in, or that a neatly turned paragraph of persuasion should do duty for a reasoned argument.

Stylistic persuasiveness and muddled thinking are well exemplified in Cupitt's discussion of the concept of 'dying to self' in *Creation out of Nothing*, a discussion which forms part of a wider examination of our 'relationship to life' under the headings of 'affirmation', 'transformation' and 'surrender'. It is in the context of 'surrender' that we are asked to consider the traditional notion of 'dying to self'. It undergoes, however, a subtle transformation in Cupitt's hands. 'Dying to self' becomes 'a dying life', and the requirement of this dying life is, 'Joyfully and without regret or hesitation to relinquish our grudges, achievements, anxieties, children, vanities, possessions, ambitions, and whatever else we may be required to give up'.[42] In this there is, apart from the minor change in terminology, nothing exceptional. However, Cupitt goes on to say:

> But religion says that the more fully we accept that we are just a transient product of the world and destined to be merged back into it, the more spiritually free and joyful we become[43]

and he further defines the dying life in terms of communication:

> If you are afraid of death and seek to save yourself from the world and protect your own selfhood, then your life will be dominated by anxiety and fear. But if you are able continually to let your own expression flow out of you and away into the world, without regret or holding back, then you will be liberated. To lose your life in this way is to save it. Life pours itself out all the time; we should do the same. To live is to pour oneself out in expressive communication, that is, to die.[44]

Dying to self has become 'dying into others', or as he expresses it elsewhere 'dying into communication'.

To a certain extent one can see what Cupitt is trying to achieve, and there is a real value in his ideas in terms of their emphasis on the interdependence of human beings on one another, and on the social and communicative, rather than purely egocentric, nature of human life. The problem is that these ideas, in themselves valuable, have been yoked in a less than satisfactory way to a specific traditional Christian idea, and the resulting amalgam, though it sounds persuasive, is inadequately thought out.

The attempt to link the two sets of ideas together is part of Cupitt's consistent effort to present his ideas as standing in a definite line of descent from traditional Christianity – using many of its terms and concepts, but transforming their meaning – and there is just enough connection between the two ideas to lend credence to Cupitt's effort.

Cupitt fails, however, because although persuasive, his thought is muddled. The traditional idea of dying to self is badly mutilated in the attempt to mould it to the contours of Cupitt's linguistic and 'expressionist' religious world. There are various problems. Firstly, the idea of 'dying to self' is uprooted from one religious thought world and implanted in another world which is fundamentally alien to it. Religion does *not* say that we are '. . . just a transient product of the world and destined to be merged back into it'. On the contrary, far from counselling the acceptance of any such idea, theistic religion, and with it Christianity, affirms precisely the opposite: that *although* we may physically be finite and ephemeral beings, yet we have an eternal potential and destiny. Dying to self belongs in this theistic context – a context having a strong doctrine of individual identity and worth, and it loses much of its power if it is implanted into a theology which understands me to be purely transient and with no eternal dimension. The whole concept of 'self' is weakened in such a thought world, and therefore dying to self becomes a less emotive and powerful concept: for how can I die to that which has no real lasting or firm identity? All Cupitt asks us to die to is a passing bundle of sensations which is hardly to be called a 'self' in the same way.

Secondly, the actual concept of dying to self does *not* hinge on letting 'your own expression flow out of you'; nor does it suggest that, 'To live is to pour oneself out in expressive communication, that is, to die'. These ideas may be valuable in themselves, but they are not the equivalent of dying to self. In the more traditional understanding, dying to self is something which takes place firstly and primarily *within* the individual and then bears fruit in that individual's living of a selfless and self-giving life with others. The actions or communications which result from it are precisely that: the result of an internal dying to self which precedes any particular expression of it. The dying to self is an internal movement of the spirit – a decision and an act of will, and in his emphasis on communication Cupitt entirely neglects this internal dimension which is primary in any traditional understanding of dying to self. The delicate balance between the inward and outward dimensions of the spiritual life has been lost in Cupitt's reduction of dying *to* self into a purely external dying *into* others.

An additional difficulty with Cupitt's transformation of the idea is that the metaphor of 'dying to self' is effectively destroyed and does not take on a new meaning of equal significance. Indeed 'death' becomes a bad metaphor in Cupitt's use of it. It is hard to see what meaning the metaphor of death has in the case of 'dying into others' or 'dying into communication' – for death is, logically, the end, rather than the beginning of communication. A powerful metaphor has been eviscerated into a resonant, but ultimately vacuous, rhetorical flourish. In this instance, as in others where his style is more persuasive than his logic, it appears that Cupitt has rather too easily convinced himself, and neglected to question whether his conclusions would appear either so self-evident or so consistent to a less committed observer.

All the criticisms of Cupitt's technique and method which have been enumerated in this chapter are, perhaps, to a large extent inevitable in a theologian of his stamp. He is a polemical writer, a man with a case to prove, and it is therefore only to be expected that his presentation might be partial and lacking in balance. The measure of this imbalance is well illustrated by the comments of a reviewer early in Cupitt's career. Christina A. Baxter wrote – perceptively at the time, and prophetically in view of more recent developments: 'Those who wish to familiarize themselves with liberal views would find Don Cupitt easy to read. Indeed, therein lies the rub, for issues are so persuasively argued that the novice might well never guess that the opposite view could be argued as coherently.'[45]

This imbalance, in all the various forms we have discussed, is undoubtedly a major shortcoming in Cupitt's oeuvre. It indicates an unwillingness to grapple seriously with the views of those who disagree with him, a failing noted by Norman Anderson in his 'Foreword' to Keith Ward's *Holding Fast to God*.[46] Such a dismissive attitude – and effective refusal to engage in constructive discussion – must be regarded as a serious flaw in the work of a theologian who, in issuing such a substantial challenge to the church and its understanding of the Christian faith, presumably wishes that same church to take seriously that challenge and respond to it accordingly. Cupitt himself makes this difficult by his approach.

That said, however, it may still be true that Cupitt – though unfortunate in his method – is justified in his views, and that the content of his arguments may be a valid one even if their manner of presentation is ill-advised. Thus it is important that in the following two chapters we turn our attention to the actual creative content of Cupitt's theology. In the next chapter we shall examine the broad spectrum of the content of his theological argument, and in the chapter following we shall look specifically at his arguments with regard to language and its relationship with reality and the possibility of an objective God.

# 6

## Contra Cupitt: Theological Validity

### I

Cupitt's method and distinctive style of approach undoubtedly have their shortcomings, as we have seen. But what of his theological ideas in themselves? Are they sufficiently compelling to command our assent even though we may sometimes baulk at the manner of their presentation? Must we, whatever our misgivings, still step resolutely forward into Cupitt's brave new world and do our best to live a satisfying religious life in its self-confessedly rarified atmosphere?

The answer to these questions will depend on the extent to which Cupitt's ideas are found to be, to use his own phrase, 'religiously adequate'.[1] As I understand the term, this means: are they at once sufficiently credible as to be intellectually acceptable, and also sufficiently spiritually fertile as to enable us to live a meaningful, creative and satisfying religious life? It should also be explained why I have chosen this criterion of religious adequacy, rather than that of faithfulness to scripture, or to Jesus, or to tradition, as the standard by which Cupitt's success is to be measured. The reason is simple in the extreme. It is that I do not consider that scripture, tradition, or even Jesus himself *can* be made the touchstone for a theology such as Cupitt's. To use any of these as the primary measure of Cupitt's work is to lay oneself open to the charge – whether justified or not is another matter – of fundamentalism, or blind conservatism and resistance to change. It may or may not be that an approach which *is* more directly related to these things will prove more religiously adequate and fruitful than Cupitt's, but this cannot, without incurring the charge of unthinking dogmatism and forfeiting the respect of Cupitt himself and his fellow radicals, be allowed to become the primary criterion for an assessment of Cupitt's work. It must be judged principally on its own terms and on its own merits, and in this task the concept of 'religious adequacy' is an illuminating one.

I believe that, in spite of the acknowledged importance of the questions Cupitt raises and the significance of the challenge which he issues to traditional Christianity, his own contribution to theology is not, in the last resort, religiously adequate. In the final chapter we shall examine what a more religiously adequate response to Cupitt's challenge might look like, but in this chapter and the next we shall outline why Cupitt's own ideas ultimately fail to solve the problems he depicts. His approach to language is a sufficiently substantial topic to require a separate chapter, and therefore in this chapter we shall confine ourselves to a number of other areas, less overarching and more specific than language, in which Cupitt's theology does not fulfil his own criterion of adequacy. For convenience these may be grouped under five broad headings: a number of internal inconsistencies in his thought; the presence of empty or redundant concepts; a tendency to employ unfounded value judgments; an unreflective use of argument and occasional ragged logic; and a number of problems with regard to ethics, a sphere to which Cupitt attaches especial importance. Naturally there are connections between these various categories, but the rough classification is nonetheless useful in the interests of clarity.

If we turn to the first of these categories then, it is ironic that Cupitt should be found to be at fault with respect to one of the criteria which he himself applies to realism: that is, the demand for internal consistency in the thought-world of any religious perspective. He is more than willing to criticize realism in this respect,[2] and yet his alternative vision is no less riddled with inconsistency. Three instances may be isolated, stemming respectively from the goal of Cupitt's religious quest; the nature of scepticism itself; and the moral consequences of his vision of faith.

Traditionally, one of the goals of the religious life is the pursuit of the transcendent. This may be understood as having various elements to it. Firstly, the effort to achieve some kind of 'vision' of the transcendent (of the divine nature and will); secondly, the living of life in a meaningful relationship with that nature and will (a personal faith in a 'personal' God); and thirdly, as a consequence of this, the transcendence of our own mortal nature to become the bearers or vehicles of God's life and love in the world (the operation of grace and the living of the risen life). In Cupitt's religious world, the first two of these elements are ruled out on *a priori* grounds – after all, if there is no 'objective' God then we cannot reasonably be said to have any vision of his nature and will, or to live in a personal relationship with him. One might imagine, therefore, that with these two elements removed the ground had been cut away from under the third element of transcendence. Far from it. Cupitt continues to invoke the notion of transcendence, although often subtly altered to 'self-transcendence',[3] and continues to refer, occasionally at least, to such traditional notions as grace, although again they are used in a subtly 'unrealistic' sense. The retention of these ideas – however they are used – is fundamentally inconsistent with the whole nature of Cupitt's religious world. The concept of *transcendence* is out of place in a world in which there is no *transcendent*. It appears as a rootless concept which is anchored to nothing, which has no touchstone against which it may be measured, and no source or inspiration for whatever values it may be held to enshrine. It is also logically and linguistically inconsistent. The very notion of transcendence *demands* the existence of another realm, world or state which is radically different from the one which I inhabit now, and it demands the possibility of my being transformed through contact with that realm. Such a realm is absent from Cupitt's thought: all that is left is this world and me within it, and it is nonsense to claim that I can be radically transformed by myself, or that *I* can transcend *myself*. It is a concept which simply makes no logical or semantic sense. Likewise the same could be said of such ideas as grace. Grace is something which theology understands as being received, and if there is nowhere and no one from whom to receive it, then I am left in the position of having to say that I create it – which is nonsense. All that is left in these instances is a profoundly unsatisfactory muddle which suggests – in so far as it suggests anything – the equally unsatisfactory idea that we are left to pull ourselves up by our own boot-straps, which is hardly an adequate religious concept.

That Cupitt himself has become dissatisfied with his previous understanding of transcendence, whether for these or for other reasons he does not explain, is made plain in his latest works, where especially in *What is a Story?* he reinstates a transcendent realm as such, albeit only as a 'fiction'. Transcendence without some concept of the transcendent has, even for Cupitt, proved ultimately unsatisfactory. Now he urges that the quest for the transcendent is a *'felix culpa*, a happy fault, a life-enhancing mistake that we need to keep on making'.[4] It is a 'mistake' because the transcendent is, he says, a fiction – it does not really exist: but it is life-enhancing because:

> . . . you need to have been jilted by God in order to stir up enough passion for you truly to love your neighbour. You need to have postulated and yearned after an infinite Perfection and ground of all value beyond the world, so that you can return into this world with a sufficient head of steam to be able selflessly to love your fellow human beings.[5]

In this there is an implied renunciation of his previous understanding of self-induced transcendence. He has acknowledged that transcendence needs the transcendent to be possible and meaningful. Admittedly, therefore, in his most recent work, Cupitt has at once tacitly acknowledged and avoided some of the shortcomings of his previous thinking, but his position remains essentially unsatisfactory. It remains so because he has merely moved from one set of inconsistencies to another. If self-transcendence is a logically inconsistent notion, then it is equally illogical to insist that we should strive after what is openly proclaimed to be a fiction. It would be more consistent to say that if the transcendent *is* indeed a fiction, then we should eschew it as it can only hold out illusions and vain hopes. There is nothing there that we can grasp. However, if this is once admitted, then one is plunged back into something like Cupitt's previous position. It is hard to be authentically religious *and* deny the existence of the transcendent. Even in his most recent thinking Cupitt has only succeeded in exchanging one illogicality for another, and, supported solely by a fiction, his latest ideas threaten to fall back into his previous inadequate position. Radicalism à la Cupitt has emphatically failed to find an approach to the central religious concept of transcendence which is 'religiously adequate'.

If Cupitt's understanding of one of the major goals of the religious quest displays the shortcomings of his radical approach so clearly, then it is less than surprising that this approach should be found to be self-contradictory in its understanding of itself. A sceptical radicalism of the sort which Cupitt espouses is founded on the historicizing and relativizing influences of culture, language and so on, and is committed to the view that we are transient, ephemeral and 'subjective' beings, living in an equally transient, ephemeral and subjective cosmos. A corollary of this view is that there are none of the traditional objective certainties left available to us; there are no 'values', no 'eternity', no objective God, and we are left to create the best and most meaningful life we can out of the flux of existence.

Cupitt, as always, is eloquent and persuasive in his advocacy of his beliefs, as when he describes them as being characterized by an 'ironical awareness', which is, '. . . an awareness that all our frameworks of understanding are merely human and can never be trusted absolutely'.[6] Similarly, he graphically portrays the time in which we live as being:

> . . . a time of dissolution, in which all human knowledge-systems and frameworks of understanding have come to be seen as disputable and transient. Human life is no longer held in and undergirded by an enduring coherent moral framework. Once only a few philosophers knew this, but now everyone knows it: it is our eschatological crisis.[7]

It is in this ontological and epistemological void that Cupitt's distinctive religious vision takes shape, and it is only in this void that Christianity can become what it has always been meant to be – an autonomous, self-chosen, self-imposed, and purely subjective and internal path of life. It is only in this void that Christianity has the freedom to become truly itself:

> . . . the special theological character of the present age is its *absence* of any impressed theological character. This freedom, this

openness and *lack of any destiny* . . . marks our own queer post-
'period'-period as the first truly *Christian* period.[8]

The difficulty with this attempt to say what Christianity is – or
should be – is that at exactly the point at which it attempts to be
creative and positive, relativism topples over into inconsistency. By
its very nature, relativism is a very efficient weapon of destruction
since it precludes the possibility of objective certainty; but this same
destructive efficiency also prevents it from being able to say anything
certain even about itself. There is something intrinsically absurd
about a relativism which has become sure of itself, for it must, if only
for the sake of consistency, leave the door open to the possibility that
it is itself only relative! It cannot, logically, even be *certain* that there
are no certainties! And it emphatically cannot seek to legislate about
what, objectively, are the conditions in which we live and what ought
to be done about them, for the simple reason that the moment it does
so it steps outside the framework of relativity and attempts to inhabit
the ground of objectivity which it has already defined as non-
existent! Relativism, it seems, is a philosophical outlook which can
be used only sparingly, and in common with philosophical
theologians such as Leszek Kolakowski,[9] I would suggest that a
thoroughgoing relativism of the kind which Cupitt employs is, in the
end, self-defeating and self-refuting: it is blatantly logically
nonsensical to hold any position which asserts, effectively, that
everything is relative *except* the statement that 'everything is relative'!
All such a position succeeds in doing is undermining its own grounds
for existence. In his employment of such an argument, then, Cupitt
finds himself not so much sawing off the branch on which he is
sitting but, even more bizarrely, attempting to sit on a branch which
he already acknowledges to have been sawn off! His position appears
to be one which is hardly tenable, let alone 'adequate'.

These inconsistencies in the theoretical and theological framework of Cupitt's vision of faith are reflected in the way in which that
faith is translated into action, and especially in the fact that there is
an inherent problem which emerges whenever a relativistic and
sceptical vision is 'cashed', to use Paul Rowntree Clifford's term,[10]
in the real world. This problem is particularly acute in the moral
realm, where it is hard to see what values might reasonably be

inculcated or promoted by a consistent and thoroughgoing relativism. What is there left when all the traditional sources and guarantors of value have been stripped away? Perhaps, more than anyone else, it was Nietzsche who came closest to a consistent following through of this line of thought when he asserted the ultimate primacy and fundamental nature of the 'will to power', and certainly 'will' in general would seem to be the only generator of value which can reasonably be posited in such a world. However, the strictly moral value of a 'will' to anything – and certainly of a 'will to power' – has been seriously brought into question by the ease with which others have since adopted and abused Nietzsche's concept, using it to justify anything from simple authoritarianism to outright Fascism. As a foundation for a system of life-enhancing values, such a radical relativism has turned out to be significantly flawed.

As a consequence of this, Cupitt, like others, shies away from pursuing relativism to its logical conclusions – in the practical realm at least. Theory and practice do not, in fact, match up. As a philosophical theory Cupitt is willing to embrace relativism; as a practical and moral tool, he is, ultimately, uneasy with it. Thus having stated that '. . . apart from us and what we do there is no moral order, nor any other kind of order in the world',[11] Cupitt can then, only one paragraph later, speak of '. . . the fundamental moral structures of existence that constitute us as persons and give us our identity'.[12] If challenged, he might argue that this is simply an unfortunate choice of words for conveying something which must be – in his world – actually less than fundamental, but even allowing this much, the fact that these are the words he actually uses itself suggests an underlying unease with a world which has no moral reference points from which to work. Even if he might, on reflection, wish to amend his words, his original sentence stands as a kind of Freudian slip of the pen, and as such retains its significance and ambiguity.

The problem of relativism and moral values is neatly highlighted in this one sentence. As it stands, the idea of 'fundamental moral structures' is an anachronism in Cupitt's philosophical and religious world – such things cannot exist; and the fact that they would seem to 'need' to exist illustrates the self-defeating nature of relativism in the moral, as in the theoretical realm. Quite simply, if you invoke 'fundamental moral structures' then you have left relativism behind, and if you cannot produce a moral world without having to use such 'fundamental moral structures' then relativism is instantly devalued as a reputable moral framework. Further problems of morality in Cupitt's world will be discussed when we examine his ethical approach in more detail, but this particular issue serves here to indicate that Cupitt's relativism is as internally inconsistent in the moral realm as it is in the theoretical.

## II

Closely related to this vein of inconsistency, in that such concepts are themselves inconsistent, is Cupitt's use of empty or redundant concepts in his argument. This frequently arises from his efforts to present his thinking as standing in a direct and credible line of descent from more traditional Christian theology. Thus he uses the traditional Christian Trinitarian structure of belief, with its references to God as Father, and to Jesus and the Holy Spirit, and also traditional Christian concepts such as 'salvation' and grace'. The problems inherent in doing this have been referred to briefly in Chapter 3, but they must now be considered more closely.

Cupitt's interpretation of God as an 'ideal' or as the sum of our values, has already been outlined at some length. The issue at stake here, though, is whether such an understanding of God is 'religiously adequate' or not; and persuasive though Cupitt is, there are a number of factors which militate strongly against its adequacy. Though separate and distinct, these factors are closely related, and all stem from the subjectivity of Cupitt's understanding of God.

First, then, being subjective, the concept of 'God', as Cupitt uses it, is intrinsically contentless. In and of itself it has no reality or substance and only acquires these as we ourselves provide them. God is thus automatically reduced to human size, and loses all potential for mystery, ineffability, or any capacity for inspiring worship or devotion – to say nothing of any kind of transcendent power. Even at a first glance, then, it is hard to see how such a 'God' can fulfil any but the most attenuated religious needs and aspirations.

The shortcomings of such a 'God' go deeper even than this. Being subjective, Cupitt's God has no substantial moral force or value. He acquires moral significance in just the same way as he acquires reality: namely – and only – when it is given to him by ourselves. Such a God may therefore be invoked to hallow whatever sort of ethical standards I may happen personally to cherish and may be seen as the focus of any number of widely differing and potentially incompatible moral outlooks. Not only is this possibility an incipiently anarchic one, but it allows for a plethora of highly individualized 'gods' none of whom is any more moral or any more 'cosmic' than its owner. Cupitt may object that this vision is not his intention, but its possibility is undeniable in any purely subjective religious world, and as a basis for a committed and fruitful religious and moral life it leaves much to be desired.

The problem of commitment is further highlighted by the impersonality of Cupitt's God. As traditionally conceived, God is a personal being, although not precisely in the sense in which we are 'persons', and the central concern of Christianity is the nature of our relationship with him. Its primary goal, indeed, is to draw us into that relationship with him, in and through Jesus Christ. By contrast, Cupitt's God is entirely impersonal, a cluster of ideals or humanly created values. The capacity for relationships has disappeared, and with it much of the inspiration to commitment. It may be argued that commitment to ideals is a possibility, but such a commitment is invariably for the sake of something – and someone – else. Thus I may be committed to honesty, for example, but that is in turn for the sake of those around me who will benefit by my honesty, and with whom I am *already* in relationship. What is missing in Cupitt's scenario is the idea of commitment to God for his own sake, and for the sake of a meaningful relationship with him, as well as for the sake of humanity to whom we turn with love in the strength of that relationship with God. Our relationship with God is grievously impoverished, and with it, I suggest, both our personal spiritual life and our capacity for loving action in the world.

Finally, Cupitt's concept of God is, to use the traditional language of philosophical theology, contingent in the extreme. He is in no sense – philosophical or otherwise – necessary. He becomes an entirely optional concept which has no existence at all over against the 'believer' – if that is any longer the right word! As such, and having been reduced to human dimensions, this 'God' is no longer the proper object of worship or of prayer, and these activities are thereby themselves devalued, and he no longer provides any hope of the radical transcendence of which religion speaks, for I know only too well that I cannot, by my own unaided efforts, transcend myself! Cupitt's God, therefore, is the bearer neither of significant religious or moral values, nor the bringer of spiritual hope, but an attenuated and impersonal concept which inspires neither affection nor devotion. Ideals may be necessary, but they are not, in themselves, sufficient to nourish the life of the human spirit. There is a good deal of justice in John Macquarrie's strictures on the American 'Death of God' theologians, which, allowing for the fact that Cupitt has retained the word 'God' but eviscerated its traditional content, would apply equally well to his position:

> They frankly accept a positivism which not only abolishes religion but also faith in God, and which reduces Christianity to an ethic centred in Jesus. I cannot call this 'radical theology', for it seems to me that a truly radical theology lives in the tension of faith and doubt, whereas here the tension has been resolved by the abolition of God; and further, one would hesitate to give the name of 'theology' to an enterprise which has rejected theology's key word, 'God'.[13]

This reduction of Christianity to 'an ethic centred in Jesus' gives rise to the emptying out of a second central constituent of Christianity, namely the figure of Jesus himself. With no objective divine point of reference – such as Jesus clearly believed himself to be related to – Jesus has to become simply a symbolic figure. There is no metaphysical dimension to his life, and if he is regarded as purely human, he needs to be invested with a radically different significance from that which he usually bears as 'Son of God' or 'Saviour', interpreted in metaphysical terms. Cupitt sets forth his understanding of this significance and the nature of Christ's 'work' very forcefully in *The New Christian Ethics*:

> In a nihilistic time when the world is disintegrating, when

everything seems hollow and when people doubt whether life is worth living, the task of Christian ethics is just to save the world by making things valuable and so creating more moral employment. It does this not by the dreary apparatus of commandments and casuistry, but simply by presenting us with its dual image of Christ crucified and exalted, worthless and glorious. Christ works as a symbol of the possibility of promoting something from a state of utter loss, defeat and bankruptcy to a state of glorious perfection. When we encounter someone whom the world regards as trash, we so-to-say lay Christ's image over that one, so that Christ imaginatively catalyses a change in the way we value that person. That is his redemptive work.[14]

This attempt to interpret the figure of Jesus as being primarily, indeed almost exclusively, a symbol of transformation fails for two reasons. First, although Jesus has always been invested with a rich symbolic value, he will not work *merely* as a symbol. The symbolic power of Jesus as a bringer of transformation rests on the possibility – to put it no more strongly than this – that he himself was transformed, that he is, after the humility of his life and the shame of his death, exalted and glorified. If this is not the case, then Jesus' own efforts to raise up and revalue others are merely a pathetic posturing in the face of ultimate defeat. If shame and death are the end of the story for Jesus, then no matter what fleeting gains there may be on the way, there can be no radical transformation of our life either, for we live it in the knowledge that all too soon, and regardless of what we may do, death and defeat and meaninglessness await us. For Jesus to function effectively as a symbol, there must be a reality behind that symbol. If symbol and reality are at odds the symbol does not work. Certainly throughout Christian history Jesus has been a powerful symbol of many things – not least transformation and revaluation – but this symbolic value has always rested on a metaphysical foundation. Cupitt removes the metaphysics, and the result is that, for all his efforts to convince us otherwise, the symbol collapses with it.

This alone would be enough to vitiate Cupitt's interpretation of Jesus, but there is a second reason why it is profoundly un-satisfactory, and this is closely related to his understanding of God which we considered earlier. We have seen that he conceives of God in wholly impersonal terms, as being an 'ideal' rather than a 'personal being'. Jesus, then, is the physical embodiment, or 'incarnation' of this ideal, and through him we are brought into contact with the transforming power of the ideal. Cupitt's skilful advocacy makes this sound an eminently plausible idea, but behind the urbane and attractive prose there still lies the fact that what Cupitt is suggesting is that we are related through personality to an impersonal ideal. Behind Jesus there is actually nothing to which we can relate on a personal level, and once again Jesus appears as a symbol with nothing beyond it. He reveals nothing in Cupitt's world. He simply presents us with a set of values, or rather, with an approach to value. Very admirable and very moral this may be, but it is not distinctively 'religious'. Cupitt's Jesus is ethically attractive, but ethics is only one strand of the religious life and not, as it might seem from Cupitt's account, its entirety.

Finally, these failings, and particularly the reduction of Jesus to an ethical exemplar, carry with them the potential for the ironic possibility that Jesus himself could become irrelevant to a Christianity which follows Cupitt's path to its logical conclusion. Once again it is John Macquarrie who expresses this possibility with commendable clarity:

> If men are adult enough or self-sufficient enough to get along without God, surely they will soon be able to get along without Jesus too. The nostalgic longings of those who once had faith may keep a place for Jesus a little longer, but soon he too will have to go. If the next generation needs any figure on which to focus its ethical aspirations, it will surely be able to find someone more up-to-date and appropriate than Jesus, for when we consider that his whole life was wrapped up in God, he is not really a very appropriate exemplar for the secular world.[15]

Although I have eschewed faithfulness either to tradition or even to Jesus as a criterion for criticizing Cupitt's views, it must still be said that a religion which could even envisage the possibility of dispensing with its founder – to say nothing of its 'Lord' – is in danger of committing suicide, and that such a religion is hardly likely to be perceived as 'adequate' to any but a few eccentric individualists.

With the author and the agent of our 'salvation', as traditionally conceived, reduced respectively to an ideal and a symbol, it is hardly surprising that Cupitt's presentation of Christianity should also exhibit serious shortcomings with regard to several of the most basic and central concepts of Christianity, most notably that of 'salvation' itself. We have already noted, in Chapter 2, Cupitt's description of salvation as a 'state of the self', and questioned whether this is an adequate understanding of it, but it is important here to consider in more detail what Cupitt means by this expression, and whether it is a religiously viable position to espouse. He outlines the essence of such an idea of salvation in *Taking Leave of God* and although this is, in terms of his later radicalism, an early work, his ideas of salvation do not seem to have undergone any major transformation since then. Thus he defines 'spirit' as '. . . the capacity to exceed one's natural capacities, the power of self-knowledge and self-transcendence',[16] which carries with it the corollary that the primary religious requirement is the imperative, '*Become spirit*!'[17] This becoming spirit and our transcending of ourselves results in:

> . . . the full completion of something which ordinarily is ours only in a very small and partial way; a completion which in the language of religion is given such names as salvation, eternal life, beatitude and so forth.[18]

Salvation is thus indeed a 'state of the self', and one which is achieved by our own transcending of ourselves.

The problem with this vision of salvation is two-fold. There is firstly a logical and semantic difficulty in the idea of transcending oneself. Logically, the options are that either I can transcend myself only by the operation of a force greater than I which takes me out of myself (the objective possibility of which Cupitt, of course, denies), or that I cannot, in truth, transcend myself at all, and that all my capacities, however exalted, are just that – my 'natural capacities'. To say that *I* transcend *myself* is a logically nonsensical middle ground which has no intellectual or spiritual content to it. Cupitt is using the traditional language of transcendence in a context which is no longer able to bear it, and the result is a logical and semantic failure.

Secondly, and equally seriously, there is the same denial of any 'relational' dimension to faith in Cupitt's approach to salvation as there is in his conception of God. The idea of a 'state of the self' implies no relationship with any other being: indeed such a thing is implicitly *denied* by the purely self-referential nature of Cupitt's phrase. There is a certain irony in this when one of Cupitt's main dislikes with regard to traditional Christianity is what he perceives as its tendency to focus on the soul of the individual at the expense of our relationship to others. He professes an acute distaste for, and mistrust of the language of mysticism with its theme of 'the flight of the alone to the Alone', but he fails to perceive that there is considerably less sense in his implied vision of 'the flight of the alone to itself'! Furthermore, his interpretation of salvation involves not merely a revision of twenty centuries of Christian thought and spirituality, but a complete jettisoning of some of its most treasured insights in the interests of a radically different understanding of many of its most fundamental beliefs. Thus the idea of salvation, in all of its many interpretations, has been held to involve, as a primary constituent, the concept of a personal relationship with God which is restored and made whole, whether in this life or in eternity or both. In Cupitt's scheme, salvation is eviscerated of this personal element, and thereby loses both its power to attract and its truth to the needs of human nature and our hunger for relationship.

There is little merit in examining exhaustively every instance of Cupitt's reduction of Christian terms and concepts to redundancy or irrelevancy, but the various instances cited here are sufficient to show that this is a persistent failing of his theology. He is attempting to do something which is, I suspect, intrinsically impossible, which is to create a radically new form of faith whilst retaining the terminology of the old. In order to lend credence to his thinking, he employs the terminology of past ages, but this is ill-suited to his task. What he wishes to say and what these terms imply – particularly in the realm of relationships – is often at odds, and the result is that his theology is sprinkled with empty or irrelevant concepts which all too often produce both logical and spiritual incoherence.

## III

We have seen how Cupitt employs traditional concepts to mean something very different from that which they originally signified, and this tendency to make things mean what he wants them to mean is further reflected in his assumptions about value: namely, that things have precisely the value which he gives them. It may be argued that this is entirely in keeping with his arguments about ethics and values, but the shortcomings of such arguments will themselves be discussed when we come to consider ethics at the end of this chapter. At this stage what is in question is not the method *per se*, but the specific ideas to which Cupitt attaches value as a result of his individualistic approach to value creation. Two of these ideas, each of them among the most central to Cupitt's entire theological schema, will be considered in detail here: autonomy, and the 'discipline of the Void'.

Autonomy is one of the key ideas in Cupitt's earlier essays in radicalism, and the strength of his demand for it, and the reasons for that demand have already been fully examined in previous chapters. The issue here is whether Cupitt is justified in several of his assumptions about autonomy, and whether it is the *summum bonum* which he considers it to be. In attempting to define autonomy in the opening pages of *Taking Leave of God*, Cupitt makes three statements about value which are open to question. He claims that 'Anyone who has tasted freedom knows that it would be a sin against one's own soul to revert to dependency'.[19] With this as his starting point, he uses autonomy to define various other values, and states categorically, '. . . what is integrity? It is one's *autonomy*'.[20] Having established the fundamental need for autonomy, there follows a lengthy review of how it is that mankind has reached the point of demanding it, and this is concluded with the statement that

> . . . once one has understood the possibility of autonomy for oneself then one is under a moral necessity to seize it and on no account ever to renounce it voluntarily.[21]

As far as the first of these statements is concerned, the value of the autonomy which Cupitt wishes to commend is largely evoked by the value-laden way in which he uses the terms which surround it, especially 'freedom' and 'dependency'. These are used in such a way that they are presented as opposites – which, from the point of view of Cupitt's argument, they are. The effect of this is to denigrate and devalue the idea of dependency, such that it acquires an entirely pejorative meaning. In doing this, Cupitt is guilty of a piece of deft sleight of hand. Freedom and dependency are not necessarily opposites, as may be demonstrated by comparing each word with the usual opposite of the other. Thus freedom is not synonymous with independence, nor is dependence synonymous with captivity. Indeed, as we shall see when considering Cupitt's third statement, there are circumstances in which freedom and dependency might even complement one another. Furthermore, in his desire to devalue the notion of dependency, Cupitt is blind to the concept of 'interdependence'. This quality is one which all human beings share not only with one another, but also with the whole of the created order, and it severely undermines the idea that any kind of dependency is, under any circumstances, a bad thing. At the very least Cupitt is guilty of attempting to make us see the world of values through his own particular pair of moral spectacles, and at the worst he is guilty of distorting values in order to suit himself.

In his identification of autonomy with integrity, Cupitt takes this wilful misrepresentation a stage further. 'Integrity' is a word full of value-laden associations, all of them positive, and by identifying it with autonomy Cupitt is attempting to transfer the positive associations of integrity to his favourite concept of autonomy. The identification is, however, a simple fallacy. Integrity does not equal autonomy. Indeed, it is completely possible to imagine a situation in which I might be entirely autonomous and behave with a complete lack of integrity. The mere fact that I am completely free from any external constraint does not in any way guarantee that my actions will be consistent with any moral good whatever. Indeed, it might be convincingly argued from history that the opposite is in fact the case! In yoking the two terms together Cupitt confuses personal moral value with a wider and more general kind of moral value. Thus it may certainly be 'good' that I should have as much freedom as possible, but my freedom or lack of it is no reflection on my own moral nature. The element of personal moral value is supplied by my integrity which may be exercised regardless of my situation.

If one wishes to link the ideas of integrity and autonomy together, it might be more convincingly argued that integrity represents a right use of oneself and one's relationships, whatever they may hold of independence or dependence. According to this analysis, autonomy itself is seen to be less overpoweringly value-laden, and integrity is considered as the quality which brings a personal moral dimension to autonomy. Such an analysis would seem to be at once more subtle and precise in its terminology, and more true to experience than Cupitt's rather simplistic equation of autonomy with integrity.

The same kind of simplistic approach to autonomy is evinced by the third of Cupitt's statements which we have chosen to examine. Again he assumes that autonomy is always an absolute good which overrides any others, and that dependence is never to be countenanced. Certainly his demand that we seize autonomy would appear to be appropriate when our subjection has been coerced: it is, in that rather literal sense, better to be free than enslaved. However, Cupitt falsely assumes that this dichotomy between slavery and freedom is always and everywhere the issue as far as autonomy and dependence are concerned. Again, as was mentioned earlier, he ignores the possibility of interdependence, and even more significantly, he fails to envisage a situation where I may, with complete integrity, voluntarily renounce a large measure of my autonomy out of affection for another person, or presumably, in the religious sphere, out of affection for God, a position expressed particularly cogently by Emmanuel Levinas:

> For me, the freedom of the subject is not the highest or primary value. The heteronomy of our response to the human other, or to God as the absolutely Other, precedes the autonomy of our subjective freedom. As soon as I acknowledge that it is 'I' who am responsible, I accept that my freedom is anteceded by an obligation to the other. Ethics redefines subjectivity as this heteronymous responsibility in contrast to autonomous freedom.[22]

Once again Cupitt's presentation of his ideas is entirely coloured by the *a priori* value-judgments which he brings to his theology – value judgments which are, frequently, not sufficiently thought through to do justice to the richness of human experience and relationships.

In making this critique of Cupitt's ideas on autonomy, I am not intending to advocate a religion based upon passivity or slavery. Such a religion is every bit as spiritually and morally abhorrent as Cupitt claims. It may, however, seriously be questioned whether autonomy is the supreme good which Cupitt imagines it to be, and given that Cupitt's strictures upon God, and indeed upon the whole structure of Christianity, are largely governed by his almost obsessive quest for autonomy, it may be that there is room for other values in religion besides autonomy, and with them, more room also for a relational and personal approach to faith and to God than Cupitt is willing to allow.

If autonomy is one of the raw materials of Cupitt's theological edifice, then what he calls 'the discipline of the Void' is one of its finished artefacts – the logical consequence of all that has gone before. He outlines both his understanding of it and its significance in *Radicals and the Future of the Church*, and it forms part of the culmination of a process which had begun nearly ten years earlier with autonomy and *Taking Leave of God*. He defines this 'discipline of the Void' very carefully, being anxious to avoid any suspicion that it involves any hankering after the past, or a searching beyond the human realm to a 'void' which any kind of 'god of the gaps' might be supposed to fill. Instead, he says, the 'void' is '. . . the experienced character of our life itself. It is the poignant insubstantiality, fleetingness or contingency of everything. It is life's own strange fusion of endlessness and transience',[23] and he is therefore

> . . . advocating a religion of life in the sense of a spiritual discipline that enables us to accept and to say yes to our life as it is, baseless, brief, pointless and utterly contingent, and yet in its very nihility beautiful, ethically-demanding, solemn and final.[24]

This certainly sounds most impressive. But what is Cupitt actually saying? When reduced to its essentials, he is simply advocating, as being in some unspecified way 'good' or religiously appropriate, a particular response to life as it appears to him to be. And his reasons for doing so are less than self-evident. It may justifiably be asked,

'Why is such a life as Cupitt depicts either "beautiful" in its nihility, or "ethically-demanding"?' Cupitt simply says that it is, and assumes that we must agree with him. In neither case is the evidence conclusive. It is not explained adequately why nihility should be considered beautiful, and one could argue equally convincingly that nihility is intrinsically ethically anarchic – or even, appropriately, nihilistic. After all, if everything else has been stripped of meaning, why should ethics alone survive?

There is a further objection, however, to this 'discipline of the Void'. Cupitt bases his argument for this 'discipline' on the assumption that it is somehow 'good' to say Yes to life in all its transience and pointlessness, and this is surely open to question. If life really *is* as Cupitt sees it, a more honest and therefore more morally 'good' response might actually be to say *No* rather than Yes to it. In the day-to-day living of life it is generally considered 'good' to say No to that which is base or useless, and why should the same principle not be applied to life in its totality. If it is as worthless as Cupitt claims, it is surely more moral to refuse it than to accept it. Cupitt is quite capable of saying *No* to an objective God, and this is morally acceptable; why not therefore say *No* equally to life, if it is as worthless as it seems to him to be? In returning different answers to these two questions, Cupitt would seem to be applying two different standards, based only, in the last resort, on value-judgments, with the result that there is no real consistency in his advocacy of the 'void' and its accompanying 'discipline'.

Once such consistency is sacrificed Cupitt becomes a slave to his own value-judgments. At the end of the section in which he discusses the 'discipline of the Void' he concludes: 'we find eternal joy in emptiness, we say an everlasting Yes to the flux. *That* is our worship.'[25] In making a statement such as this, Cupitt has left behind the world of common sense, and is carried away by his own rhetoric of the 'discipline'. We may be forced to accept emptiness, but neither religion nor human nature constrains us to find joy in it, and for most people life is an attempt to bring order to the flux, and not merely to say Yes to it as it stands. Again one feels that if the world really *is* as Cupitt proclaims, it would be more realistic to launch a protest against it, or say No to it. In a spiritual sense Cupitt looks rather like a would-be suicide who fears to take the final step, and in that refusal there is an implicit admission that the world is *not* in fact as worthless as he would have us believe. His eschewing of the final step appears as an unacknowledged and unconscious act of hope and as a paradoxical statement of faith in a life and a universe which, he would have us believe, do not merit such hope or faith.

As with the 'good' of autonomy, Cupitt is seduced by his initial assumptions and value-judgments into reaching conclusions whose implications have only been sketchily thought through, and indeed, his 'discipline of the Void' is, when examined in detail, a concept which is at once flimsy and paradoxical. In its refusal to reach its own logical conclusions it is, as it were, 'divided against itself', and thus carries within itself the seeds of its own destruction. Cupitt's whole interpretation of faith rests upon these insufficiently examined value-judgments and assumptions about the 'goodness' or 'rightness' of such concepts as 'autonomy' and the 'discipline of the Void', and this interpretation is therefore as open to question as are the value-judgments upon which he bases it.


# IV

Closely allied to Cupitt's assumptions and value-judgments – though distinct from them – is his tendency to argue in an unreflective way and to espouse some rather ill thought-out ideas. Perhaps the most basic and glaring instances of his unreflective style, stemming possibly from the speed at which he writes, are those occasions on which he simply fails to notice that the evidence he adduces for a particular point can equally well be used against him. That is, he presents an idea and sees only one possible interpretation of it, when in fact, without amending the argument at all, another interpretation is equally possible.

Thus in *Radicals and the Future of the Church* he criticizes objective theism on the grounds that it is no more than a projection, and he claims that this option is no longer viable for the modern consciousness which now sees through this projection and sees the cosmos as it really is – empty and without meaning. He argues that

Once you have got into the habit of noticing the way *all* people naïvely first project their own values and cultural conceptions upon the cosmos, and then claim that the cosmos backs them up, you can no longer do it for yourself. You see only too clearly that every claim to cosmic backing is just ideological.[26]

For the present I am not concerned with the accuracy of this statement, but merely with its somewhat two-edged nature, for what Cupitt fails to see is that this same statement may equally well be used against his own position. Others may use projection – unconsciously of course – to derive 'cosmic backing' for their views, but Cupitt and those like him may use projection to derive what might be called a 'negative cosmic backing' for their views. They may simply be projecting their bleakness on to the cosmos – and lo and behold, it obligingly reflects back the fact that their bleak views are entirely justified! It is the old story of the optimist and the pessimist: the optimist believes that this is the best of all possible worlds; the pessimist fears that this may be so. The same data may be interpreted in two diametrically opposed ways. And if this is so, then, of course, the spectrum of projection as a criticism of objective theism is laid to rest. Once projection can be applied to anything and everything it ceases to have any critical function or power. At the most it can only assert that we can no longer know what is or what is not projection, and if that is the case, then I am once again quite entitled to hold my views and assert that they are no more likely to be a projection of my desires than any other position is. Cupitt fails to see that projection theory, as a critical weapon, is ultimately vitiated by its double-edged nature. It is just as likely to cut the one who wields it as it is to cut the intended victim.

Serious though it is, this shortsightedness concerning projection theory is merely a defect in one very specific area of Cupitt's theological vision, and the problem of his unreflectiveness is much more acute when it threatens to undermine the foundations of his entire scheme. This is the case with the title of *The Long-Legged Fly*, a title which stands as a symbol for the world-view and approach to spirituality which Cupitt is trying to delineate. He writes in the 'Author's note' which he prefaces to the book:

I take the pond skater as an image of religious thought in an age of thoroughgoing reductionism. It is light, resourceful, fast-moving and well able to survive. The tendency in many quarters is to reduce reality to, or to model reality as, no more than a field of vibrations or differences: packets of wavelets in the texture of space-time, ripples of sensation on the surface of the human body, patterned pulses in an electrical circuit, a sideways play of signs. It seems meagre; but the pond skater makes a world out of such minimal materials, and so must we. Like the pond skater's world, our theology will have to be perfectly horizontal.[27]

This vision of the human world as 'perfectly horizontal' is the governing factor in the theology which Cupitt then develops in the remainder of the book, and this theology is deliberately intended to be as two-dimensionsal as the spiritual world in which he says we live. The problem with Cupitt's image of the pond skater is simply that it does not work. Admittedly, as with any picture or model, one must be careful not to press it too far, but nonetheless Cupitt does seem to be wilfully blind to another dimension of even a pond skater's existence, let alone our own. Granted, the pond skater's world may appear to be two-dimensional, and may even appear to the pond skater to be so, but what Cupitt does not acknowledge is that the reality of that apparently two-dimensional world is actually largely created by the heights above and the depths beneath. It is from these other realms that both food and danger come, although indeed the pond skater may never notice them until they break through into its two-dimensional world. Thus although Cupitt might attempt to use the pond skater as an image of our life, it is an image which is entirely inappropriate as a vehicle for his vision of our world. Indeed it largely vitiates such a vision by suggesting, implicitly, that far from being accurate, such a two-dimensional vision as Cupitt's simply ignores – either wilfully or accidentally – the other dimensions of life, such as the realm of the spirit, which are, whether we notice them or not, actually the dimensions which mould and indeed create the conditions of our life here on earth. The pond skater's world is potentially more theistic than Cupitt perceives. In the broad sweep of his thought as well as in its details, Cupitt is as blind to the ambiguities of his own position as he is alert to the shortcomings of others.

Arising directly out of this insufficiently reflective manner of thinking comes a persistent raggedness of logic which constitutes another serious flaw in Cupitt's theological oeuvre. Again this may partly stem from the speed at which he writes, but haste is at best a partial excuse for illogicality and lack of rigour. This raggedness manifests itself in a variety of ways: in Cupitt's understanding of the idea of meaning; in a poor use of analogy in which the analogy is insufficiently thought through; and in the drawing of some very dubious inferences from his own arguments.

The first of these is very simply demonstrated. In his efforts to give meaning to our actions, and especially our moral ones, Cupitt is hampered by what he perceives as the inherent meaninglessness and absurdity of our whole existence. This has the effect of threatening to reduce any action – however apparently 'good' – to the status of being merely an absurd and insignificant ripple on the surface of things. Clearly this is not an adequate basis for an ethically meaningful approach to life, and Cupitt therefore attempts to find a solution to this problem. He does so by appealing to an implicit relationship between scale and values. He admits that it is '. . . clear that my own particular ethical deed cannot stand alone',[28] and he therefore asserts that 'If it is to be delivered from absurdity it needs to be taken up into some larger whole'.[29] He later fleshes out this statement somewhat by adding that:

> To overcome this sense of absurdity the individual needs to be able to see herself as belonging to a larger community whose entire production taken together is ethically comprehensive. Her little work is saved from absurdity by being incorporated into a whole to which it contributes and from which it draws meaning.[30]

As a solution to the problem of absurdity, this is itself absurd. Cupitt provides no reason why the whole should be less absurd than each of its parts taken individually, except that it is bigger and more 'comprehensive'. Indeed, given his world view, it is hard to see what reason he could provide, and so the problem still remains. If the cosmos is intrinsically meaningless, then it is hard to see why all our actions taken together should become meaningful when individually they are merely absurd. Ethically meaningful action within an inherently absurd system is a contradiction in terms. Far from solving the problem of absurdity, all that invoking numbers and an increase in scale and comprehensiveness does is to raise the problem of absurdity to the power$^x$. Cupitt wishes us to believe that the whole is greater than the sum of its parts, but it is hard to see how this can be so when the whole has already been stripped of intrinsic worth, and depends entirely on the parts (themselves absurd) to invest it with meaning. It is illogical in the extreme to argue that absurdity can give meaning to emptiness, and this is precisely what Cupitt is attempting to do.

The same illogicality underlies Cupitt's poor use of analogy, especially when he draws these analogies from the realm of art. Their failure is particularly damaging to Cupitt's cause as he is very fond of seeing the whole of the religious life as an artefact, and comparing the religious life with the artistic life. The fact that his analogies are often inadequate or inaccurate casts doubt on the entire voluntarist approach which Cupitt bases on this supposed similarity between religion and art.

Thus Cupitt uses an analogy from art to illustrate the degree to which he claims that we 'create' our own God. In a passage quoted previously he remarks: 'Your God has to be, let's be blunt about it, your own personal and temporary improvisation.'[31] In support of this he cites the plurality of interpretation which art affords, and claims the same plurality for the religious life:

> The only true God is your own god, your personal god, the one who takes up his abode in your heart as a result of your own personal reading and appropriation of the Christian faith. The nature of writing is such that not even Shakespeare himself could have the power or the right to impose upon us, permanently, just one official, orthodox and authoritative reading of his works. Even if he had tried to do it, we would still fall to arguing about how to interpret his interpretation, for interpretation just is incurably plural and changeable; and even those who wish most determinedly to resist the implications of what I am saying cannot deny that the Holocaust has made *The Merchant of Venice* a different play and that feminism has made *The Taming of the Shrew* a different play.[32]

This sounds very plausible indeed and I would agree with Cupitt that all of us do have our own particular interpretation of God. What Cupitt conveniently ignores, however, is that in our interpretation of art – regardless of what changes of perception we may have had wrought in us by time and circumstance – we are still interpreting something which is *given*. Yes, our interpretation must be creative as well, but we cannot change the basic picture, play, or musical score itself. So too with God. Theology must be creative and responsive to its own time and place, otherwise it will atrophy and die, but it may still be argued that however creative it must be, it is nonetheless in the business of interpreting a *given* reality, rather than of creating that reality in the first place. Cupitt's analogy works well as far as the need for creativity is concerned, but like the examples of projection theory and the title of *The Long-Legged Fly* mentioned earlier, he does not see that this same analogy can equally – or even more convincingly – be used to support the givenness of God as it can his createdness.

Analogy is suspect, however, not only when Cupitt is advocating voluntarism, but also when he uses it to criticize realism in religion. He begins by assuming that realistic religion intends to present, in the interests of 'truth', a copy of the way things really are 'out there'. This copy, he maintains should, in the interests of that same 'truth' be as exact as possible. A problem arises, however, when the copy becomes too exact. Initially he uses the idea of a map to illustrate this:

> A one-mile-to-the-mile three-dimensional map of Cambridge that exactly reproduced all the detail of Cambridge would in effect *be* Cambridge, and cease to be a *map* at all. By the same reasoning, when the copy gets to be a truly exact replica the status of the original is also threatened, because we can no longer tell which of them is which, or which of them has precedence. So the copying-ideal of truth if pressed hard enough may defeat itself by undermining both the copy and the original.[33]

Lest this be thought to be too mechanical a model to use, he later cites the case of 'Super-Realism' in art in which the artist: '. . . sets out to make a work more real than reality itself, and thereby upsets our sense of reality'.[34] The result of this is that: 'When the artist makes something that creates the illusion of reality, the work also makes reality seem to be an illusion.'[35]

As so often with Cupitt this sounds extremely plausible and persuasive until one realizes that it is not in fact an appropriate or a logical argument. By means of it Cupitt castigates religion for doing something which religion itself – and certainly Christianity – does not *claim* to do, and which it actually freely proclaims is impossible anyway. Realism in religion and religious language does not claim to be able to copy or image or define God accurately, and only if it were to make such a claim would the charge of incipient super-realism have any foundation at all. On the contrary, running throughout both Judaism and Christianity is the conviction that God *cannot* be known, and even less pictured or described, as he is in himself. Indeed, it is ironic that it should be Cupitt who brings this charge when, at a previous stage in his career he was an ardent champion of the classical *via negativa*. Cupitt should know, better than many, that the most that Christianity claims is that we can have some notion of what God *might* be like if we could see him as he is. Such a position simply is not super-realism. It is, at the most, a hesitant realism which is, furthermore, permanently conscious of its own shortcomings. Cupitt's charge is inappropriate: realism and super-realism are not interchangeable terms, but denote two entirely different perspectives and outlooks.

The charge is not only inappropriate. It is also logically unsound in the manner in which Cupitt employs it. He uses the example of the map of Cambridge, and claims that an exact three-dimensional one-to-one model of Cambridge would, in effect, '*be*' Cambridge. Thus he claims, the logical end of any attempt to copy is super-realism. To a certain extent his arguments may be plausible as far as inanimate objects are concerned – although even then there would still be other factors to take into account which might vitiate his argument, such as the position of 'Cambridge' or its lack of population! In the case of animate things, though, even the possibility of mistaking copy for reality disappears. I may make as exact a copy of my cat as I possibly can, but the fact remains that I shall have no difficulty in identifying which is copy and which is reality – and nor, incidentally, will my cat! The copy remains a copy in this instance, no matter how accurate it may become. To suggest, therefore, that we can copy God to such an extent that we can fail to distinguish copy from reality is quite simply ludicrous. The logic of super-realism has been pushed to an illogical extreme. Once again Cupitt's fondness for analogy has led him into a logically untenable position.

Analogy is, in effect, a method of drawing parallels between one situation and another, of inferring one thing from another; and given the inadequacies of his use of this method of argument, one is hardly surprised when he compounds this error by drawing unsound inferences from his own arguments and analyses. Like his prose, Cupitt's analysis of situations always has the merit of clarity, and his incisiveness is frequently illuminating. The same clarity tends to lend credence to the conclusions which he draws from his analysis, and it is only on reflection that one realizes that although the analysis may be sound enough, the inferences and conclusions are as suspect as his analogies have been shown to be.

This is exactly the case with his examination of the cultural construction of our thought in *Creation out of Nothing*. He takes science – popularly supposed to be the most 'factual' of subjects – as his example, and he comments that it is '. . . difficult for science to accept that it is itself a cultural construction.[36] Of the fact that science is, and must be, such a cultural construction there is, he says, no doubt. In support of this he cites what has happened to our appreciation of nineteenth-century science during the past one hundred years:

> A large literature has demonstrated that, for example, nineteenth-century medical men, in their pronouncements about such vital topics as Woman, insanity, adolescence, childbirth and so forth, were enforcing purely local cultural values. They thought that what they were saying was 'scientific', in the sense of being naturally and extra-culturally True, but in retrospect it is clear that they were acting as cultural policeman. Nobody considering the evidence today could deny that much or most of nineteenth-century medicine has thus been decentred, in the sense that it has been shown that it was something rather different from what it thought it was.[37]

And he adds that the same fate will 'in all probability' befall the sciences of today.

It is not Cupitt's analysis which is at fault here. He may well be *right* in his claim that today's science will, in practice, turn out to be largely, if not entirely, culturally conditioned and therefore appear to future generations rather as nineteenth-century science appears to us. This is not in dispute. What is less certain is the inference, or at least the implication, that this *must* necessarily be so. The one does not follow logically from the other. The *fact* that a thing is so does not convert into the proposition that it necessarily *must* be so. And indeed, the fact that a thing has in practice turned out in the past to be so does not constitute a valid reason why we should not at least *attempt* to make it otherwise. It is, in a different context, an instance of the same besetting fault in logic which leads Cupitt to assume that bad practice on the part of the church, however widespread, constitutes a failure in essence or somehow vitiates the entirety of the church's doctrine and faith. Outspoken against realism he may be, but taken together, and covering as they do such a wide spectrum of Cupitt's ideas, these various failings of logic and argument do not inspire confidence in the adequacy of Cupitt's own religious vision.

## V

The greater part of this chapter has been concerned with the intellectual inadequacies of Cupitt's position, but a religion must also be adequate according to a number of other criteria, not least with regard to its ethical implications. This Cupitt clearly realizes since he attaches a substantial importance to the moral realm, and reserves much of his most outspoken criticism of realism for its perceived ethical inertia. The question arises, therefore – is Cupitt's own ethical approach one which meets, to an acceptable degree at least, his own criterion of 'religious adequacy'?

One of the foundations for any ethical vision is the existence of some kind of concept of 'value', and Cupitt's approach to ethics is suspect even at this basic level. The central thrust of *The New Christian Ethics* is that we need to get rid of the old 'fictions' about eternal values, objectivity, souls and so on, and set about the truly Christian task of 'creating' value. The old foundations for value are increasingly recognized as projections – attempts to make ourselves at home in an alien and impersonal cosmos – and once this recognition takes place, the system '. . . no longer works in the old way because we are not at heart realists any more'.[38] That is, once we know how the old 'fictions' work, they in fact cease to work, and we cannot employ them any longer.

The problem with Cupitt's response to this is that it is self-defeating, since the creation of value *ex nihilo* is equally a projection, or at least, as he freely admits, a convention:

> Since we know damned well that our life is *objectively* worthless, since there is no objective point of view upon us of any moral consequence to us, then it's all up to us and we are entirely free to establish, if we can, the convention that each human life is unique and of infinite worth. Established, it's true – as true as anything can be.[39]

Thus all Cupitt does is to substitute a new fiction for the old ones, and if they did not work then neither does his, especially since, just as he says of the old values, we know it to be a fiction from the outset. The underlying worthlessness of Cupitt's cosmos makes it very difficult to accept the existence of any human values within it, except as a rather pathetic attempt to convince ourselves that our actions do have some significance after all. It is rather like talking to someone suffering from senile dementia and humouring their fantasies about what is happening around them – except that in this case we are in the curious position of being both the sufferer from senility and the comforter!

Arising also out of the demise of objectivity is the issue of what 'value' actually means in such a world; an issue which Cupitt fails to resolve satisfactorily. Initially he attempts to side-step the problem by claiming that in any society 'value' is there already, and that all we have to do is to '. . . criticize, to re-interpret and to re-assess what we already have'.[40] This assertion is unsatisfactory for two reasons. First, it gives to 'value' a degree of givenness and objectivity which is not strictly available to it in Cupitt's world. It begins to sound like an *a priori* concept, and this has already been ruled out. And secondly, it does not answer the question of what 'value' actually is, or what grounding it has. What criteria are available to establish whether this 'value' is of any 'value'? What, in the end, does 'value' mean, except that we have, collectively, agreed to see the world in a way which is convenient to us or which makes us feel good?

At a later stage, Cupitt does admittedly attempt to address this problem more fully. He defends his notion of value on the grounds that it does have some tangible moral content. He claims again that value is simply inherent in life:

> As I have argued in detail elsewhere and here, every sense-datum, every flicker of the life-energy, every event in us is already a micro-evaluation. And language is already everywhere steeped in evaluations. Culture as a whole is a collectively-evolved and very complex evaluation of life.[41]

This idea is then developed in a religious context in an attempt to give content and purpose to the value he describes:

> Religion is not content simply to accept culture's current grading. It thinks the overall score is too low. So religion is a systematic attempt to save the world by marking up the worth of whole ranges of people and things that culture has marked down. So far as this can be done successfully, it will greatly enhance everybody's joy in life. It will not only be the rehabilitated losers who will gain. We all gain, because ignorance, neglect, prejudice and repression make the world greyer for everyone.[42]

This is, however, not a justification of value, but simply a value-judgment! For all his efforts, he has still failed to give any clear definition to the notion of value. Perhaps he would claim that it is what makes life better and less grey for all of us. But this is disputable. I may claim, contrary to Cupitt, that because it does not directly affect me, the condition of other people's lives is of little interest to me and therefore of little 'value' so far as I am concerned. Alternatively, if I claim that they do have a 'value' even though they do not affect me, then I am invoking an understanding of value which is greater than I am, and perhaps even greater than my particular culture, and this would seem to lead inexorably back towards a more 'objective' understanding of value than Cupitt is willing to allow.

There is, it seems, no satisfactory content which can be given to the idea of 'value' within the vision of the world which Cupitt inhabits.

It is virtually inevitable that a broadly similar set of problems should arise with regard to the concept of 'truth' – another pillar of any ethical system or schema. In Cupitt's creationist ethical world, 'We make truth and we make values',[43] and the most that can be said of anything is, as we saw earlier, that once established, something is '. . . true – as true as anything can be'.[44]

If this is the most that can be said of truth, then it is not actually saying very much. Once again it leaves unanswered, or even worse, avoided, the issue of what truth actually is, apart from another fiction; and it falls into the same trap between meaningless subjectivity and incipient objectivity as value has been shown to do. Am I free to attempt to persuade you that *anything* may be true? If so, then 'truth' is so debased as to be meaningless, since truth and falsity depend solely upon our agreement on the matter; and conversely, if not, then one is appealing to a notion of 'truth' which is larger than I am and which threatens to return again to the forbidden realm of objectivity! Again, it seems, subjectivity – even when dressed up as creationism – is not a sufficient basis on which to construct an adequate, or indeed even a meaningful view of ethics.

The consequences of the lack of content in such concepts as 'value' and 'truth' which Cupitt's thoroughgoing creationism engenders, are also damaging in themselves. The most significant consequence is that Cupitt is in danger of vacating the central ground of ethics. According to most understandings of the subject, ethics is concerned to a large extent, though not admittedly exclusively, with an understanding of right and wrong. Cupitt's ethics simply opposes value and lack of value as, respectively, the up-and down-sides of the ethical balance. We have already seen that the content of 'value' in Cupitt's world is open to dispute, but whatever it may be, Cupitt makes it quite explicit that it is not the same thing as right and wrong. He argues that we need to be cured of a 'sense of sin',[45] and '. . . get rid of the "sin" and "guilt" that still blight many people's lives',[46] and with this as his avowed intention it is no surprise that he is also intent on showing the redundancy of the entire concept of 'wrong', first in cosmic terms and then in more human terms, concluding that:

It makes no more sense to suppose that we could be shown to be basically wrong in our description-and-evaluation of our world than it does to suppose that we could somehow show wasps that their view of the world is basically wrong for them.[47]

At first sight Cupitt's picture is attractive. It sounds more affirming and less critical than much of traditional ethics, and indeed one would have to agree with him that Christian ethics has often been weighted too heavily with the ideas of sin and guilt. However, one suspects that this is a classic example of the baby having followed the bath water, for in his efforts to get away from the extremes of the past, he has moved too far in the opposite direction. To have any force at all, ethics must offer some convincing reason why I *should* live my life in a certain way or according to certain standards, and if it does not do this, then it is not deserving of serious attention. At a very basic level, we 'know' the difference between right and wrong, and ethics is almost integral to human life. We may have too much guilt, but that does not prevent it from being an appropriate reaction under certain circumstances. When Cupitt undercuts the ideas of right and wrong he therefore runs the risk of emptying ethics of its significance. If as he says, there is no right or wrong, but only value or lack of it, then I am free to choose what I value, and ethics has no content beyond personal choice. If, on the other hand, he wishes to assert that it *matters* what I choose, because one thing is *better* than another, then ideas of right and wrong are threatening to creep back in at the back door, and all Cupitt has done is to give new names to old concepts. Once more subjectivity does not succeed in solving the problems which it creates.

Finally, apart from its inherent shortcomings, a number of which have been examined here, Cupitt's ethics suffers from the fact that it is linked to another dimension of his thinking which we have already seen to be inadequate – his demand for autonomy. Thus he criticizes traditional Christian ethics for its heteronomy, its demand for passivity above all else, and its concern primarily with the 'inner purity' of the individual rather than with his or her actions.[48] Traditional Christianity is destructive of freedom and creativity, and Christianity had become, by the sixteenth century, 'morally impotent',[49] and has remained largely so ever since. We have already had cause to question whether autonomy is the supreme good which Cupitt suggests, and the same criticism holds good here with regard to the ethical autonomy which he demands. But equally, his own position is undermined also by the fact that his critique of traditional Christian ethics is unjust. Cupitt's slave-mentality Christian is a caricature of the truth. As so often he is correct to the extent that he diagnoses a frequent failing of Christian ethics. Christianity has had, certainly in some of its less felicitous manifestations, a tendency to demand nothing but slavish obedience,[50] but this is not, as Cupitt supposes, the essence even of traditional ethics. There has always been a strand in Christian thought which has valued the ethical creativity and striving of the individual, and it is a strand which has deeply biblical roots. It is, for example, hard to interpret the parable of the talents in a way which does not lay high stress on the creativity and effort of the individual. Similarly, St Paul, for all his occasional legalism, nonetheless displays a consistent conviction of the essential freedom of life in the Spirit. Occasionally – or even frequently – these insights may have been neglected or lost in Christian practice, but this fact, however lamentable, does not vitiate the essence of the Christian ethical endeavour. The debate between heteronomy and autonomy is not so one-sided, and nor are the scales quite so weighted in favour of autonomy as Cupitt maintains.

On a wide variety of issues then, both intellectual and ethical, theoretical and practical, Cupitt's theology has been examined according to his own criterion of 'religious adequacy'. Its intellectual and logical shortcomings have been sketched, and its ethical impracticability and lack of content have been outlined. Both in his technique and method, and in the content of his theology, then, Cupitt has been found wanting. There remains, however, one vital aspect of Cupitt's argument, and that is the supposed inescapability of language. For if Cupitt is correct in this respect, and language and its constraints are indeed inescapable, then for all the shortcomings of his position, it may still be that we are fundamentally trapped in the kind of theological world which Cupitt delineates, and must therefore simply make the best of it as he attempts to do. Does Cupitt's vision triumph in the end simply because, whatever its imperfections, he is merely presenting things as they are, and whatever we may think about it, there is, in reality, no escape from this vision? To this final possibility, and with it to the underlying question of language, we must now turn.

# 7

# Contra Cupitt: Language and Reality

I

Language is, as we have noted on several occasions, fundamental to Cupitt's theological schema. Indeed, as stated at the conclusion of the previous chapter, it is the key to the success or failure of Cupitt's endeavour. Quite simply, if he is right about the nature of language, then, for all its imperfections, his theology represents a plausible response to the purely human, de-objectified and linguistically bounded world which he depicts; but if he is wrong with regard to language, then a more 'realist' approach to theology remains a live option, and 'creationism' becomes little more than an interesting, though rather flimsy, theological idiosyncrasy.

In his discussions of language, Cupitt's command of his medium is – fittingly – outstanding, and he is, as ever, superficially extremely persuasive. Beneath this veneer there are, however, a number of flaws in his reasoning which cumulatively cast doubt on the accuracy of his assessment of both language and reality and the relationship between them. These flaws may be conveniently categorized as arising successively from Cupitt's initial framework of thought and assumptions about religious language; his understanding of the nature of language both in general terms and specifically in connection with God; his consequent failure to conceive of an 'outside' to language; and the questionable wisdom of any alliance between theology and linguistic analysis, together with the issue of whether Cupitt's own interpretation of deconstructionist thought in particular is even an accurate one.

In the construction of any argument, the premisses from which one starts are of prime importance, and it is therefore, from Cupitt's point of view, unfortunate that his case should rest upon an inadequate understanding both of how Christians have traditionally spoken of God and of the nature of 'meaning'. As far as God is concerned, Cupitt makes, as we have seen, certain assumptions about realism. Of these the most important is that when we speak of God we are demanding a one-to-one correspondence of language with reality 'out there', and are, in fact, defining God or making a copy of him in language. Thus he says – and one could cite a wide variety of other passages also – that realism implies that

> ... theory in science, ethics, religion and so on is thought of as being true insofar as it 'clothes in words' or replicates in language the structure of an intelligible reality out there, be it a physical law, a divine attribute, or an eternal moral verity. The Intelligible as captured in our thought and re-presented in language is a photocopy of the pre-existent Intelligible out there.[1]

In making this statement, and others like it, Cupitt fails to make a vitally important distinction between 'referring' and 'defining'. He assumes that religious language is intended to be 'factual' and either does not see, or does not acknowledge, that religious language is, and always has been, largely metaphorical; and by means of metaphor one can, of course, refer to something without in any sense claiming to be defining it. As Janet Martin Soskice notes, this distinction has a long and honourable pedigree, including among its defenders both Anselm and Aquinas.[2] She comments that the 'agnosticism of our formulations' preserves us from the charge of attempting to define God, and she concludes, importantly, that:

> ... this separation of referring and defining is at the very heart of metaphorical speaking and is what makes it not only possible but necessary that in our stammering after a transcendent God we must speak, for the most part, metaphorically or not at all.[3]

Her critique of Cupitt in this respect is very telling, for she understands more clearly than he does the nature of religious language, and in her appreciation of it the shortcomings of Cupitt's presentation are graphically highlighted. We shall examine her critique of Cupitt in more detail shortly, but before proceeding any further with this discussion of language – and of metaphor in particular – it is perhaps useful to establish what cognitive status may reasonably be ascribed to metaphorical language in general and to metaphorical religious language in particular. Once this is established, we shall then be in a position to speak of metaphor in the context of language and reference without confusion as to whether or not it can be said to be cognitively precise.

An excellent starting point for this issue of the cognitive status of metaphor is Richard Swinburne's discussion in *Revelation*. Early on in the book he discusses lucidly the kinds of 'truth' which may be ascribed to statements and the criteria for deciding upon the truth or falsity of a particular sentence. With respect to metaphorical sentences he examines carefully their claim to truth value:

> ... all sentences have border areas for their truth – when the curtains are blue-green, it is in many contexts as near to the truth to say that 'The curtains are green' is true as to say that it is false. Metaphorical sentences simply have wider border areas than most other sentences, in that there are wider areas in which there is not the kind of agreement in application ... if a sentence is to have a truth-value. Sometimes, however, it must be acknowledged, it is just so unclear what kind of comparison is being made by a metaphorical sentence that it cannot be said to have a truth-value. However, I would claim, given that the sentence occurs in the course of a conversation or a passage of writing with a clear subject-matter, a metaphorical sentence is normally such as to be true under some conditions of the world and false under others.[4]

Through this analysis he presents a case that metaphorical sentences are capable of having a truth-value just the same as any other kind of sentence, although he acknowledges that we may need to invoke a wider range of factors such as context – in addition simply to the words themselves – in order to establish the 'truth' or otherwise of a metaphorical sentence. We may need to be a little more careful in our assessment than with so-called 'literal' sentences, but metaphor may be a bearer of truth in areas and in ways in which more literal language is, in the last resort, inadequate.

Much later on in his book, Swinburne deftly illustrates this with regard to the metaphorical language in the creeds. He cites concepts such as Jesus 'ascending' and 'coming down' and sitting 'at the right hand of the Father', and argues, quite reasonably, that these must be interpreted metaphorically, and he provides a sample metaphorical interpretation of each phrase, such as that, for example, the idea of 'coming down' implies not physical downward movement, but rather the 'taking on [of] human limitations, including a human body with the limitations on what could be done and known through it.'[5] In each case there is a definite content or 'truth-value' to the metaphor, and there is no sense in which metaphorical language can be dismissed as non-referential or non-cognitive merely because it is not literal in its reference.

Such would be my own understanding of the cognitive status of metaphor, and that of Janet Martin Soskice whose arguments we shall be studying in some detail. Metaphor is capable of imparting cognitive information – it has a real cognitive status – although not in a literal sense. Thus in the creeds we are given real and meaningful information about, for example, Christ and his work in both incarnation and ascension, but not in a literal physical sense of movement up and down in space; and metaphor succeeds in enabling us to 'picture' – and indeed to understand – both incarnation and ascension more clearly than the constraints of more literal language would succeed in doing. It may be argued, therefore, that metaphor not only has a real cognitive status, but that it may be on occasion actually a more effective vehicle for imparting con-ceptual understanding than literal language.

With this perception of metaphor in mind, we may return to Janet Martin Soskice's critique of Cupitt's views of language. She takes as an example of his usage, and of his misunderstanding of the distinction between referring and defining, his claim that when Christians say that 'God is spirit' they are 'giving a description of God'. She traces, with remarkable insight, the process by which different models for thinking about God arise and become part of the religious language of a community:

In this way, over time, there comes into being a rich assortment of models whose sources may be unknown but which have been gradually selected out by the faithful as being especially adequate to their experience. This accumulation of favoured models, embellished by the glosses of generations, gives the context for Christian reflection and provides the matrix for the descriptive vocabulary which Christians continue to employ in attempts to describe their experience. This accretion of images, all of them hesitant and approximating, yet confirmed by generations of belief, constitutes much of what Christians call revelation.[6]

In saying 'God is spirit' then, Christians are not, as Cupitt claims, defining God – nor are they even attempting to do so. But rather, as Janet Martin Soskice concludes:

> This use of 'spirit' is one which sits in a particular context and tradition; its sense is not given by rigid definition, but by considering the way in which the term is variously used in the community and tradition, and importantly the way it is used in Christianity's sacred texts.[7]

If, as I believe she is, Janet Martin Soskice is correct in her distinction between referring and defining, then much of Cupitt's critique of realism loses its force, as he is found to be criticizing something (i.e. a purely literal understanding of language) which does not exist.

## II

It is not merely in his premisses about language – which this lack of distinction between referring and defining makes plain – that Cupitt is misguided. His entire understanding of what language is and how it works, especially in the religious realm, is open to serious criticism. Increasingly in his more recent books, from *The Long-Legged Fly* onwards, he has advocated the self-reflexive nature of language. That is, that language simply refers us to more language, and not to some other reality behind it:

Look up a word in the dictionary. There you find that its origin, its history and its various uses and meanings are all explained in terms of other words. Some of these may be unfamiliar to you, so you go on to look them up as well – and so you find yourself browsing, wandering back and forth through the book indefinitely. One word leads to another, and so on forever.[8]

Meaning is thus 'relative and differential',[9] and, 'The fatal illusion is to believe that we can pierce the veil and find more-real and unchanging verities behind it.'[10] In order to make his meaning plainer, he takes the example of the colour orange, and argues that orange cannot be defined in isolation, but only in relation to other colours such as red and yellow. There is no one-to-one mapping of reality in language.

Cupitt is by no means entirely wrong in this analysis of language and reality, but neither is he entirely accurate. I would not wish to deny the importance of language in our interpretation of our environment, and even at times in our creation of it, but I would not agree that because there is no one-to-one mapping of reality in language there is therefore no way we can step outside language to perceive a reality behind it, or even use language to perceive that reality. The choice is not the all-or-nothing one which Cupitt presents. He takes a very simple example of a dictionary and its definitions, and he is wise to do so, for it is easier to establish the nature of language with regard to straightforward usages and everyday things and experiences than it is to begin from the complexities of theological debate: what is true in one realm can, in principle, be posited of the other. Thus in answering Cupitt we may take an equally simple example. Again if one stays within the world of the dictionary, there are dictionaries, for adults as well as children, which contain pictures; and there are many specialized 'dictionaries' such as motor-part lists which consist almost exclusively of pictures. These pictures are of greater or lesser accuracy in depicting the objects to which they refer, but in no case is there – or is there ever intended to be – a one-to-one mapping of the object in question. Yet there is clearly a definite relationship between the word 'cow' or 'half-shaft', the picture or diagram of it, and the real object as and when we may encounter it. Language is self-reflexive, one word is dependent on more words for our understanding of it, but only to a limited degree. There is also a clear referential element in language which relates it to a realm beyond it. Again, we may return to the distinction between referring and defining. Cupitt assumes that language, if it is not reflexive, must 'define' reality and this, in spite of the fact that we speak in terms of a 'definition' given in a dictionary, is too narrow an understanding of the function of language. Language *can* and *does* refer us to reality – to a realm *beyond* language – in a meaningful and tolerably consistent fashion, although not necessarily exactly. This inexactitude is something which Cupitt will not allow. He insists that it is one thing or the other, all or nothing, whereas it may well be nearer the truth to suggest that the nature of *all* language (and not just religious language) is ultimately metaphorical: it connects us with something outside itself with sufficient accuracy for all practical purposes; it 'refers' quite adequately, although rarely, if ever, with one-to-one accuracy.

If this is so, and if Cupitt is therefore in error in his conception of the nature and function of language, then we may equally well take issue with his somewhat dogmatic statements on the function of religious language and the possibilities which are open to it.

His attitude to language about God is similar to his attitude towards language in general: that is, he is concerned to show that it refers not to any being outside itself, which we call God, but is intended rather to evoke in us a set of aspirations and hopes, and to guide us in a way of living. In that sense it is again reflexive, for it never gets beyond itself to anything else. Again one could examine many different passages from a variety of books, but there is a useful extended discussion of this argument in *The World to Come*. He discusses four 'levels' of religious language: 'physical anthropomorphism', 'social anthropomorphism', 'personal anthropomorphism', and 'images of boundlessness'.[11] Each of these is discounted as a way of talking about God: the first because it is clear that it does not and cannot apply 'literally' to God; the second and third because in various ways they 'shape piety and set goals before us' rather than 'inform us'; and the final level because at this point the language itself becomes paradoxical, pointing to negatives, and while the images may 'sign post the path' they do not 'describe its destination'. Whichever level of religious language we employ then, there is no meaningful sense in which we can talk 'about' God. Language, if it will not work on a one-to-one correspondence model – as we have agreed that it will not – will not work at all in pointing beyond itself. The problem with language about God is similar to the problem of language in the dictionary, and Cupitt argues that we cannot make the movement from language about God to God himself. Language, whatever its subject, remains just that – language, and no more.

However, we have already seen how Cupitt's understanding of language is limited by his insistence that it must work on a one-to-one mapping or not at all, and that his approach is questionable in its accuracy. The same criticism holds good also, therefore, with regard to religious language. He claims, quite rightly, that religious language does not and cannot accurately map things or events in the world 'out there': but though this is true, there is no reason why, for all his protestations to the contrary, religious language may not still have some meaningful contact with such a realm, or why it should not genuinely 'refer' in some less than perfect fashion, to the objects of which it speaks, God included. Because it does not do everything is no reason why it must do nothing.

Furthermore, there is no intrinsic reason why language always has to bear the same relation to that of which it speaks. It may be quite coherently argued that there is what one might call a variably asymmetric relationship between language and reality. By this I mean that language and the reality which it maps are on a moving continuum, and the relationship between them is more or less exact – though always meaningful, being a difference of degree and not of kind – depending upon the object of language. Thus if I describe the half-shaft mentioned earlier, the relationship between language and reality is virtually one-to-one, in that I can enable you to build up in your mind an accurate picture of a half-shaft, even if you have never seen one before. This exactitude diminishes as one proceeds along the spectrum: for example, cow; animal; goodness; God; each of these being less specific and less susceptible of accurate description than the last, and language consequently becoming less literal and more metaphorical in the process. This increasingly inexact and metaphorical use of language does not mean that it ceases to refer to something beyond itself, but merely that, precisely as we suggested earlier, it does indeed 'refer' to, rather than define the objects of which it speaks. Thus our images of God may still be held, without incoherence, to refer to God, although admittedly in a more or less inadequate fashion. Cupitt's assertion that they simply do not refer to anything except ourselves and our states of mind cannot be allowed to pass unchallenged.

David Walker takes issue with Cupitt on this same subject, although he bases his objection on the 'intention' of religious language to refer beyond itself. He too objects to Cupitt's insistence that statements about God are essentially statements about the believer himself, and he illustrates his objection with reference to the statement, 'God is love'. He agrees with Cupitt that

> ... if it is to be made with any degree of personal integrity, the statement 'God is love' must be a statement about myself, my intentions and moral resolves as well as about what is believed to be 'other' than myself. St John's reminder that he is a liar who says he believes in and loves the God of love and yet hates his own brother only too clearly demonstrates that statements about God are simultaneously morally prescriptive statements about ourselves.[12]

But he argues that such statements are not 'merely' statements about ourselves. He draws a comparison between the statement 'God is love' and the statement, 'The Liberal Alliance is the only way forward for Britain'. The two statements are similar in form, and the second one is quite clearly both a statement about the individual and his commitment to a particular view or opinion, *and* an '"objective" claim concerning the particular political party in question', although admittedly not 'objective' in the sense of being 'one made by a detached, neutral observer'.[13] Equally, he argues, the statement 'God is love' is both a statement about ourselves, and an 'objective' claim – although again admittedly from a 'subjective' standpoint – about God himself. Such statements, he concludes, aim

> ... at being what John Macquarrie has called an 'existential-ontological' statement; that is a statement about man and his existence which at the same time purports to refer to that ultimate

reality which is infinitely beyond man and his world as well as being that in which his existence is rooted. Thus, it is a statement which is 'objective' as well as 'subjective'; one concerned with what is transcendent over, as well as immanent within, the self.[14]

With regard both to the nature of the relationship between language and reality, and as a result of David Walker's argument from the *intention* of language to refer beyond itself, Cupitt's contention that language is entirely self-reflexive is found to be less conclusive than his compelling prose style enables it to appear. Janet Martin Soskice is therefore justified in her defence of critical theological realism, and in her conclusion – similar to my own above – that

> . . . the theist can reasonably take his talk of God, bound as it is within a wheel of images, as being reality depicting, while at the same time acknowledging its inadequacy as description.[15]

The falsity of Cupitt's picture of language and reality, and therefore the greater adequacy of the alternative we have sketched, is clearly demonstrated by a consideration of some of his latest work. In *Creation out of Nothing* he discusses the nature of reality in the light of his understanding of language; and in *What is a Story?* he addresses, among others, the issue of religious language and its talk of God – precisely the two areas which we have discussed in more general and theoretical terms above. An examination of these two books provides a concrete illustration of the points raised in that discussion.

In *Creation out of Nothing*, then, he discusses the nature of 'reality' and traces what he sees as its movement from being an entity of the 'first order' to one of the 'second order'. Originally reality came first, and knowledge copied it, but now he says, the order is reversed, and what we see as reality is in fact determined by our knowledge:

> What the physical universe is for us depends upon and is determined by the current state of our physical sciences and by our view as to the status of scientific knowledge. I look up into the sky, and current astronomical theory determines what I see. I see, for example, empty space and not blue glass. Theory shapes perception. Reality doesn't come first and then get itself copied by

our knowledge; rather, reality becomes itself for us in our knowledge of it.[16]

The consequence of this is

> ... that reality never gets fully closed or fixed, but goes on being contested endlessly. The world is an argument that never gets settled. So there is no objectively-determinate real world that could ever be finally fixed in language.[17]

The key both to the accuracy of these statements, and to their ultimate inadequacy, lies in the words 'for us'. The phrase slips in almost unnoticed in the first of these quotations, and is then equally surreptitiously omitted from the second. For the first statement is, as far as it goes, correct. What we see as reality is inevitably governed – perhaps even dictated – by our own cultural linguistic and scientific ethos and knowledge. There is, presumably, no other way in which we could see things, other than through the medium of our time and circumstances. As it stands, the first quotation is a statement about ourselves and our perceptions of reality, rather than reality itself. However, the second quotation elides the words 'for us' and purports to be a statement about the nature of reality itself – that what we see in fact constitutes reality, not just 'for us' but as the only reality there can be. Cupitt may be convinced of this, but there is no philosophical or linguistic justification for such a shift of perspective, and what Cupitt loses sight of is that it may be that our perceptions of reality, though fleeting and culture-bound, *are* nonetheless better or worse approximations to a reality which is outside of, and beyond us and 'other' than us. Our perceptions may be just that – *our perceptions* of reality and no more, and this may still be so even if, owing to the conditions of our life and knowledge, we can never know, appropriate, or even approach this reality in any other way. Cupitt jumps from a statement about the way we see things to a statement to the effect that the way we see things is the only reality there can be, simply because it is the only one we can know. Such a jump is not defensible, and nothing he says is in any logical way destructive of the reality of 'reality' itself, but refers only to our ability or inability to perceive it. What we see may even possibly be all that matters to us, though this too is open to dispute (as illustrated by my remarks on *The Long-Legged Fly* above); but even this does not preclude the possibility that reality itself may be independent of our seeing of it. For all Cupitt's protestations to the contrary, language, and with it our perceptions of reality are demonstrably not coterminous with reality itself.

Similar problems arise when Cupitt considers specifically religious language and its claim to speak about God. In *What is a Story?* he begins from the straightforward observation that every narrative must have a narrator. This causes no problem when the narrator is a single 'I' or even a number of individual 'I's' as in a considerable amount of modern fiction. In this case, the narrator or narrators simply tell their own story, partial and incomplete as it is, and no problem of perspective is involved. Difficulties arise, however, when the narrator absents himself from the story and stands, as it were, behind it, becoming what Cupitt calls the omniscient narrator. Such a narrator inhabits a realm which does not exist. Cupitt uses the opening verses of Genesis to illustrate his point, and remarks:

> Who's talking? Where does this text present itself as coming from? Every narrative must have a narrator who tells the tale from a certain standpoint, but the standpoint from which these sentences purport to emanate is one that the narrative itself assures us does not exist and could not exist.[18]

The problem does not go away even if, as has often been the case, we assert that God is ultimately the author, and that human beings merely penned the story on God's authority: 'Can God really cease to coincide with himself, objectify himself, and write about himself as it were from the outside?'[19] If such an omniscient standpoint is impossible, then we must admit that objectivity has deserted us, and that even the omniscient narrator is merely a grandiose way of writing fiction. Thus he concludes:

> . . . doctrinal talk about 'what God has done' cannot help but be situated on the sort of fictioned-past timescale that is conjured up by phrases like 'In the beginning', 'Once upon a time' and 'In those days'. Not that there is anything wrong with such talk: while

it cheerfully admits its own human, fictional, 'non-realist' status, it is fine; but when it starts claiming more than that it makes itself absurd.[20]

Religious language, like any other language, is, Cupitt argues, equally unable to point beyond itself to any reality other than language. God is, and must remain, a linguistic fiction.

We have seen already, though, that Cupitt's claims about language are by no means unassailable, and the same is true with regard to religious language. Here again, as in so many other contexts, he posits only two options and attempts to establish an 'either-or' choice between the two positions: in this case, the omniscient narrator, which is shown to be absurd in its claims to complete objectivity, or an admission that every story, including those told by such a narrator, is outright fiction. But these do not have to be the only options. Cupitt is once again glossing over or avoiding the distinction between referring and defining. He misses the largely metaphorical nature of religious language, and he does not admit the possibility of what we have called a variably asymmetric relationship between language and reality.

In response to Cupitt, then, we may invoke those same ideas, and insist that our language is not coterminous with reality. Theology does not have to work in either of Cupitt's two ways. It is, simply, not faced with the 'either-or' choice which he wishes to offer it. Because of the nature of language it can still say – fully admitting the impossibility of a truly omniscient narrator – that by whatever means, it still at least *attempts* to speak of an objective reality called God. All its devices, including the omniscient narrator, are not spurious efforts at a pretence to objectivity, but merely parts of the effort to speak, however haltingly, of that of which we cannot adequately conceive. The omniscient narrator may be a 'fictional' standpoint, and language may always be only human, but it can coherently claim a reference, even if inexactly, beyond itself.

An argument such as this delivers theology and religious language from Cupitt's charge of absurdity, since it freely admits the frailty of our vision, whatever grandiose devices we may use to present that vision. But for all this frailty, it is still able to claim a measure of objectivity and realism. All is not merely fiction. Cupitt's presentation of religious language is as questionable as his presentation of language in general.


### III


A major part of Cupitt's mis-representation of language in general and religious language in particular is bound up with his assumption that language is inescapable, and with the fact that this intrinsic inescapability renders any attempt to speak of anything beyond language absurd. Clearly this is akin to the points raised in the previous section, but it deserves a separate discussion as it raises a slightly different question about language. In the previous section we dealt with the nature of the relationship between language and reality, and we now have to consider how language affects our own standing *vis-à-vis* that reality. For it may be, even if we admit the linguistic possibility of such a reality beyond language, that it remains entirely irrelevant to us because we ourselves are imprisoned within language and are therefore unable to enter into any meaningful relationship with it.

This is indeed Cupitt's position. We can, he says, 'act only in language', and are '*made* of signs'.[21] Language 'goes all the way down', and there is '. . . no thinking which is not couched in some kind of language, and no apprehension of the world which is not language-like, [and therefore] everything is filtered through language'.[22] As a result, language is indeed inescapable, and there is no sense in our thinking that we can know anything else:

> . . . the world only takes on a definite shape through our organizing activity, as we wrap it up in language. It is chaos made cosmos by language, or rather, first appears as cosmos *in* language. So there aren't two orders which can be compared with each other, but only one.[23]

Much of this makes good sense, and yet, again here as in so many instances, Cupitt's vision is marred by a fatal failure of perception. He claims that since language is inescapable, we cannot *know* anything outside it, and that this renders the possibility of any such 'outside' meaningless to us. But the two parts of his argument are not necessarily causally connected. We may admit that language is inescapable – although as we shall see, even this is open to dispute – but even so this does not render talk of things 'outside' or 'beyond' it meaningless. Certainly if we cannot escape language in order to view the world 'as it is in itself', then it is meaningless to talk of such knowledge, but Cupitt makes the mistake of confusing knowledge with belief. Christianity, strictly speaking, does not claim to *know* objectively whether God is objectively real (and its talk of 'knowledge of God' is a personal and subjective interior knowledge which is of a different order entirely); rather it simply *believes* that he is, and this remains a viable position even if we cannot ourselves escape from the world of language and relativity. Language may be a constraint upon us and upon our knowledge, but it is not an *a priori* constraint upon what can or cannot, may or may not exist, nor upon our relationship to such things, except to say that we cannot *know* them as they are in themselves, a fact which Christianity readily admits anyway.

Contrary to Cupitt, then, we can rationally posit, and speak of, a realm beyond language and place ourselves in a meaningful relationship with it, regardless of whether we ourselves can escape from language. Even more than this, though, we may proceed to challenge Cupitt's contention that language *is* inescapable. It may be argued that vital and far-reaching though language is, it does not constitute the whole of even our own human realm, and if we can get beyond language even here, then our previous arguments for a realm beyond language become even more compelling.

One of the favourite means by which Cupitt challenges us with the inescapability of language is through the realm of our thought and supposed 'inner life'. Thought, he argues, is logically secondary to language since it is merely silent speech, and there is no 'inner life' other than this. We are each simply 'the sum of . . . [our] social relations', and there is no extra-linguistic realm which we inhabit even within ourselves. The argument is, for his purposes, neatly clinched by the remark: 'If perchance you dispute this thesis then . . . kindly step forward and state your objection in some other medium than language',[24] the fact that this cannot be done constituting the final 'proof' of Cupitt's thesis.

We may question, however, whether the circle is quite as neatly closed as Cupitt suggests. No doubt he is indeed asking us to do something impossible, but this does not render a non-linguistic realm or non-linguistic thoughts equally impossible. It is merely that – inevitably – such a realm or such thoughts are not of the same order as linguistic thoughts, and Cupitt is asking us to conduct a rational linguistic type of argument in a medium which is not of this kind at all. We cannot 'state' objections as such in any other medium; the only 'argument' which we can use is simply to point to the manifestations of this other non-linguistic realm and argue that they themselves are a standing denial of Cupitt's thesis. Thus, Susanne Langer claims a non-linguistic, but communicatory status for pictures. These, she says, are not merely fleeting perceptions, but a symbolic and logical means of communication which is not linguistic.[25] Similarly, although Cupitt attempts to include music in the realm of language,[26] we may argue that this is stretching the limits of language a little too far and that Cupitt is simply using 'language' rather imprecisely to cover any form of communication. If this is so, then again Langer argues cogently that music has an ability to communicate *precisely* at the point at which language ceases.[27] It is reflections such as these which, among others, lead Janet Martin Soskice to her commendably precise definitions in *Metaphor and Religious Language*, in the course of which she argues not only that metaphor *is* linguistic, but that other forms and patterns of thought *are not*. For her, at least, the possibility of non-linguistic thoughts is self-evident: 'Clearly we have non-linguistic thoughts'.[28] The actual presence of non-linguistic thoughts is hard to prove, since in this effort to prove their existence we must fall into linguistic thoughts and indeed language itself in the attempt to communicate them, and therefore, whatever their reality may be, we fall into Cupitt's trap. We have, however, prised open Cupitt's closed circle somewhat and done the most that can be done in language, which is to open up once more the possibility that such thoughts may exist, though we cannot define them within language. This achievement in itself adds weight to the previous remarks concerning our ability to relate to a reality outside of language, since, within ourselves at least, we can apprehend the existence of an equally non-linguistic realm. In this instance too, Cupitt has over-estimated the ubiquity of language.

Finally with regard to his assessment of language, he places too high a stress not only on the inescapability of language, but also on its straightforward *importance*. He takes issue with the religious significance often found in silence, and contends that since language and communication make us essentially what we are, we are committed, in the interests of religion, to as much communication as possible: 'Holiness is garrulity is humanity is communication is the Logos. Saints are gossips, talk is life.'[29] Of the relative merits of silence and speech he concludes:

> . . . the notion of silence as a specially important and religiously-valuable region outside language and ontologically prior to it can now be seen to be a mistake, just another form of death wish. The most frivolous gossip is holier, wiser and deeper than silence. Socrates, the Buddha and Jesus are all remembered as chiefly *talkers*.[30]

One might wish to agree with him that silence is not necessarily 'ontologically prior' to speech, although equally one might argue against him that nor is language ontologically prior to silence, for there seems no good reason why they may not both be given the same ontological status and be allowed to be merely different from, rather than 'better than' or 'prior to' each other. But whatever view one takes of the relationship between them, it is, to say the least, illogical to suggest that there is any 'value' religious or otherwise in language *per se*. Value inheres in whatever it is that is communicated through speech, and not merely in speech itself. Language, *per se*, is not that important. Quite apart from the fact that Cupitt seriously misrepresents Jesus in casting him as 'chiefly a talker' – the silence and hours of solitude of Jesus were in fact the things which fed his more public acts such as talking – it would be more reasonable to suggest that language is only important when we have something meaningful to say, and indeed what is remembered about Jesus is not the *quantity* of his speech, but its *quality*. Language, it appears, is neither so inescapable nor so significant in itself as Cupitt asks us to believe.

## IV

By now doubt has been cast on many of Cupitt's assumptions and arguments about language, often by means of a discussion of particular examples of Cupitt's work. There is, however, a final question to be raised about his approach to language, and this is, more generally, the wisdom – and the logic – of theology contracting such a close alliance with any kind of linguistic analysis, especially in view of the fact that as theology is inevitably couched in language, it will, if it is not careful, find itself the junior partner in any such alliance; and to this may be added the question of whether Cupitt's understanding and use of linguistic philosophy does, in fact, interpret its essential position accurately.

Janet Martin Soskice provides a useful analysis of the problems which lie in store for theology if it follows too closely the canons of literary critical theory. She examines the school of literary criticism which has concentrated on 'meaning' rather than on 'reference' or 'truth', and she cites as examples of the genesis of this kind of criticism, C. K. Ogden and I. A. Richards.[31] Among more recent critics she singles out Karsten Harries, who, citing one of Cupitt's favoured gurus Jacques Derrida

> . . . goes so far as to argue that the purpose of some of the poet's metaphors is to weaken and break down the referential function of language in order to let us become absorbed in the poem. The poet's object is to direct us away from reality and to escape from the referentiality of language into the 'world' opened up by the aesthetic object.[32]

Such an approach is not necessarily out of place in the purely literary world, and Janet Martin Soskice further allows that 'Theologians have, quite rightly, been influenced by literary criticism.'[33] However, although the Bible is a book, and in that sense a literary artefact, the world of theology is nonetheless a different one from the world of literary fiction, and she concludes that

> . . . in view of the scepticism implicit in some literary approaches to meaning and metaphor, one cannot but wonder if those

theologians who uncritically take over their mode of analysis may find they have made a bad alliance.[34]

One can see the reasons for her unease. The separation of 'meaning' and 'reference' may be all very well in a purely literary world, but it creates problems for theology, bringing in as it does, as an *a priori* assumption – drawn from literature and *not* theology – the idea that there can be no objective referents for the concepts and ideas expressed in theology. 'God', for example, has only the meaning which theology or spirituality gives him, and the word 'God' can have no objective referent. Not only does this prevent theology from making any claims to what Janet Martin Soskice calls 'reality depiction'[35] but it does so for no good reason: there is no intrinsic reason why theology should uncritically take over what is, after all, only one strand – and a hotly disputed one – in the world of literary critical theory. Not only may it be a 'bad alliance', it is not even a necessary one.

There is, however, a further problem in connection with meaning and reference which Janet Martin Soskice does not touch upon, and this is the difficulty and self-contradictoriness, from which any theology such as Cupitt's must suffer, of attempting to exclude certain areas of reference from language whilst including others. What Cupitt is asserting is that language cannot refer to another world than this one, but can refer to this one, and this is ultimately an untenable assertion. It is untenable because unless you invoke some sort of verification principle – an idea which has been long since discredited anyway[36] – then if language cannot refer to one world, it cannot logically refer to *any* world at all, including this one: and this is nonsense, not philosophy! You cannot arbitrarily define the limits of language in this way, and if language is held to refer at all, then the possibility remains open that it refers, in however an unsatisfactory fashion, not only to the everyday world about us, but also to other realities and entities outside or beyond this world. Again, the gap between 'meaning' and 'reference' opened up by some literary theorists is found to be unsuited to the realm of theology, and theology can with some justice demand that if the nature of language is to be referential, then *its* language is to be understood in this manner also.

Furthermore, in this context of meaning and reference, there is the question of whether or not it makes any sense to use ostensibly referential language in a non-referential way. In other words, is Cupitt's separation of meaning and reference within theology not only unnecessary and self-refuting, but also simply illogical and eccentric? John Searle suggests that it is. Speaking of Wittgenstein in conversation with Bryan Magee he commented on the relationship of 'language games' and reality – 'meaning' and 'reference' under other names – and he remarked:

> The reason why people play the language game of religion is because they think there is something outside the language game that gives it a point. You have to be a very recherché sort of religious intellectual to keep praying if you don't think there is any real God outside the language who is listening to your prayers.[37]

By continuing to use the traditional language of religion in an exclusively non-referential sense, Cupitt is producing, in the end, neither good philosophy nor good theology, but remains perched precariously somewhere between them, irritating both and fulfilling the legitimate demands of neither.

Finally, it may be seriously questioned whether Cupitt, in his borrowings from, and adaptation of French post-structuralist philosophy, has adequately understood both this philosophy itself and its implications for theology. Cupitt's conviction of the ubiquity and inescapability of language has been discussed in detail elsewhere, and needs no recapitulation here. His position would seem to be somewhat akin to that espoused by Baudrillard, whose outlook is deftly characterized by Christopher Norris:

> Baudrillard is perhaps the most extreme instance of this 'post-modern' drive to extend the aesthetic . . . to the point of collapsing away every last form of ontological distinction or critical truth-claim . . . For there is simply no point in maintaining such distinctions so Baudrillard would have us believe – in a world where 'false' appearances go all the way down, and where the only available measure of 'truth' is the capacity to put one's ideas across to maximum suasive effect.[38]

If this is indeed what the bulk of French post-structuralism is saying, then all of the various criticisms enunciated above with regard to Cupitt would apply equally well to those in following whom Cupitt has developed his ideas. To these criticisms might be added also the particularly telling analysis by Roy Bhaskar of the philosophical confusion which such a position entails. He notes that what is needed is a clear distinction between:

(a) the principle of *epistemic relativity*, viz that all beliefs are socially produced, so that knowledge is transient and neither truth-values nor criteria of rationality exist outside historical time and (b) the doctrine of *judgmental relativism*, which maintains that all beliefs are equally valid in the sense that there are no rational grounds for preferring one to another. I accept (a), so disavowing any form of epistemic absolutism, but reject (b), so upholding judgmental rationality against irrationalism . . . Relativists have mistakenly inferred (b) from (a), while anti-relativists have wrongly taken the unacceptability of (b) as a reductio of (a).[39]

Other thinkers too have castigated the irrationalism of the excesses of this kind of thinking,[40] and J. G. Merquior[41] has shown the impossibility of abandoning all absolute standards and values without impaling oneself on the horns of the relativists' epistemological dilemma which was outlined in Chapter 6.

However, such an extreme position is *not* characteristic of the majority of post-structuralist (and largely deconstructionist) thinkers whose influence Cupitt acknowledges, and in particular it is not characteristic of the work of Jacques Derrida. Thus, I believe, Cupitt will be found to be misrepresenting deconstruction in the service of his own arguments just as much as he has misrepresented Christianity. He has adopted a number of unfortunate 'slogans' from modern French philosophy such as, 'there is only the text', 'there is no outside', and 'language goes all the way down', and he has failed to appreciate that when viewed in its entirety, and in particular as practised by its more rigorous exponents, deconstruction is not as free-wheeling and purely negative as Cupitt would like to think, and that it is also, in a way that Cupitt himself is not, more cautious about its own claims and more conscious and critical of its own provision-ality.[42]

Undoubtedly the most famous and influential figure in the development of deconstruction has been Jacques Derrida, and his understanding of the implications of deconstruction is significantly at odds with Cupitt's. Indeed, in an interview with Richard Kearney he complains at some length about precisely the kind of misrepresentation of deconstruction of which Cupitt is guilty. The passage is important enough to deserve full quotation:

> There have been several misinterpretations of what I and other deconstructionists are trying to do. It is totally false to suggest that deconstruction is a suspension of reference. Deconstruction is always deeply concerned with the 'other' of language. I never cease to be surprised by critics who see my work as a declaration that there is nothing beyond language, that we are imprisoned in language; it is, in fact, saying the exact opposite. The critique of logocentrism is above all else the search for the 'other' and the 'other of language'. Every week I receive critical commentaries and studies on deconstruction which operate on the assumption that what they call 'post-structuralism' amounts to saying that there is nothing beyond language, that we are submerged in words – and other stupidities of that sort. Certainly, deconstruction tries to show that the question of reference is more complex and problematic than traditional theories supposed. It even asks whether our term 'reference' is entirely adequate for designating the 'other'. The other, which is beyond language and which summons language, is perhaps not a 'referent' in the normal sense which linguists have attached to the term. But to distance oneself thus from the habitual structure of reference, to challenge or to complicate our common assumptions about it, does not amount to saying that there is *nothing* beyond language.[43]

These complaints have been echoed by several informed commentators on deconstruction such as Christopher Norris.[44] Thus 'reference' may certainly be more problematic than traditional philosophy has often supposed, but it is by no means irrelevant or outmoded, and the same may be said of 'truth'. Once again, Derrida expresses his position succinctly as being one in which the difficulties surrounding 'truth' are acknowledged, but 'truth' itself is not thereby devalued or destroyed:

> . . . the value of truth (and all those values associated with it) is never contested or destroyed in my writings, but only re-inscribed in more powerful, larger, more stratified contexts . . . and . . . [within] those contexts (that is, within relations of force that are always differential – for example, socio-political-institutional – but even beyond these determinations) that are relatively stable, sometimes apparently almost unshakeable, it should be possible to invoke rules of competence, criteria of discussion and of consensus, good faith, lucidity, rigour, criticism and pedagogy.[45]

Admittedly, Derrida is one of the most rigorous of the post-structuralist thinkers, and his ideas have been interpreted in a rather less disciplined fashion by some of his admirers, especially in America, but nonetheless he is by no means alone in maintaining a concern for truth and reference, however problematic they may be. Paul de Man, who was much influenced by Derrida, is equally painstaking and non *laissez-faire* in his approach. He comments with regard to reference (and with interpolations by Jonathan Culler) that:

> 'To understand primarily means to determine the referential mode of a text . . . and we tend to take for granted that this can be done . . . As long as we can distinguish between literal and figural meaning, we can translate the figure back to its proper referent.' To identify something as a figure is to assume the possibility of making it referential at another level and thus to 'postulate the possibility of referential meaning as the *telos* of all language. It would be quite foolish to assume that one can lightheartedly move away from the constraint of referential meaning.'[46]

Similarly, with regard to truth, he comments that: '. . . no reading is conceivable in which the question of its truth or falsehood is not primarily involved',[47] and, just as with Derrida, this rigour is reflected by his more informed commentators and critics:

Rumours that deconstructive criticism denigrates literature, celebrates the free associations of readers, and eliminates meaning and referentiality, seem comically aberrant when one examines a few of the many examples of deconstructive criticism.[48]

In the hands of its most outstanding practitioners and advocates, then, deconstruction would appear to be rather different from that which Cupitt imagines it to be. Both Derrida and de Man (and others also) understand deconstruction as being an approach which, whilst it may complicate issues of reference and truth, and may even sometimes lead to paradox, nonetheless does not – either in theory or in practice – undermine reference and truth as intelligible concepts. They remain – and they remain vital – even if we perhaps have to be a little more careful or cautious in our use of them.

Such an understanding of deconstruction as this radically alters its potential relationship with theology. It means that deconstruction does not, as Cupitt seems to imply, 'settle' the question of God in favour of his non-existence, but rather it simply highlights the difficulties in talking meaningfully of God or of metaphysics generally – difficulties of which Christianity has never anyway been entirely unaware. John D. Caputo delineates this understanding of the relationship between deconstruction and theology with particular clarity:

The role of difference/*différance* is to establish the conditions within which discourse functions. It founds (and un-founds, undermines) languages, vocabularies, showing how they are both possible and impossible, that is, incapable of a closure which would give them self-sufficiency and a feeling of success in nailing things down. So difference/*différance* establishes the possibility (and impossibility) of a language which addresses God, even of one which invokes the dissonances of negative theology – even as it establishes the possibility (and impossibility) of a discourse in which God is denied. It does not settle the God-question one way or another. In fact, it *un*settles it, by showing that any debate about the existence of God is beset by the difficulties which typically inhabit such debates, by their inevitable recourse to binary pairs which cannot be made to stick.[49]

Interestingly, and significantly, he then proceeds to challenge Mark Taylor's 'a/theology' in terms which would be equally appropriate to Cupitt's use of Derrida's ideas – in other words, that deconstruction has been hailed as an antagonist of theism and that Derrida has been fitted into the 'familiar death of God story', rather than recognizing the position of 'armed neutrality' which deconstruction *actually* takes up between the claims both of theism and atheism.[50]

In conclusion, then, we may say that not only do all the previous criticisms expressed in this chapter hold good for Cupitt's own position, but that it can equally be argued that he is either substantially misusing the concepts of deconstruction, or that he has radically misunderstood them – neither of which possibilities does anything to instil confidence in his exposition of his own ideas based on this misreading.

In the course of this chapter and of the previous two, we have seen, therefore, that Cupitt's work suffers from substantial defects of both technique and method and theological content, and that his vision of the role of language is by no means the only possible interpretation of reality. His efforts to dismiss the objectivity of religion on *a priori* linguistic grounds fails, and we – and theology – can escape from the bars of his linguistic prison. If such a thoroughgoing radicalism is ultimately unsatisfactory, the question remains that given the justice of much of Cupitt's critique of traditional Christianity, what kind of – admittedly critical – realism might be developed in opposition to voluntarism; and what are the grounds for suggesting that such a critical realism might be more 'adequate' both intellectually and religiously than voluntarism? To this crucial question, we must finally address ourselves.

# 8

# The Reinstatement of Realism

## I

We have established in the foregoing three chapters that Cupitt's theological vision is substantially flawed in a number of vital areas, and that we are not imprisoned within the human linguistic realm, this realm not being the closed circle that Cupitt imagines it to be. There is, therefore, clearly room for an alternative theological approach to Cupitt's, and it is the intention of this chapter to outline such an approach and to indicate why it is to be preferred to Cupitt's voluntarism. Thus in the first section we will consider the intellectual foundations for critical realism and seek to establish that it is a theological option worthy of serious attention, and then in the succeeding sections we shall argue that a critical realism of this sort is more adequate both religiously and philosophically than a non-objective and non-metaphysical approach to Christianity.

In arguing against Cupitt for the viability of critical realism, it is worth recalling Cupitt's method of attempting to refute realism, which is, as we have seen, not so much to construct a case against it as simply to deny the possibility of it as a respectable or coherent theological option. A typical statement of his position would be that 'Religious activity must be purely disinterested and therefore cannot depend upon any external facts such as an objective God or a life after death',[1] with the corollary that 'Objectifying religion is now false religion, for it no longer saves.'[2] We have seen also Cupitt's tendency to equate realism with fundamentalism, and it is therefore hardly surprising that he fails to take adequate account of the possibility of critical realism, but merely dismisses it as an unsatisfactory half-way house suitable only for those who lack the courage to move further.

In opposition to this rather dismissive attitude there is, however, a growing body of opinion in the theological world which favours a more sympathetic and constructive re-examination of critical realism, feeling that Cupitt is at once insufficiently attentive to its possibilities and, indeed, now rather dated philosophically speaking, in his outspokenly anti-metaphysical stance. It was on these grounds, in fact, that Keith Ward issued the first substantial challenge to Cupitt in *Holding Fast to God*. He opens his attack on Cupitt by saying that:

> I . . . think that belief in such a God [an objective metaphysical one] is not at all out of date or intellectually disreputable. In fact, it is more intellectually defensible and morally necessary now than may have seemed possible, at least among English-speaking philosophers, forty years or so ago.[3]

And he comments also that: 'As I see it, C[upitt]'s views have been outdated by rapid advances in philosophy and the natural sciences.'[4] In the course of his monograph Ward expounds and expands these two statements. He describes the demise of logical positivism with its anti-metaphysical presuppositions,[5] and argues that Cupitt is locked into just such an outdated positivist frame of mind, and he establishes that the traditional arguments for God's existence are by no means as dead as Cupitt would have us believe.[6] Most significantly of all, though, he demonstrates that not only is metaphysical thinking not outdated, but that it is actually a necessary and inevitable part of any coherent response to the world. He does so by arguing that the denial of metaphysics is itself a metaphysical statement – in that it expresses a view concerning the 'real nature of things', which is the subject matter of metaphysics – and that therefore such a denial is immediately self-refuting! (In this there is a curious echo of Cupitt's own recent discovery that 'not to have a master narrative is still also to have one'.[7]) This perception of the necessity for some kind of metaphysics is, after a period of decline, now gaining ground again, both in the philosophical world and in the mind-set of ordinary individuals. Thus '. . . reflective people are again looking for an overall view, which will hold together all the different areas of human knowledge and experience in a coherent whole'.[8] Such an estimate of the renewed place of metaphysics in modern philosophical thought is borne out by both the title and the detailed content of Iris Murdoch's latest work, *Metaphysics as a Guide to Morals*. Indeed, her espousal of a metaphysical frame of reference is particularly significant since, like Cupitt, she rejects the idea of an objective God, preferring instead to speak of 'the good'. An insistence on metaphysics, it appears therefore, is not merely a rearguard action on the part of conservative theologians anxious to safeguard the objectivity of God, but a live option in contemporary philosophy, regardless of religious affiliations. Metaphysics is therefore a realm in which the theologian can claim an interest and a stake without the need for any special pleading whatever. Certainly the use which a theist will make of metaphysics will be distinctive, but the coherence of a metaphysical understanding of religion is no longer seriously challenged by the best of modern philosophy. The theologian can once again enter the realm of metaphysics without appearing either dated or foolish.

A further interesting aspect of this renewed interest in metaphysics in both theology and philosophy is that it has arisen partly in reaction to the anti-metaphysical polemic of the positivists and their descendants. They may initially have threatened the existence of metaphysics, but they are now, through the inadequacy and superficiality of their own alternatives to it, ironically at least partially responsible for its resurgence. The manner in which this has transpired was deftly highlighted by Janet Martin Soskice in a recent interview in the *Church Times*. In his article about the interview Paul Handley comments:

> In general, though, she detects that theology is beginning to be taken more seriously, in response to the rise of post-modernism: 'nihilism with a sharper edge – this whole idea that maybe Nietzsche was right, meaning that if God is dead it's not just the death of God but the death of absolute values. How is any value to be grounded or constituted if all we have around us is a great teeming confusion, a bareness? What then is the ground of not only our moral judgment, but also our artistic judgment, our literary judgment?'[9]

Objective metaphysical theism is regaining its credibility for the simple reason that the difficulty of constructing a meaningful and fulfilling approach to life without positing the existence of some objective source of value and meaning has been graphically illustrated by the various reductionist and broadly 'subjective' theologies of the recent past. Their spiritual atmosphere is now increasingly seen as being too thin to support life, and serious theologians – Janet Martin Soskice and Keith Ward among them – are appreciating and exploring afresh the somewhat neglected merits of objectivity and metaphysics.

What this return to objectivity means for theology is that there is, more surely than for some decades, once again a secure intellectual foundation for a realistic understanding of theology. The possibility and value of such a theological method is cogently argued by Brian Russell in his article, 'With Respect to Don Cupitt'. He criticizes Cupitt for the manner in which he argues, much as we have done earlier in this study. He dislikes Cupitt's method of argument which '. . . functions by claiming to establish mutually exclusive alternatives, and then to show the logical impossibility of one of the two alternatives, thus leaving the other to reign supreme',[10] and he denies that the theologian (or indeed the ordinary believer) is faced with a straight choice between what he calls '. . . ontological Idealism and naïve or literal Realism'.[11] There is a third possible path which avoids the contentlessness of the one, and the intellectual and moral pitfalls of the other. This third method is that which we have called 'critical realism', and Russell claims that such a method allows us to acknowledge the inadequacy of our understanding of God, and yet enables us to formulate a genuine objective content which avoids the credulousness and moral repugnance which Cupitt quite rightly abhors in a more fundamentalist or literal realism.

Clearly there is not sufficient space here to examine the consequences of critical realism for every one of the major Christian doctrines or symbols, for that would entail the construction of an entire systematic theology! However, the merits of critical realism may be at least briefly sketched by examining one of the doctrines which Cupitt most dislikes in its literal realist form – that of the Atonement. Cupitt's critique of this doctrine with its morally repugnant theories of sacrifice or substitution or vengeance or deceit has been examined at length elsewhere in this study, as has also his alternative to it, and we have seen that whilst Cupitt certainly avoids the morally dubious consequences of traditional atonement theories, he simply exchanges moral dubiety for spiritual vacuity. Deprived of all objectivity and metaphysics, the atoning death of Christ loses much, if not all, of its powerful spiritual content, and we have seen too that the 'salvific' consequences of Christ's death are also emptied of meaning once salvation becomes simply a 'state of the self'. If, then, Cupitt's alternative is no more satisfactory than the literal realism which he effectively discredits, what other alternative might there be?

In answering this question it is necessary first of all to indicate some of the differences between what I have called 'literal realism' and 'critical realism'. The major problem with literal realism, as Cupitt perceives, is that it tells a story which equates physical events with metaphysical effects on a more or less one-to-one basis. That is, it reads into the events of a story a definite and exact record of God, his activity, his 'moods', and his relationship and dealings with the human race. In doing this it encounters a host of problems, some directly and others more indirectly. Directly it tends to anthropomorphize God to a dangerously unbalanced extent by claiming too great a degree of absolute knowledge, and attempting to explain what God is 'doing' at every stage in the story. Equally it tends to cling to an outmoded world view, both in terms of natural science (i.e. in its interpretation of such passages of scripture as Genesis 1), and in terms of its wider understanding of the cosmos in which the earth often seems still to be suspended between the forces of heaven and hell in the manner of the old 'three-decker' universe. Less directly, although springing from these problems, it tends to find itself in a situation of moral dilemma as a result of its attempts to 'explain' exactly God's dealings with us – as Cupitt clearly depicts in his discussion of the atonement.

If, therefore, it is to be any more successful than such a standpoint, a more critical realism must do at least three things. It must avoid making simplistic and unfounded statements about God or about metaphysical 'events'; it must produce a vision or theory which is consonant with our understanding of ourselves and with our knowledge from other disciplines; and it must avoid falling into contradiction or over-anthropomorphism in its talk of God and his actions. If it is successful in these things, whilst still providing a meaningful picture of God's relationship with his creation, then it is likely to be true that such a position will avoid also the attendant moral errors of literal realism.

It may be objected here that in dealing specifically with the atonement, there is a danger that issues of 'critical realism' and its cognitive and explanatory claims may be confused with the related, but strictly separate issues of morality. In answer to this objection, I would argue that the two areas are, in this instance, though separable, actually closely allied. I propose, therefore, to examine the whole picture, whilst yet distinguishing between these two elements.

A critical realist approach will then, in accordance with the remarks above, attempt to get away from theorizing about God and his actions in an anthropomorphic way (and therefore from proposing a simplistic one-to-one correspondence between physical events and metaphysical effects); and it will attempt to formulate some theory which still relates events and metaphysics (to do otherwise is to sacrifice realism entirely), but without being reduced to naïve and potentially idolatrous speculation about what God can or cannot, must or must not, feel and do. In other words it will attempt to interpret the events of the Christian story – in this case the passion and crucifixion – in such a way as to safeguard the freedom of God and to acknowledge the shortcomings of our own knowledge, whilst yet still affirming that the events are significant on a metaphysical as well as on a merely physical plane – that they are effective rather than merely symbolic.

Thus critical realism acknowledges a limit to our knowledge as far as God is concerned, in that it does not leap to detailed metaphysical conclusions about God on the basis of physical events; but in terms of human cognition it still emphasizes that we can see or know or feel the activity of God through these events and through the effects which they have upon us.

Let us look, then, at the atonement, acknowledging for the present that in order to provide a full picture the cognitive and moral issues, although separate, must be considered together, since it is likely that a more sensitive cognitive theory will also result in a more satisfactory moral position. These two strands of critical knowledge and moral consequences will then be separated later on for the purpose of a closer analysis.

In order to discover what a critical realist vision of the atonement might look like, the question must be asked as to what it is that is supposed to be achieved by Christ's death, and what is supposed to be changed by it? In much traditional theology of the sort to which Cupitt objects, the answer has been given that what is achieved is our reconciliation with God by the cancelling out of our sins, which, through the cross, God forgives; and that what is changed by Christ's death is principally God's attitude towards us, which becomes one of mercy rather than one of wrath. The problems with this sort of interpretation are manifold and Cupitt rightly exposes the casuistical efforts of literal realists to explain away the very poor light in which God appears in almost any such understanding of the atonement.

In contrast to this, one possible critical realist approach – and others may wish to propose an alternative – would begin from the assumption that what is achieved by Christ's death is indeed our reconciliation with God, but through the showing forth of his love which *always* forgives, rather than through a once-for-all event of forgiveness; and that what is changed by it is principally our understanding of, and attitude towards God. Such an approach would suggest – in keeping with the central message of the gospel – that God always loves us, but it would add that we need to be assured of this and to know it within ourselves in order to come to be in a relationship with him; just as on a purely human plane, we need to know that we are loved before we can feel entirely at ease with another person. This eternal love of God for his creation was expressed most fully and most graphically in the acceptance and forgiveness of the worst that humankind can do to God – to reject him, and to attempt to kill his love in the person of his Son, Jesus Christ. Thus the cross does not, according to this view, *bring about* a forgiveness which was not there before, but rather it *enacts* and *re-presents* the forgiveness which has always been there at the heart of God. God's attitude towards us, therefore, does not change as it is held to do in more traditional models of the atonement. What does change is our attitude towards God: in seeing our forgiveness acted out before us and the evil we can do annihilated in the life of the resurrection, we then have the confidence to approach God in the *knowledge* that he loves us and is able to transform our lives, and thus by our change of attitude we are reconciled with him.

Having sketched, albeit briefly, an alternative model of the atonement, we are now in a position to isolate the issues of cognition and morality in order to see how they differ and yet how they are related in my understanding of critical realism as applied to this particular – and particularly thorny – doctrine of the atonement.

My presentation of realism is 'critical' in this instance pre-dominantly in its approach to the issues of human knowledge and understanding. In common with all realist theories it assumes, of course, *some* cognitive content – that we can know something of God and of what his intentions are. However, there are perhaps four aspects of this critical realism which render it very different from, and ultimately more satisfactory than any literal interpretation. First, it avoids the trap of anthropomorphizing God and attributing to him changeable emotions and the need for restitution and the placating of his feelings. In contrast to this, my interpretation assumes and states only the fundamental and inexhaustible love of God for his creation – something which we *must* assume to be true of God if he is to be worthy of our love and worship in the first place. No exalted claims are made for our understanding or articulation of that love, but merely that – if we assume that he exists at all – God must be first and foremost love if he is indeed to be God and not a cosmic despot. To attribute such love to God does not anthropomorphize him, for the simple reason that we have already acknowledged the in-adequacy of our words and thoughts to comprehend God, and God's love is allowed to be *his* love (and therefore beyond our comprehen-sion), and not merely *our* love transferred to him.

Secondly, this more critical realism does not assume a compli-cated series of metaphysical transactions going on in order to bring about our forgiveness and salvation. Such metaphysical speculation is seen as naïve and not susceptible of adequate substantiation. Once again this interpretation rests only upon the one basic assumption about God and his nature – that of love. Of course, it may be argued, this is just as much of an assumption as those of literal realism or those of atheism. However, since any theological position or atheological position whatsoever rests on its most basic assumptions – none of which can be 'proved' beyond all question – there is no reason to single out the assumption of God's love as being less reasonable than any other. Indeed, it can be argued that it is the most reasonable of all assumptions about God: it is a necessary assumption in that, as we indicated above, if God is not love then we have no reason to worship or love him even if he exists, and he ceases to be 'that than which nothing greater can be conceived'; and it is an assumption which is borne out by the story which speaks at every point of a love stronger even than death itself.

Thirdly, a critical approach does not read into Christ's death all the complex typology of sacrifice, or give a spuriously precise metaphysical definition to such things as St Paul's ideas of the 'Old' and 'New Adam'. They can still hold 'truth', but in a metaphorical rather than a metaphysical sense. Critical realism, as I understand it, certainly proclaims that we are redeemed and renewed by Christ's death, but not primarily on a cosmic metaphysical plane. Rather, the redemption and renewal take place on a personal spiritual plane through knowing ourselves to be loved to the uttermost, regardless of our imperfections and evil, and by being, through that knowledge, renewed and set free by the power of that love.

And finally, in this context of knowledge and understanding, this sort of critical realism is also more consonant with our modern psychological perception of ourselves as beings in need of love and reconciliation (it is no accident that 'alienation' has been a key word this century, both within theological circles and outside them), and with our understanding of the psychologically more creative effects of affective attraction and freely given love as against the potentially damaging psychological effects of an atmosphere of guilt, punishment and fear.

In this psychological dimension of realism, there is also a clear link with the moral consequences of critical realism which form a part – although a secondary one – of the overall picture. For the moral consequences of critical realism are to be preferred also to those of literal realism, in that critical realism does away with the moral repugnance of the atonement to which Cupitt, following Coleridge, so strenuously objects. As a theory it no longer implies that God is fickle or vengeful, or that a series of morally underhand dealings is necessary for our salvation. Certainly this is merely a consequence of a different – and, I believe, superior – cognitive framework, but the two aspects are nonetheless substantially related and deserve, as here, to be considered together.

I would argue, therefore, that a model of the atonement such as I have proposed here is materially different from the older theories of sacrifice or substitution but it is equally objective and equally metaphysical, whilst at the same time it avoids the problem of making God appear to exist on a morally lower plane than his creatures. A critical realism such as this represents, therefore, a viable alternative to both literal realism and subjective voluntarism, and avoids the worst extremes of both, whilst also using the best insights of both: namely, the objective content of the one, and the need for an internalized attitude to faith recognized by the other. A critical realist interpretation of the atonement insists both on the objectivity of God and on the need for our reconciliation with him, and yet at the same time places the locus of change and reconciliation within the human heart, as Cupitt himself insists that it must be. Realism, it appears, does not have to be the inert, slavish, morally repugnant credo which Cupitt so heartily – and rightly – despises.

In this context of the intellectual foundations for realism, it is worth asking, finally, whether, if realism does not *have* to be the sort of realism which Cupitt depicts, he is really 'taking leave' of the *Christian* God at all. Certainly he is taking leave of a particular conception of God, and he is outspoken in his denunciation of the excesses of literal realism as we have seen. But is the crushing and despotic God of whom he takes leave really the God of Christianity, or merely a travesty of the nature of God as Christianity at its best understands him to be? Keith Ward suggests that this is indeed the case. He examines a number of Cupitt's statements about the nature of the God of whom he is taking leave and then comments:

The God whom C [and so throughout] cannot abide is not the Christian God, the God revealed in Christ; and the real God is very like C's religious ideal, except that he exists. C's arguments for taking leave of God have missed the point, by simply talking about the wrong God. I hope that we would all take leave of his God, but I hope also that few would be tempted to think that his God was either the traditional Christian God or the God of living Christian experience.[12]

If Ward is correct, as I believe he is, then the fact that Cupitt is taking leave of a gross misrepresentation of the Christian God provides another compelling reason why a renewed and critical realism is a viable option for the Christian theologian. We have admitted in the first part of this study that Cupitt is frequently justified in his criticisms of literal realism and its consequences, but the real God of Christian experience does not have to be approached in such fundamentalist terms. Again we have examined the place and role of metaphor in religious language, and offered a theory of the relationship between language and reality and therefore between language and God. Thus what is at fault may not be 'God' as such, but merely certain of our ways of apprehending and speaking of him. Critical realism, as we have argued, offers an approach which maintains the objective reality of God without falling into the trap of claiming a literal correspondence between our language and the God of which it speaks. As critical realists we may well take leave of Cupitt's caricature of God, but 'hold fast', in Keith Ward's phrase, to the enduring Christian experience of the 'real' God. Given then, that this alternative both to literal realism and thoroughgoing voluntarism exists and is worthy of serious attention, what are its merits, both spiritually and theologically? It is to these related questions that our attention must now turn.

## II

We have established that critical realism is a viable option intellectually, and we shall return in the following section to consider some of the ways in which it is preferable philosophically, in its faithfulness to reality and experience, to voluntarism. But the heart of any religion lies not just in its theoretical foundations, but in its practice – the daily experience of worship, prayer and ethical consequences in the lives of its adherents. If then, we hope to press the claims of critical realism with any success, it is important to demonstrate its more evidently 'spiritual' merits as well as its intellectual coherence. On what grounds then, can it be asserted that critical realism is indeed more 'religiously adequate' than Cupitt's alternative? It would of course be possible to treat exhaustively of every possible dimension of the religious life, but in the interests both of brevity and the avoidance of tedium, I propose to examine three particular areas, each of them of fundamental significance in any religious outlook. These are first, the 'goal' whether implicit or explicit of the different approaches to spirituality; secondly, the ethical consequences of each approach to religion; and thirdly, what might be called the 'attitudinal' perspective of each approach, that is, the underlying attitude to life which it envisages as the most appropriate or commendable.

With regard to the first of these areas, we have noted Cupitt's objection to the idea that spirituality is to be pursued for the sake of reward or for the avoidance of punishment. In response to this objection he attempts to argue that spirituality should be pursued for its own sake, and that the goal of the religious life is just that – spirituality itself. The difficulty with this is that in trying to get away from a spirituality which concentrates on its consequences for the individual, which he rightly sees as an odiously ego-ridden perspective, he dispenses with any 'objective' realities in the spiritual life. At a first glance it sounds a plausible solution: once there is no objective God to reward us or punish us, then all such base incentives to spirituality are removed, and it may then be pursued entirely for its own sake. In this assumption there is, however, a fundamental error, for the language which Cupitt uses will not bear the weight of the ideas he is expressing. If I say that I pursue spirituality for its own sake then the sentence has no real content – a problem we have seen with much of Cupitt's theological world – for what does spirituality matter if there is no one for it to matter to? Thus if one wishes to recommend its pursuance it must be because it matters, and if it matters, it matters to me. To say then that I pursue spirituality for its own sake is tantamount to saying that I pursue it for the sake of my own spirituality – which is an equally egocentric perspective to the one from which Cupitt was originally attempting to escape! As Rowan Williams astutely remarks: '. . . religious language collapses in upon itself when it tries to make spirituality a religious goal'.[13]

Cupitt has thus reached an impasse. He has perceived a major problem with regard to a certain religious outlook, but has in his solution to it ironically re-created the same problem in a different guise. A critical realist approach is far better equipped to solve this problem than Cupitt's voluntarism can ever be, for the simple reason that it is almost impossible to see how the error into which Cupitt falls can be avoided if a non-objective spiritual realm is the only one which is to be countenanced. Spirituality *needs* an objective referent in order to avoid the egocentrism which Cupitt so much detests. Certainly it must also avoid the other extreme of a 'reward and punishment' mentality, but a critical realism is well equipped to achieve this also. A critical realist approach to spirituality begins from the dual acknowledgment that whilst we can speak meaning-fully of God, and even make statements about his nature, yet we cannot equate our statements with the reality of which they speak: our language about, and understanding of God is always inadequate. God is therefore in no danger of being reduced to human size. He is not a God who operates according to our limited perceptions of justice and mercy, reward and punishment, and there is equally acknowledged to be no way in which we can ever aspire, morally or spiritually, to the stature or perfection of the God whom we worship. By this means the motive of 'self-preservation' is once again removed from spirituality, since we cannot by our own efforts effect our salvation or improve our standing with God: and yet the objective reality of God is not impugned either. So what is the 'goal' of the religious life according to such an understanding? This goal is in fact, intimately bound up with the imperfect manner in which we conceive of God. We see beyond us, however dimly, a source of beauty, truth, holiness and the like, and we are drawn towards it precisely *for its own sake*, simply because it is what it is. Again it is Rowan Williams who aptly characterizes the essence of such an approach when he says of 'good' actions that:

> They are performed not with the motive of winning salvation, not in obedience to a command, but as expressions of the desire and pursuit of the beauty of God.[14]

According to this view, spirituality is pursued for the sake of a 'goal' outside of ourselves, not slavishly but voluntarily, and both the objective reality of God and, incidentally though not unimportantly, the free choice of the human soul are respected. Spirituality *needs* an objective referent in order not to become solipsistic:

To be what it [the spiritual life] is it must give up reserves and conditions in surrender to the dark purpose of an unknown God: as we have noted, it cannot safely image the condition to which it aspires. God as that to which the silence and abandonment of contemplation is directed abides as a corrective to subtle forms of complacency and spiritual eudaemonism.[15]

The ability of critical realism to insist at once upon the objective reality of God and the inadequate and metaphorical way in which we understand and speak of him, offers a spiritual way which avoids the extremes both of egocentrism and contentlessness, and which reflects a coherent though partial understanding of God, and a meaningful vision of our relationship with him. It therefore achieves the 'adequacy' for which Cupitt strives, and which he fails – as any purely subjective religious perspective must fail – to attain.

The second of our chosen areas follows on naturally from the first, though it is distinct from it, and this is a consideration of the ethical consequences of religion when conceived subjectively and objectively. Here, as in the realm of spirituality, Cupitt creates as many problems as he solves by his insistence on the subjectivity of the moral realm. Just as with spirituality he is concerned to escape from the danger of absorption with the individual and the benefits which may accrue to me if I act morally. The prospect of reward is not an adequate – or even a worthy – incentive for the highest moral behaviour. Like spirituality, morality must be pursued for its own sake, and so Cupitt champions the concept of 'disinterestedness'. We shall return to the question of whether this is in itself the overriding good which Cupitt claims, but here the issue is whether or not Cupitt even achieves this standpoint in his own thinking, and whether indeed such a standpoint of disinterestedness is even a possibility in the subjective world which Cupitt inhabits.

Rowan Williams provides an excellent critique of disinterestedness and his argument is worth following in some detail. He notes the difficulty of defining disinterestedness when there are '. . . finally no moral goals outside the self or the will',[16] and it is clear that there must always be an inherent problem in achieving disinterestedness in a moral world which begins and ends with *me*. The problem is intractable: certainly I may attempt not to be influenced in my moral choices by my own desires or selfish needs, but if the *goal* of my moral efforts is my own disinterestedness, then I am immediately thrust back into the egocentric perspective from which I am trying to escape. The goal of the moral life cannot be anything to do with *me* or *my* state – even my own disinterestedness – if it is to avoid an ultimately egocentric dimension. As Rowan Williams remarks:

> . . . If *disinterestedness* is itself the goal, if there are not goals beyond the self, how do we distinguish this from an ultimate narcissism, from the kind of elevated eudaemonism Mr Cupitt occasionally lets slip . . .'[17]

And he concludes, illuminatingly:

> Disinterestedness can only issue as a by-product of the moral life: as a goal in itself, it cannibalizes all other goals, and enjoins that we attend to ourselves (including our possible future selves).[18]

To be fair to Cupitt, he himself does not let the matter rest here. He perceives the danger of his position, and the possibility of precisely this line of criticism, and so he invokes the language of traditional religion with its talk of God as a way of escaping from the trap of egocentrism and giving the moral life a goal external to ourselves. Superficially it sounds a plausible enough solution, but once again, his language collapses in upon itself when one remembers that God has already been totally 'de-objectified' and internalized and reduced to an ideal, or to the sum of *our* ideal values. Thus even invoking God (when he is defined like this) only succeeds in returning us into ourselves again. A closely-argued paragraph from Rowan Williams illustrates the problem clearly:

> To say 'God is to be loved for His own sake' and mean 'the state of absolute spiritual liberty is to be desired for its own sake' does not solve the problem of how we may disinterestedly pursue purity of heart. We know perfectly well (according to Cupitt) that there are no moral constraints external to the will, and so no moral goals external to the self. In the last analysis, we shall still evaluate our

acts and choices according to how much nearer they bring us to 'divine consciousness'; we are still acting *for the sake* of our own purification. Mr Cupitt in fact accepts that disinterestedness best makes sense when moral striving is provided with an imaginative focus beyond our present self-consciousness. But how can this be effective when such a focus is acknowledged to be simply a fantasy of what I might in principle be?[19]

As with spirituality, morality *requires* a goal outside of the individual self in order to be fully meaningful and to deliver us from the prison of ourselves and our own desires, and this exteriorized goal of the moral life is something which Cupitt's entirely interior and subjective religious vision is ultimately – and inevitably – unable to provide. By contrast, it may be argued that this is precisely what critical realism is capable of providing, and yet without veering to the opposite extreme of reducing the moral life to one of slavish obedience to a divine despot: a matter of '. . . working to rule, and keeping your head down and your nose clean',[20] as Cupitt calls it. The success of critical realism in the moral realm again stems from its acknowledgment of both the 'truth' and the partial and inadequate nature of our statements about God. Unlike a more fundamentalist approach, it does not try to assert that we have received from the divine hand a set of inflexible, perfect and universally applicable laws for every conceivable moral situation. It asserts instead that we, like all who have gone before us, have a fragmentary and limited vision of the divine perfection which has issued in all of the various moral frameworks which we inherit, and which reflect our imperfect strivings after the perfection of God himself. Our part in the moral task is therefore seen as a continuation of this imperfect striving, an attempt always to refine our moral understanding and so to perceive as clearly as we are able what – in the conditions of this earth on which we live – best reflects our admittedly still inadequate vision of God's perfection and truth. The striving is always for a perfection outside ourselves, pursued at last genuinely *for its own sake* and yet there is always room also for the kind of moral creativity which Cupitt demands, in that ethics is a perpetual search for an ever clearer understanding of what the 'good' might be, and a permanent creative effort to translate our vision of God into coherent and consistent human terms. It achieves, indeed, that goal which Cupitt desires, that of freeing us from our egocentricity, and it does so precisely by retaining an objective moral vision – namely the perfection of God, however dimly perceived – of the kind which Cupitt's rarified religious atmosphere will not admit. In a critical realist perspective then, morality is intimately related to spirituality in that both stem from the same vision of God, and this inhering together of the different parts of the religious life constitutes a further important pointer to the superior adequacy of a critical realist understanding of Christianity.

Finally, in this section, there remains to be considered what we have termed the underlying 'attitudinal' outlook of these various perceptions of the religious life, and we return again therefore to the concept of 'disinterestedness'. The question here, though, is not so much whether Cupitt is able to achieve it or not, but whether, in more general terms, such an attitude is even as desirable or appropriate as the basis for the living of a truly religious life as Cupitt suggests.

Whether such an attitude is desirable or appropriate will depend, at least in part, on what the essential character of this life is seen to be. If, for example, like the majority of Buddhists – and a number of other Eastern religions – one feels that the world is, in its essence, primarily a place of trial, of suffering, or of evil, then perhaps disinterestedness might be acknowledged to be a reasonable response to it, although even then one may question whether it is necessarily entirely laudable. However, such is not, and has never been, the Christian view either of creation or of our life within it. Admittedly there is suffering and evil in abundance in our world and Christianity has never made light of these things. But they are not seen to be constitutive of the underlying essence of things. Rather, they are a deviation from it. Christianity has always held the universe to be, as God's creation, a place with the capacity for good and for joy. It has taken as its basic attitude towards the universe the oft-repeated words from Genesis 1: 'And God saw that it was good.' Evil and suffering undoubtedly mar the goodness and joy of our life, but the vision and possibility of goodness in creation is there nonetheless, and depends only upon our response to God and his goodness to actualize it in human lives.

With a vision of life such as this, 'disinterestedness' begins to seem less than satisfactory as a response to it. As Keith Ward comments:

> Suppose we think that the world, when transformed by clear knowledge of God, does offer the prospect of endless joy; then surely it becomes irrational to say that we should be absolutely uninterested in this, as in anything else. Surely the only rational thing to do is to desire it with all the passion at our disposal, to 'hunger and thirst' after a glimpse of this God, this pearl of infinite value.[21]

Our response to such a world will be the very opposite of disinterestedness: '. . . total interestedness, commitment to a positive good, passionate involvement to disclose the true object of desire to all, not renunciation of all desires'.[22]

Such an attitude towards our life is not only consistent with the nature of creation as Christianity perceives it, but also with the central revelatory event and theological tenet of the Christian faith: the incarnation. A critical realist vision of faith would see in the incarnation the supreme example of 'interestedness' – God's interestedness in his creation. And what is revealed in the incarnation is a God who is passionately committed to the well-being of his people. This commitment is revealed not only in the more metaphysical aspects of the incarnation, such as our reconciliation with God, which we discussed earlier, but also in the physical words and deeds of Jesus. For Jesus was not 'disinterested': he too was passionately committed to the people he walked and taught among, feeling compassion for their lostness and sickness, healing them, and weeping with them and for them. Disinterestedness is not only an illogical response to our world, but also radically unfaithful to the character of Jesus himself. Once again, in the closeness of the links between such a world view and the realms of spirituality and ethics, the consistency of a critical realist approach is highlighted, and its superior adequacy both in interpreting our life and enabling us to live a fulfilling spiritual and moral life is thereby reinforced.

We have seen then that a critical realist understanding of religion is both intellectually possible, and religiously appropriate, and in the final section of this chapter we shall return to the intellectual and philosophical dimension and consider what might be termed 'the question of truth'. In a sense, we are brought full circle. Having begun from an intellectual perspective we have, in our discussion of the religious merits of interestedness and disinterestedness touched on the question of what sort of religious life is appropriate to the character of the world as we perceive it to be. We turn now therefore to the question, both religious and intellectual, of the faithfulness to reality – and therefore the 'truth' – of these different understandings of religion.

### III

In the construction of the case for a realist interpretation of religion, strength is given to the position of theological realism by the recognition that it is not alone in demanding such a response to the universe. In spite of a vociferous minority, there is a large body of scientific opinion which asserts that the universe simply '*is*', independently of our observation or interpretation of it and, just as in theology, there is a growing movement towards critical, rather than literal realism in the scientific world. Janet Martin Soskice outlines the basis for such an attitude particularly clearly:

> The conviction that to make sense of scientific practice one must regard certain non-observational theoretical terms as about 'things' and their powers and not simply, in the instrumentalist fashion, as convenient fictions for the ordering of observables, is the impetus for a critical scientific realism the basic principle of which is that scientific investigation gives us access to structures that exist independently of us. Although the critical realists concede that these powers and structures may never be susceptible to direct observation by us and, in that sense, remain 'transcendent', they none the less regard scientific explanation, even in its reliance on models or analogues, as being reality depicting.[23]

Such a critical scientific realism does not claim an error-free exactitude and certainty for itself either:

> . . . it is part of the attraction of the critical realism we have been discussing that it need not hold that the terms of a mature science mirror the world in an unrevisable fashion. Its terms are seen as representing reality without claiming to be representationally privileged.[24]

In these two important respects then – that it claims to depict the reality of the universe of which it speaks, and which is a reality independent of science itself, and that it acknowledges its own inadequacy and the fragmentary nature of its insights – scientific critical realism is very much akin to theological critical realism. In this it provides at least a measure of support for the conviction that our perceptions or our language are not the only reality, but that there is a reality beyond and over against us which exists in its own right, independent of what we may say of it or do about it.

Further, and possibly even more far-reaching support is given to the critical realist position in that it reflects the way in which we instinctively perceive the world around us. Critical realism is in tune with our daily experience of living, and does not require any convoluted mental gymnastics, of the kind which Linda Woodhead finds so damaging,[25] in order to explain itself. Brian Hebblethwaite articulates this common-sense strength of realism succinctly:

> Many minds, including many non-religious minds, instinctively resist these trends [away from realism]. Common-sense conviction that the world about us consists of things and kinds of things that are what they are prior to and quite apart from any observation and thought, and are discovered to be what they are by the learned and self-correcting use of fallible human faculties, is a conviction that for the most part survives sceptical assault.[26]

He admits too the provisionality and inexactitude of our theories and knowledge of the world:

> Admittedly, the theories in terms of which the natural sciences expand and systematize our knowledge of the world are partial, provisional and revisable human constructions. So, for that matter, are the human languages themselves in which we

formulate and express both our common sense and our scientific understanding of the world. Yet the function of both language and scientific theory is to articulate and advance awareness of what there is – first and foremost of what there is in any case, quite apart from human knowledge and human interests.[27]

Here again, the realism which is being advocated is seen to be a critical one in the sense especially of being self-critical, aware of its own failings, and attempting always to refine its insights and approach more clearly the reality about which it seeks to speak.

Critical realism, therefore, rests on a conviction – shared by a substantial body both of theologians, philosophers and scientists, as well as many lay people – of what might be called the 'is-ness' of things: the conviction that they simply 'are' in and of themselves, a view echoed not only by those writers whom we have cited, but by a variety of others including a very clear statement of this 'is-ness' by F. C. Happold in his book *Religious Faith and Twentieth Century Man*.[28] Critical realism is therefore seen to be in keeping with a growing reaction against what C. D. Broad referred to as 'silly theories',[29] and in line with an 'animal faith' in the reality of things outside our own intellect of the kind which George Santayana defends.[30] Critical realism is, it is argued, more true to our daily experience of life and to our most basic instincts about life – as well as more in keeping with other realms of knowledge such as the scientific – than the more abstruse speculations of idealist, voluntarist or positivist philosophers and theologians.

This observation leads on to the second area in which critical realism may be held to be truer to the nature of reality than Cupitt's alternative: that is, the need for a religion to have the potential for universal appeal. A religion needs, as we have seen, to have its roots in a realm which makes real connections with people's daily life and experience, and, if it is to claim to be a plausible response to reality, it must also have the ability to be a religion for all people, and not merely for an eclectically minded intellectual minority. Here again Cupitt's voluntarism is open to question. The most telling critique of Cupitt's views according to this criterion of universality is advanced by John Hick. He argues that a path such as Cupitt's is only open to a particular kind of highly intellectual and self-aware spirituality, and that the vast majority of people are inherently unable to travel the spiritual path which Cupitt has mapped out. This being so, they are all doomed to die in a state of unenlightenment, unfulfilment or 'non-salvation', and there is also in Cupitt's world no possibility of any greater fulfilment for them thereafter. Thus Hick comments:

> The kind of non-realist religiousness advocated by such contemporaries as D. Z. Phillips and Don Cupitt offers, then, welcome news for the few which is at the same time grim news for the many. It is for this reason that it has to face the charge of an unintended elitism.[31]

Hick acknowledges that this unwelcome pessimism is not actually an argument for the falsity of Cupitt's position as such – he could, possibly, be right. But it is a reason why Cupitt's position:

> . . . cannot credibly claim to represent the message of the great spiritual traditions. For it proposes such a reversal of their faith, from a cosmic optimism to a cosmic pessimism, as to offer a radically different vision.[32]

We cannot, in this instance, perhaps claim that critical realism is 'right' and that Cupitt is 'wrong', but we can claim that it is truer to the spiritual needs of the whole of humanity: for if a few need fulfilment or salvation, then so do we all. Critical realism is 'truer' both representationally and salvifically than Cupitt's voluntarism is capable of being.

We have argued, then, for the superiority of critical realism both in terms of reality depiction and in terms of its religious adequacy, and suggested that it is to be preferred, both intellectually and spiritually, to any non-realist interpretation of religion. To say this is not to deny the very real problems inherent in realism, especially if it is to avoid toppling over into a literal realism of the sort which I, equally with Cupitt, would reject as intellectually, spiritually and morally repugnant. A critical realism therefore has to acknowledge and learn to live with its own shortcomings, and perpetually achieve the precarious balance of affirmation and negation in its statements about God and about the spiritual life. It has to interpret the events both of scripture and of life in a way which does justice both to the otherness and sovereignty of God, and to human creativity and freedom; and it has to find in its worship of an objective God the springs of a loving service to the world, a task which demands that it achieve a balance between the interior life of the spirit and the manifestation of that life in our lives in the world.

In view of all these constraints and potential pitfalls it cannot be argued that critical realism is a naïve or lazy option. It demands perpetual awareness and self-criticism, and an openness to the newness of religious experience. But, precisely in its need for awareness and self-criticism it avoids the tendency of voluntarism – which we have discussed above – simply to replace one problem with another, often indeed the same problem in another guise. Critical realism, it may be coherently argued, is, for all its acknowledged imperfection, more internally consistent and more 'truthful' to reality and human experience than a non-realist approach to religion. It is, therefore, on both of these grounds, to use Cupitt's own word once more, a more 'adequate' religious perspective than his own.

# Conclusion: Cupitt in Perspective

During the course of this study, it may perhaps appear that the underlying attitude to Don Cupitt has changed from the first part to the second part: that his views are presented in an apparently sympathetic light in the one, and then subjected to several harsh and searching criticisms in the other. This disparity between the two parts is to a large extent inevitable, given the aims of this study.

Thus, I believe, as I have indicated previously, that Cupitt's challenge to realism is an important one and deserves to be taken seriously by the mainstream of Christian theology. Iris Murdoch's summary of his significance for Christian theology is not inappropriate:

> . . . Cupitt is a very brave and valuable pioneer and a learned and accessible thinker, who stirs up thought where it is most needed. He speaks *directly*, as few do, about the *necessity of new thinking* about God and religion as something which concerns us all.[1]

In order, therefore, to understand the nature of his importance and challenge correctly it has been necessary to spell it out in some detail, and to present it in such a way as to acknowledge its full force. Cupitt asks some penetrating questions with regard to the way in which we interpret the Christian story, and with regard also to many of the most basic elements of Christian doctrine and practice, such as prayer, morality, salvation and the like.

Equally, however, although freely acknowledging the significance of his questions – and indeed of many of his criticisms of traditional Christianity – I also believe him to be fundamentally wrong in his response to the problems of orthodoxy, and especially in his abandonment of objectivity in religion in a search for a 'post-modern' spirituality. It has therefore been necessary to refute his claims in some detail, and to assert the intellectual and spiritual coherence of critical realism in opposition to his views. There is insufficient space in a study of this nature to construct a point-by-point answer to Cupitt, and with it a full systematic theology. The purpose of the latter part of this study has been, rather, to outline the case against Cupitt and for realism at some particularly salient points in the debate. Many of the inadequacies of Cupitt's position have been highlighted, and the bones of a substantial case for critical realism have been presented. These may be fleshed out in their turn elsewhere.

The task of responding to the many sceptical and reductionist approaches to religion – for Cupitt's is by no means the only possible one – is a vital one for theology and one which has been curiously neglected for some time. Many theologians have continued to construct theological systems or patterns of ideas without appearing to notice that others are attempting to dig away the ground from under their feet. The cause of realist theology is most helpfully served not by ignoring, but by meeting the challenges which both other disciplines, and radical theologians such as Cupitt, present to it. The importance of not merely constructing a realist theology but of confronting the challenge of anti-realism is forcefully expressed by Janet Martin Soskice:

> A form of critical realism is advocated for theology, not because it is the only cogent position, but because so much of the Christian tradition has been undeniably realist in sensibility, and because it is important to defend a version of theological realism, given the anti-realist drift of so much modern philosophical theology.[2]

However, even to say this much is not ultimately sufficient. It stresses the importance of the task facing realist theology, but it fails to say *why* that task is so important – other than to preserve realist theology, which is something of a circular argument!

In conclusion, then, I propose to offer, at least briefly, an analysis of *why* it is that realism needs to be defended against anti-realism; an analysis which, at the same time, indicates what is perhaps the most fundamental difference of all between Cupitt's anti-realist and a genuinely critical realist position – apart, of course, from the obvious fact that one of them asserts that God is an 'ideal' and the other that he is 'real'.

The difference between realism and Cupitt's anti-realism lies, I would suggest, in their starting points. It is interesting that in *Jesus and the Gospel of God* Cupitt, for the first time, expresses an interest in what he calls the category of the 'purely religious', and he insists on the need for this in direct opposition to the categories of metaphysical thought:

> To throw off the legacy of Christendom however, and return to the teaching of Jesus and the primitive faith requires not only that we rescue Jesus from dogmatic captivity, but that we rescue God from metaphysical captivity . . . And the primitive Christian faith, if and when we rediscover it, will also come as a total surprise. What we need today is not the transposition of the remains of Christendom into some liberal or humanist framework of ideas, but something more drastic, a reaffirmation of the purely religious categories in which Christianity first came into the world.[3]

There is, it must be admitted, a laudable aim behind this in Cupitt's concern for the primarily spiritual – rather than organizational, hierarchical, or power-oriented – values of Jesus and of the Christianity which he founded. However, in the succeeding few years, and beginning with *Taking Leave of God* in the following year, this 'purely religious' dimension became, as we have seen in his demand for the internalization of God and the complete subjectivity of all Christian doctrine and practice, the overriding factor in Cupitt's approach to faith. And in this he differs fundamentally from a more realistic conception of faith. Cupitt, for the best of reasons, begins from a concern with religion; with the purely spiritual; with the spiritual state of the individual, and his theology is geared to that end. He excises the potentially complicating factors of 'God', a real 'objective' and therefore intractable cosmos, and a degree of metaphysics; and the result, as we have argued, is pure but vacuous, and marginalizes any possible concern for an appropriate or 'true' response to reality.

By contrast, realism, in its more critical manifestations, begins – as we asserted in the previous chapter – from the perceived structure of reality; from its 'is-ness', from the 'facts' of the Christian story, and from our knowledge and experience of ourselves as persons in need of relationship and salvation. In the process it may occasionally become soiled or get its hands dirty, and its insights may, of course, sometimes be wrong. But this in no way invalidates the significance of its undertaking, which is to evolve a meaningful response to the cosmos and to a creator perceived both within and beyond it; to develop a coherent spiritual life which enables us to live fulfilling lives in relationship to both cosmos and creator; and to exercise both our creativity and freedom in that relationship whilst looking to God for their ultimate fulfilment conceived of as 'redemption' or 'salvation'. In this difference, and in the greater 'adequacy' of realism for which we have consistently argued, lies the need for that realism to maintain its cause against anti-realism: that is, that by doing so it is engendering a more 'adequate' and fulfilling spiritual – and therefore also material – life for the great mass of humankind, whose well-being is of prime importance to a realistic Christianity, for it cannot renege on this undertaking without playing false to the God which it claims to worship, and who is envisaged as the creator and lover of all. Realism must assert its own position if it is to remain true to itself and to the perceived character of its God.

The vital importance of this endeavour is aptly characterized by Dorothy Emmet when she comments that:

> Religion loses its nerve when it ceases to believe that it expresses in some way truth about our relation to a reality beyond ourselves which ultimately concerns us.[4]

Realism needs at once to take cognisance of the very real challenge of anti-realism, and to respond actively and creatively to it. If it does not do so, it will be false to itself, and may quite possibly perish by default. If it succeeds in responding in this way, then although the debate may never be entirely resolved, it will be one which will prove ultimately fruitful for Christianity, and may be a means by which a critical realist theology and spirituality will find that in being roused to the challenge, realism is itself better equipped than previously to provide an adequate religious response to the modern world. For all Cupitt's faults, it may be ironically, that in the force of his challenge to realism, he will, if it responds to that challenge, have served his beloved cause of 'religious adequacy' more substantially and enduringly than he himself might either have guessed, or perhaps even have wished!

# Notes

Full publication details of the books cited will be found in the Bibliography

## Introduction

1. James Barr, *The Bible in the Modern World*, and *Fundamentalism*.
2. Gustavo Gutierrez, *A Theology of Liberation*.
3. See, for example, the selection of writers and countries represented in *Frontiers of Theology in Latin America*, ed. Rosino Gibellini.
4. David Sheppard, *Bias to the Poor*.
5. See, for example, such works as Rosemary Radford Ruether, *Mary, The Feminine Face of the Church* and Krister Stendahl, *The Bible and the Role of Women*.
6. Jurgen Moltmann, *The Crucified God*.
7. Paul Rowntree Clifford, *Politics and the Christian Vision*.
8. Margaret Kane, *Gospel in Industrial Society*.
9. *Lux Mundi: A Series of Studies in the Religion of the Incarnation* ed. Charles Gore.
10. *Soundings: Essays Concerning Christian Understanding* ed. Alec Vidler.
11. *The Myth of God Incarnate* ed. John Hick.
12. For example Don Cupitt, *Crisis of Moral Authority*, first issued in 1972 and reissued in 1985.
13. Scott Cowdell, *Atheist Priest? Don Cupitt and Christianity*, p. 73.
14. Keith Ward, *Holding Fast to God*.
15. Brian Hebblethwaite, *The Ocean of Truth*.
16. David L. Edwards, *Tradition and Truth*, ch. 3.
17. Cowdell, *Atheist Priest?*
18. Don Cupitt, *Christ and the Hiddenness of God*, Preface to the 2nd edn, p. 9.

## 1 Roots in Orthodoxy

1. Scott Cowdell, *Atheist Priest?*, p. ix.

2. E.g. Keith Ward, *Holding Fast to God*; Brian Hebblethwaite, *The Ocean of Truth*.
3. Cowdell, p. xiii.
4. Quoted on back cover of the second edition of *Crisis of Moral Authority*.
5. Don Cupitt, *Explorations in Theology 6*, p. vii. Cupitt's italics.
6. Ibid., p. viii.
7. Don Cupitt, *Christ and the Hiddenness of God*, 2nd edn, p. 6.
8. Ibid., pp. 42–3.
9. Ibid., p. 43.
10. Ibid.
11. Don Cupitt, *The Leap of Reason*, 2nd edn, p. 37.
12. Ibid., Cupitt's italics.
13. Ibid., p. 66.
14. Ibid., p. 66.
15. Ibid., pp. 72–3.
16. Ibid., p. 77.
17. John Macquarrie, *Twentieth-Century Religious Thought*, 4th edn, pp. 34–5.
18. St Augustine, *Confessions*, I.4.
19. Cupitt, *The Leap of Reason*, p. 92.
20. Ibid.
21. Cupitt, *Christ and the Hiddenness of God*, p. 213.
22. Ibid.
23. Don Cupitt, *Jesus and the Gospel of God*, p. 92.
24. Ibid., p. 93.
25. Ibid., p. 93.
26. Ibid., p. 99.
27. Ibid., p. 99.
28. Ibid., p. 99.
29. Lloyd Geering, *Faith's New Age*, p. 165.
30. Don Cupitt, *Crisis of Moral Authority*, p. 118.
31. Don Cupitt, *The Worlds of Science and Religion*, pp. 102–3.
32. Ibid., p. 103.
33. See, for example, G. W. Allport, *The Individual and his Religion*, pp. 24–6, 116.
34. Cupitt, *The Leap of Reason*, pp. xii–xiii.

## 2  Objections to Orthodoxy

1. John Macquarrie, *Jesus Christ in Modern Thought*, p. 265.
2. Don Cupitt, 'The Last Man', in *Explorations in Theology 6*, pp. 59–64 (p. 61).
3. Ibid.
4. Ibid.

5. Ibid.
6. Ibid., p. 62.
7. Don Cupitt, 'The Original Jesus', in *Explorations*, pp. 65–69 (p. 65).
8. Ibid., p. 69.
9. Ibid., p. 69.
10. Don Cupitt, 'Myth Understood', in *Explorations*, pp. 70–78 (p. 78).
11. Ibid.
12. Don Cupitt, *Jesus and the Gospel of God*, p. 18.
13. Ibid., p. 21.
14. Don Cupitt, *Christ and the Hiddenness of God*, p. 8.
15. Don Cupitt, 'The Ethics of this World and the Ethics of the World to Come', in *Explorations*, pp. 98–109 (p. 106).
16. Ibid., p. 108.
17. S. T. Coleridge, *Aids to Reflection* (1825), 'Aphorisms on Spiritual Religion', Bohn edition (1901), p. 103. Quoted in Don Cupitt, *Crisis of Moral Authority*, p. 21.
18. Cupitt, *Crisis of Moral Authority*, p. 28. Cupitt's italics.
19. Ibid.
20. Ibid., p. 29.
21. Don Cupitt, *The New Christian Ethics*, p. 5.
22. Cupitt, *Crisis of Moral Authority*, p. 45.
23. Cupitt, *The New Christian Ethics*, p. 20.
24. Emil Brunner, *The Mediator*, pp. 595–6. Quoted in Michael Ramsey, *The Gospel and the Catholic Church*, p. 131.
25. Cupitt, *Jesus and the Gospel of God*, p. 22.
26. Ibid., p. 23.
27. Ibid., p. 43.
28. Ibid., pp. 86–7.
29. Iris Murdoch, *Metaphysics as a Guide to Morals*, p. 56.
30. Janet Martin Soskice, *Metaphor and Religious Language*, p. 140.
31. Don Cupitt, *Only Human*, pp. 204–5.
32. Ibid., p. 205.
33. Feuerbach, *The Essence of Christianity*, p. 26.
34. Ibid., p. 249.
35. Cf., for example, Cupitt, *Crisis of Moral Authority*, pp. 78–9, p. 119.
36. Cupitt, *Crisis of Moral Authority*, pp. 119–120.
37. Ibid., pp. 7–8.
38. Don Cupitt, *Taking Leave of God*, p. 129.
39. Ibid.
40. Ibid., p. 158.
41. Ibid., p. 159.
42. Ibid., p. 159.
43. Don Cupitt, *The World to Come*, p. 98.

44. Ibid.
45. Don Cupitt, *The Long-Legged Fly*, p. 158.
46. Don Cupitt, *Radicals and the Future of the Church*, p. 97.
47. Ibid., p. 173.
48. T. S. Eliot, 'The Hippopotamus', in *The Complete Poems and Plays of T. S. Eliot*, Faber & Faber 1969, pp, 49–50.
49. *We Believe in God*, A report by the Doctrine Commimssion of the Church of England.
50. *Children in the Way*, A report on Children in the Church, for the General Synod Board of Education.
51. Cupitt, *Taking Leave of God*, p. 5.
52. Cupitt, *The World to Come*, p. xi.
53. Cupitt, *Christ and the Hiddenness of God*, p. 166.
54. Ibid., p. 154.
55. Ibid., p. 162.
56. Ibid., p. 162.
57. Ibid., p. 164.
58. Ibid., p. 164.
59. See, for example, D. Z. Phillips, *Religion Without Explanation*.
60. Cupitt, *Christ and the Hiddenness of God*, p. 167.
61. Cupitt, *Explorations*, p. viii.
62. Rupert Brooke, 'Heaven', in *Collected Poems*, Sidgwick & Jackson 1918; 3rd edn 1942, pp. 132–33.
63. Feuerbach, pp. 106–7.
64. Lloyd Geering, *Faith's New Age*, p. 141.
65. Feuerbach, p. 184.
66. Ibid.
67. Freud, *The Future of an Illusion*, in The Pelican Freud, Vol. 12, p. 233.
68. Freud, *Psychopathology of Everyday Life*. Quoted in J. N. Isbister, *Freud: An Introduction to his Life and Work*, p. 210. Freud's italics.
69. Freud, *New Introductory Lectures on Psycho-Analysis*. Quoted in Isbister, p. 215.
70. Emile Durkheim, *The Elementary Forms of the Religious Life*, p. 206.
71. Cupitt, *The World to Come*, p. 71.
72. Freud, *The Future of an Illusion*, p. 233. Freud's italics.
73. Cupitt, *Radicals and the Future of the Church*, p. 167.
74. Ibid.
75. Cupitt, *The Long-Legged Fly*, p. 155.
76. Ibid.
77. Ibid.
78. Cupitt, *The New Christian Ethics*, p. 27.
79. Ibid., p. 60.
80. Ibid.

81. Geering, pp. 141–2.
82. Troeltsch, *Protestantism and Progress*. Quoted in Geereing, p. 254.
83. Cupitt, *Taking Leave of God*, p. 14.
84. Ibid., p. 98.
85. Ibid., p. 43.
86. Ibid., p. 43.
87. Cupitt, *Only Human*, p. 211.
88. Cupitt, *Taking Leave of God*, p. 126.
89. Don Cupitt, *The Sea of Faith*, 2nd edn, p. 59.
90. Cf., for example, Cupitt, *Only Human*, p. 136.
91. Cupitt, *Only Human*, p. 212.
92. Cupitt, *Taking Leave of God*, p. 126.
93. Ibid.
94. Cupitt, *The New Christian Ethics*, p. 36.
95. Cupitt, *Taking Leave of God*, pp. 115–6.
96. Cupitt, *The World to Come*, p. 74.
97. Cupitt, *The New Christian Ethics*, p. 41.
98. Ibid.
99. Cupitt, *Christ and the Hiddenness of God*, pp. 66–7.
100. Cupitt, 'The Meaning of Belief in God', in *Explorations*, pp. 54–58 (p. 57). Cupitt's italics.
101. Cupitt, *Jesus and the Gospel of God*, p. 94.
102. Cupitt, *Taking Leave of God*, p. 9.
103. Ibid.
104. Cupitt, *Creation out of Nothing*, p. ix.
105. Ibid., p. x.

## 3  Departure from Orthodoxy

1. Cf., for example, Don Cupitt, *Radicals and the Future of the Church*, ch. 2.
2. Don Cupitt, *Christ and the Hiddenness of God*, p. 7.
3. Ibid., p. 22.
4. Ibid., p. 23.
5. Don Cupitt, *Jesus and the Gospel of God*, p. 43.
6. Ibid.
7. Don Cupitt, 'The Meaning of Belief in God', in *Explorations in Theology 6*, pp. 54–58 (p. 57).
8. Ibid.
9. Cupitt, *Explorations*, p. viii.
10. Don Cupitt, *Taking Leave of God*, p. 34.
11. Ibid., p. 38.

12. Richard Swinburne, *Revelation: From Metaphor to Analogy*, p. 162.
13. Cupitt, *Taking Leave of God*, p. 38.
14. Ibid., p. 51.
15. Ibid., p. 51.
16. Ibid., p. 13.
17. Ibid., p. 96.
18. Ibid., p. 96.
19. Ibid., p. 127.
20. Ibid., p. 127.
21. Ibid., p. 141.
22. Ibid., p. 166.
23. Ibid., p. 166.
24. Ibid., p. 166.
25. Ibid., p. 166.
26. Jonathan Swift, *Gulliver's Travels*, Book 4.
27. Cupitt, *Taking Leave of God*, p. 166.
28. Ibid.
29. Don Cupitt, *Only Human*, pp. 178–9.
30. Ibid., p. 202.
31. Don Cupitt, *The Sea of Faith*, 2nd edn, p. 264.
32. Cupitt, *Only Human*, p. 181.
33. Don Cupitt, *The World to Come*, p. 63.
34. Ibid., p. xiii.
35. Ibid., p. xiii.
36. Ibid., p. 7.
37. Ibid., p. 11. Cupitt's italics.
38. Ibid., p. 10.
39. Ibid., p. 38.
40. Ibid., p. xvii.
41. Cupitt, *Only Human*, p. 212.
42. Cf., for example, Cupitt, *The World to Come*, p. xi.
43. Cupitt, *The World to Come*, p. 4.
44. Ibid., p. 13.
45. Ibid., pp. 60–61.
46. Ibid., p. 26.
47. Ibid., p. 157.
48. Ibid., p. 156.
49. Cupitt, *Only Human*, p. xi.
50. Ibid., p. 194.
51. Ibid., p. 195.
52. Don Cupitt, *The New Christian Ethics*, p. 6.
53. Don Cupitt, *The Long-Legged Fly*, p. 37. Cupitt's italics.
54. Ibid., p. 20. Cupitt's italics.

55. Ibid., p. 158.
56. Ibid., p. 153.
57. Ibid., p. 159.
58. Ibid., p. 162.
59. Ibid., p. 162.
60. Cupitt, *The New Christian Ethics*, p. 94.
61. Cupitt, *Radicals and the Future of the Church*, p. 55.
62. Ibid., p. 55–6.
63. Ibid., Chapter 2.
64. Cf., for example, *Radicals and the Future of the Church*, p. 168 on the place of the imagination in theology and ethics; and p. 170 on the place of art in the religious community.
65. Don Cupitt, *What is a Story?*, p. 67.
66. Ibid., p. 134.
67. Ibid., p. 138.
68. Ibid., p. 139.
69. Ibid., p. 154.
70. Ibid., p. 154.

## 4 *The Case against Realism*

1. Within the Church of England alone, one may cite the current divisions on the ordination of women, and the uncertainty surrounding the church's stance on marriage and divorce for example, as instances of its own internal confusions and tensions.
2. The letters page of the *Church Times* affords examples almost weekly of disputes about the church's position in the world, and its potential for escapism, as well as its use or abuse of its resources.
3. Don Cupitt, *Taking Leave of God*, p. ix.
4. Don Cupitt, *The Long-Legged Fly*, p. 13.
5. Ibid., p. 18.
6. Ibid., p. 19. Cupitt's italics.
7. Scott Cowdell, *Atheist Priest?* p. 58.
8. David L. Edwards, *Tradition and Truth*, p. 86.
9. Ibid.
10. Cf. Keith Ward, *Holding Fast to God*, ch. 2.
11. Bryan Magee, *Men of Ideas*, p. 131.
12. Don Cupitt, *Radicals and the Future of the Church*, p. 37. Cupitt's italics.
13. Cupitt, *Taking Leave of God*, p. 1.
14. Cf., for example, Cupitt, *Taking Leave of God*, p. 2.
15. Don Cupitt, *What is a Story?*, pp. ix–x.
16. Ibid.

17. Cupitt, *The New Christian Ethics*, p. 9.
18. Cupitt, *The Long-Legged Fly*, p. 8.
19. Don Cupitt, *Creation out of Nothing*, p. 45.
20. Cupitt, *Taking Leave of God*, p. 98.
21. Cupitt, *What is a Story?*, p. 154.
22. Cupitt, *Radicals and the Future of the Church*, p. 55.
23. Cupitt, *The World to Come*, p. 140.
24. Stewart R. Sutherland, 'En Route for the Ineffable', Review of *The World to Come, Times Literary Supplement*, 28 May 1982, p. 574.

## 5  Contra Cupitt: Technique and Method

1. Don Cupitt, *The Sea of Faith*, 2nd edn, pp. 217–18.
2. Cf., for example, Don Cupitt, *Taking Leave of God*, pp. 5, 158–9; *The World to Come*, p. 7; *The Long-Legged Fly*, pp. 157–8.
3. Don Cupitt, *The New Christian Ethics*, p. 41. Cupitt's italics.
4. As examples one might think of the concern of natural theology to stress the goodness of creation; the Christian patronage of the creative arts; the social reforms pioneered by philanthropic Christians; and the renewed twentieth-century interest in the relationship between faith and healing, both personal and social.
5. Cupitt, *Taking Leave of God*, pp. 6–7.
6. Ibid., pp. 115–6.
7. Cupitt, *The New Christian Ethics*, p. 67.
8. Don Cupitt, *Christ and the Hiddenness of God*, p. 167.
9. James Mark, Review of *Taking Leave of God, Theology*, 84 (1981), 211–213 (p. 212).
10. Graham Slater, Review of *The World to Come, Expository Times*, 194 (1983), (p. 188).
11. Cf., for example, Cupitt, *Taking Leave of God*, pp. 156–9.
12. Cupitt, *Taking Leave of God*, pp. 4–6, 98–9.
13. Father; shepherd; husband; lover etc.
14. Cf., especially, Cupitt, *Taking Leave of God*, pp. 85–7.
15. Scott Cowdell, *Atheist Priest?* p. 63.
16. Cupitt, *Taking Leave of God*, p. 87.
17. Ibid., Chapter 2.
18. Cupitt, *The Long-Legged Fly*, pp. 150–1.
19. Don Cupitt, *Radicals and the Future of the Church*, p. 14.
20. Cupitt. *Taking Leave of God*, p. 43.
21. Ibid., p. 164.
22. Cupitt, *The Sea of Faith*, p. 59.
23. Cupitt, *The New Christian Ethics*, p. 71.

24. Cupitt, *The Sea of Faith*, p. 59.
25. See, for example, such different theologians as John Macquarrie, John Hick and Maurice Wiles, all of whom would assert their reasons for preferring a critical realism to a purely subjective approach to religion.
26. Among theologians a typical expression of such a position would be found in the work of scientific theologians such as John Polkinghorne and John Habgood, and philosophical theologians such as Keith Ward.
27. David L. Edwards, *Tradition and Truth*, p. 76.
28. Maurice Wiles, Review of *The Sea of Faith*, *Theology*, (May 1985), p. 232.
29. John A. T. Robinson, 'Man's Last and Highest Parting', Review of *Taking Leave of God*, *The Times Literary Supplement*, 5 December 1980, p. 1376.
30. Cupitt, *Taking Leave of God*, p. 39.
31. Cf., for example Isaiah's call in Isa. 6.1–6 as a prime example of this.
32. Wiles, Review of *The Sea of Faith*, *Theology*, (May 1985), p. 233.
33. Don Cupitt, *What is a Story?*, pp. 88–9.
34. Ibid., pp. 101–2.
35. Wiles, Review of *The Sea of Faith*, *Theology*, (May 1985), p. 233.
36. Cupitt, *The World to Come*, pp. 84–5. Cupitt's italics.
37. Cupitt, *The New Christian Ethics*, p. 15. Cupitt's italics.
38. Ibid., p. 16.
39. Cupitt, *Radicals and the Future of the Church*, p. 17.
40. Ibid.
41. The Reformation and Vatican II would be very different examples of major movements within the church; and alongside this the church has always – although admittedly not always at the time – come to value the work of critical and intelligent theologians.
42. Don Cupitt, *Creation out of Nothing*, p. 155.
43. Ibid.
44. Ibid.
45. Christina A. Baxter, Review of *Explorations in Theology 6*, *Churchman*, 94, No. 2 (1980), p. 163.
46. Norman Anderson, 'Foreword' to Keith Ward, *Holding Fast to God*, p. v.

## 6 Contra Cupitt: Theological Validity

1. Cf. Don Cupitt, *Taking Leave of God*, ch. 9.
2. A common example being its insistence, on the one hand, of the goodness of God; and on the other hand, the moral dubiety of the actual effects of this God on the believer: ie tyrannical and crushing.
3. Ie., Cupitt, *Taking Leave of God*, p. 9.
4. Don Cupitt, *What is a Story?*, p. 139.
5. Ibid., p. 141.

6. Don Cupitt, *The World to Come*, p. 84.
7. Ibid., p. 119.
8. Don Cupitt, *Radicals and the Future of the Church*, p. 99. Cupitt's italics.
9. Leszek Kolakowski, 'It's all relative, except . . .', Review of *Only Human*, *The Times Literary Supplement*, 8 August 1985, p. 854.
10. Paul Rowntree Clifford, *Politics and the Christian Vision*. Clifford uses this term to indicate the translation of thought into action. Doctrine, theory or vision is 'cashed' when it is put into practice.
11. Don Cupitt, *Only Human*, p. 128.
12. Ibid., p. 129.
13. John Macquarrie, *Principles of Christian Theology*, revd edn, p. 158.
14. Don Cupitt, *The New Christian Ethics*, p. 130.
15. Macquarrie, p. 159.
16. Cupitt, *Taking Leave of God*, p. 88.
17. Ibid., p. 91. Cupitt's italics.
18. Ibid., p. 96.
19. Ibid., p. 4.
20. Ibid., p. 4. Cupitt's italics.
21. Ibid., pp. 19–20.
22. Richard Kearney, *Dialogues with Contemporary Continental Thinkers*, p. 63.
23. Cupitt, *Radicals and the Future of the Church*, p. 142.
24. Ibid., p. 143.
25. Ibid., p. 145. Cupitt's italics.
26. Ibid., p. 167. Cupitt's italics.
27. Don Cupitt, *The Long-Legged Fly*, Author's note.
28. Cupitt, *The New Christian Ethics*, p. 160.
29. Ibid.
30. Ibid.
31. Cupitt, *Radicals and the Future of the Church*, p. 14.
32. Ibid.
33. Ibid., p. 160. Cupitt's italics.
34. Ibid., p. 161.
35. Ibid., p. 161. Cupitt's italics.
36. Don Cupitt, *Creation out of Nothing*, p. 169.
37. Ibid.
38. Cupitt, *The New Christian Ethics*, p. 36.
39. Ibid., p. 13. Cupitt's italics.
40. Ibid., p. 44.
41. Ibid., p. 134.
42. Ibid., p. 134.
43. Ibid., p. 4.
44. Ibid., p. 13.
45. Ibid., p. 23.

46. Ibid., p. 27.
47. Ibid., p. 109.
48. Cf. ibid., p. 13, as a good example of this.
49. Ibid., p. 22.
50. One might think, for example, of the church of the Middle Ages; or, as a more modern example, of the stamping out of the Roman Catholic Modernists during the early years of this century.


7 *Contra Cupitt: Language and Reality*

1. Don Cupitt, *The New Christian Ethics*, p. 11.
2. Janet Martin Soskice, *Metaphor and Religious Language*, p. 140.
3. Ibid.
4. Richard Swinburne, *Revelations: From Metaphor to Analogy*, pp. 46–7.
5. Ibid., pp. 159–161.
6. Janet Martin Soskice, p. 153.
7. Ibid., pp. 153–4.
8. Don Cupitt, *The Long-Legged Fly*, p. 13.
9. Ibid., p. 21.
10. Ibid., p. 20.
11. Don Cupitt, *The World to Come*, pp. 151–3.
12. David A. Walker, 'Truth and Objectivity: A Response to Don Cupitt', *The Expository Times*, 97, No. 3, (1975), 75–79 (p. 76).
13. Ibid., p. 77.
14. Ibid., p. 77.
15. Janet Martin Soskice, p. 141.
16. Don Cupitt, *Creation out of Nothing*, p. 56.
17. Ibid., p. 60.
18. Don Cupitt, *What is a Story?*, pp. 120–1.
19. Ibid., p. 123.
20. Ibid., p. 124.
21. Don Cupitt, *Radicals and the Future of the Church*, p. 54. Cupitt's italics.
22. Ibid., p. 86.
23. Ibid., p. 55. Cupitt's italics.
24. Ibid., p. 86.
25. Susanne Langer, *Philosophy in a New Key: A Study in the Symbolism of Reason, Rite and Art*, Harvard University Press 1942, pp. 96–7.
26. Cupitt, *Creation out of Nothing*, p. 159.
27. Langer, p. 233.
28. Janet Martin Soskice, p. 18.
29. Cupitt, *Radicals and the Future of the Church*, p. 62.
30. Ibid. Cupitt's italics.

31. Janet Martin Soskice, p. 98.
32. Ibid.
33. Ibid.
34. Ibid., pp. 98–9.
35. Ibid., p. 99.
36. For a good theological discussion of the self-refuting nature of the verification principle, see, for example, Keith Ward, *Holding Fast to God*, pp. 18ff.
37. Bryan Magee, *The Great Philosophers*, p. 345.
38. Christopher Norris, *What's Wrong with Postmodernism*, p. 23.
39. Roy Bhaskar, *Scientific Realism and Human Emancipation*, Verso 1986. Quoted in Norris, *What's Wrong with Postmodernism*, p. 98. Bhaskar's italics.
40. Cf. for example, Norris, *What's Wrong with Postmodernism*, and John M. Ellis, *Against Deconstruction*, Princeton University Press 1989.
41. J. G. Merquior, *Foucault*, 2nd edn, pp. 146–7.
42. Cf. Richard Kearney, *Dialogues with Contemporary Continental Thinkers*, p. 125.
43. Kearney, pp. 123–4. Kearney's italics.
44. Norris, *What's Wrong with Postmodernism*, p. 154, and Christopher Norris, *Derrida*, pp. 53–4.
45. Jacques Derrida, *Limited Inc.*, 2nd edn, ed. Gerald Graff, Northwestern University Press, Illinois, 1989, p. 146. Quoted in Christopher Norris, *Deconstruction: Theory and Practice*, p. 156.
46. Paul de Man, *Allegories of Reading*. Quoted in Jonathen Culler, *On Deconstruction*, p. 249.
47. Paul de Man, *Blindness and Insight*. Quoted in Cullen, p. 274.
48. Cullen, p. 280.
49. John D. Caputo, 'Mysticism and Transgression: Derrida and Meister Eckhart' in *Continental Philosophy II: Derrida and Deconstruction* ed. Hugh J. Silverman, p. 28. Caputo's italics.
50. Caputo, in Silverman, pp. 28–9.

## 8  The Reinstatement of Realism

1. Don Cupitt, *Taking Leave of God*, p. 10.
2. Ibid., p. 5.
3. Keith Ward, *Holding Fast to God*, p. 1.
4. Ibid.
5. Cf. ibid., p. 15.
6. Ibid., ch. 2.
7. Don Cupitt, *What is a Story?*, p. 154.

8. Ward., pp. 28–9.
9. Paul Handley, '"Profile" of Janet Martin Soskice', *Church Times*, 20 November 1992, p. 8.
10. Brian Russell, 'With Respect to Don Cupitt', *Theology*, (January 1985), 5–11 (p. 9).
11. Ibid.
12. Ward, p. 31.
13. Rowan Williams, '"Religious Realism": On Not Quite Agreeing with Don Cupitt', *Modern Theology*, 1:1 (October 1984), 2–24 (p. 17).
14. Ibid.
15. Ibid.
16. Ibid., p. 11.
17. Ibid., p. 11. Williams' italics.
18. Ibid., p. 11.
19. Ibid., p. 12. Williams' italics.
20. Don Cupitt, *The New Christian Ethics*, p. 5.
21. Ward, p. 80.
22. Ibid.
23. Janet Martin Soskice, *Metaphor and Religious Language*, p. 120.
24. Ibid., p. 132.
25. Linda Woodhead, 'This World Too', Review of *The Time Being*, *Church Times*, 19 June 1992, p. 12.
26. Brian Hebblethwaite, *The Ocean of Truth*, p. 104.
27. Ibid., p. 105.
28. F. C. Happold, *Religious Faith and Twentieth Century Man*, pp. 35–6.
29. Cited in John Macquarrie, *Twentieth-Century Religious Thought*, 4th edn, p. 190.
30. George Santayana, *Scepticism and Animal Faith*, cited in Macquarrie, p. 237.
31. John Hick, *An Interpretation of Religion*, p. 207.
32. Hick, p. 208.

## Conclusion

1. Iris Murdoch, *Metaphysics as a Guide to Morals*, p. 456. Murdoch's italics.
2. Janet Martin Soskice, *Metaphor and Religious Language*, p. 137.
3. Don Cupitt, *Jesus and the Gospel of God*, pp. 92–3.
4. Dorothy Emmet, *The Nature of Metaphysical Thinking*, cited in John Macquarrie, *Twentieth-Century Religious Thought*, 4th edn, p. 277.

# Bibliography

There is an excellent and exhaustive bibliography included in Scott Cowdell's study of Don Cupitt, and I have therefore included in this bibliography only those items which have been directly relevant to the planning and writing of this thesis. For convenience these have been placed under a number of headings.

## (a) Books by Don Cupitt

*Christ and the Hiddenness of God*, Lutterworth Press 1971; Second Edition, SCM Press 1985
*Crisis of Moral Authority*, SCM Press 1972; Second Edition 1985
*The Worlds of Science and Religion*, Sheldon Press 1976
*The Leap of Reason*, Sheldon Press 1976; Second Edition, SCM Press 1985
*Who was Jesus?* (with Peter Armstrong), BBC Books 1977
*Explorations in Theology 6*, SCM Press 1979
*Jesus and the Gospel of God*, Lutterworth Press 1979
*The Nature of Man*, Sheldon Press 1979
*The Debate about Christ*, SCM Press 1979
*Taking Leave of God*, SCM Press 1980
*The World to Come*, SCM Press 1982
*The Sea of Faith*, BBC Books 1984; Second Edition SCM Press 1994
*Only Human*, SCM Press 1985
*Life Lines*, SCM Press 1986
*The Long-Legged Fly*, SCM Press 1987
*The New Christian Ethics*, SCM Press 1988
*Radicals and the Future of the Church*, SCM Press 1989
*Creation out of Nothing*, SCM Press 1990
*What is a Story?* SCM Press 1991
*The Time Being*, SCM Press 1992
*Rethinking Religion*, St Andrew's Trust, Wellington, NZ 1992
*After All*, SCM Press 1994

*(b)  Contributions by Don Cupitt to Symposia*

'Theology and Practice' in M. C. Perry (ed), *Crisis for Confirmation*, SCM Press 1967

'One Jesus, Many Christs' in S. W. Sykes and J. P. Clayton (eds), *Christ, Faith and History*, CUP 1972

'How We Make Moral Decisions' and 'God and Morality' in G. R. Dunstan (ed), *Duty and Discernment*, SCM Press 1975

'Natural Evil' in Hugh Montefiore (ed), *Man and Nature*, Collins 1975

'The Christ of Christendom' and 'A Final Comment' in John Hick (ed), *The Myth of God Incarnate*, SCM Press 1977

'Jesus and the Meaning of God', and 'Mr Hebblethwaite on the Incarnation' in Michael Goulder (ed), *Incarnation and Myth*, SCM Press 1979

'The Jesus of Faith and the Christ of History' in Durstan R. McDonald (ed), *The Myth/Truth of God Incarnate*, Morehouse-Barlow, Connecticut 1979

'Kant and the Negative Theology' in Brian Hebblethwaite and Stewart Sutherland (eds), *The Philosophical Frontiers of Christian Theology*, CUP 1982

'A Tale of Two Cities: The World to Come' (with J. A. T. Robinson) in John A. T. Robinson, *Where Three Ways Meet*, SCM Press 1987

'Faith Alone' in Peter Eaton (ed), *The Trial of Faith*, Churchman 1988

The Introduction to William Hale White, *The Autobiography of Mark Rutherford and Mark Rutherford's Deliverance*, Libris 1988

A Response, in David L. Edwards, *Tradition and Truth*, Hodder & Stoughton 1989

'The Abstract Sacred' *The Journey*, Usher Gallery, Lincoln 1990

'The God Within' in Dan Cohn-Sherbok (ed), *Tradition and Unity*, Bellew Publishing 1991

'The Bible and the God of Israel' in Dan Cohn-Sherbok (ed), *Using the Bible Today*, Bellew Publishing 1991

'After Liberalism' in D. W. Hardy and P. H. Sedgwick (eds), *The Weight of Glory*, T. & T. Clark 1991

'Unsystematic Ethics and Politics' in Philippa Berry and Andrew Wernick (eds), *Shadow of Spirit*, Routledge 1992

'Anti-realist Faith' and other contributions in J. Runzo (ed), *Is God Real?*, Macmillan 1993

'The Last Judgement' in Leo Howe and Alan Wain (eds), *Predicting the Future* CUP 1993

'Nature and Culture' in Neil Spurway (ed), *Humanity, Environment and God*, Blackwell 1993

'The Faith of a Radical Christian' in Neville Glasgow (ed), *Frontiers*, St Andrew's Trust, Wellington, NZ 1993

'Explaining Religious Experience' in Dan Cohn-Sherbok (ed), *Glimpses of God*, Duckworth 1994

## (c) Articles by Don Cupitt

'What do we mean by "The Church"?', *Theology* 64, 1961, 275–281
'Four Arguments against the Devil', *Theology* 64, 1961, 413–415
'Mansel and Maurice on our Knowledge of God', *Theology* 73, 1970, 301–311
'God and the World in Post-Kantian Thought', *Theology* 75, 1972, 343–354
'How we Make Moral Decisions', *Theology* 76, 1973, 239–250
'God and Morality', *Theology* 76, 1973, 356–364
'Christian Existence in a Pluralist Society', *Theology* 77, 1974, 451–459
'Up in Arms', in *Words: Reflections on the Uses of Language*, BBC Publications
    1975, 97–104
'The Leap of Reason', *Theology* 78, 1975, 291–302
'The Finality of Christ', *Theology* 78, 1975, 618–628
'Christian Ethics Today', *Crucible*, July–September 1976, 104–107
'Religion and Critical Thinking – I', *Theology* 86, 1983, 243–249
'Religion and Critical Thinking – II', *Theology* 86, 1983, 328–335
'A Reply to Rowan Williams', *Modern Theology* 1:1, 1984, 25–31
'A Sense of History', *Theology* 89, 1986, 362–366
'Is Anything Sacred?' Christian Humanism and Christian Nihilism, *Religious Humanities*, Autumn 1990, 151–159


## (d) Books by Other Authors

Allport, G. W., *The Individual and his Religion*, Constable 1951
Archbishop's Commission, The, *Faith in the City*, A Report by the Archbishop's
    Commission, Church House Publishing 1985
Barr, James, *The Bible in the Modern World*, SCM Press, 1973
——, *Fundamentalism*, Revised Edition, SCM Press 1981
Bowie, Malcolm, *Lacan*, Fontana Press 1991
Clifford, Paul Rowntree, *Politics and the Christian Vision*, SCM Press 1984
Cowdell, Scott, *Atheist Priest? Don Cupitt and Christianity*, SCM Press 1988
Culler, Jonathan, *On Deconstruction*, Routledge & Kegan Paul 1983
Derrida, Jacques, *Writing and Difference*, Routledge & Kegan Paul 1978
——, *Dissemination*, The Athlone Press 1981
Descombes, Vincent, *Modern French Philosophy*, CUP 1980
Doctrine Commission, The, *Christian Believing*, A Report by the Doctrine
    Commission of the Church of England, SPCK 1976
——, *Believing in the Church*, A Report by the Doctrine Commission of the
    Church of England, SPCK 1981
——, *We Believe in God*, A Report by the Doctrine Commission of the Church of
    England, Church House Publishing 1987
Durkheim, Emile, *The Elementary Forms of the Religious Life*, Second Edition,
    Unwin Hyman 1976

Edwards, David L., *Tradition and Truth*, Hodder & Stoughton 1989
Feuerbach, Ludwig, *The Essence of Christianity*, Eliot, Harper & Row, New York & London 1957
Freeman, Anthony, *God in Us: A Case for Christian Humanism*, SCM Press 1993
Freud, Sigmund, *Pelican Freud, Vol 12*, Penguin 1985
Geering, Lloyd, *Faith's New Age*, Collins 1980
General Synod, The, *Children in the Way*, A Report for the General Synod Board of Education, The National Society and Church House Publishing 1988
Gibellini, Rosino, ed., *Frontiers of Theology in Latin America*, SCM Press 1980
Gore, Charles, ed., *Lux Mundi: A Series of Studies in the Religion of the Incarnation*, John Murray 1889
Gutierrez, Gustavo, *A Theology of Liberation*, Revised Edition, SCM Press 1988.
Habgood, J., *A Working Faith*, Darton, Longman & Todd 1980
——, *Confessions of a Conservative Liberal*, SPCK 1988
Happold, F. C., *Religious Faith and Twentieth Century Man*, Penguin 1966
Hebblethwaite, Brian, *The Ocean of Truth*, 1988
Hick, John, *The Existence of God*, Macmillan 1964
——, *An Interpretation of Religion*, Macmillan 1989
——, ed., *The Myth of God Incarnate*, SCM Press 1977
Isbister, J. N., *Freud: An Introduction to his Life and Work*, Polity Press 1985
Kamuf, Peggy, ed., *A Derrida Reader: Between the Blinds*, Harvester Wheatsheaf 1991
Kane, Margaret, *Gospel in Industrial Society*, SCM Press 1980
Kearney, Richard, *Dialogues with Contemporary Continental Thinkers*, Manchester University Press 1984
Koyama, Kosuke, *Mount Fuji and Mount Sinai*, SCM Press 1984
Kurzweil, Edith, *The Age of Structuralism*, Columbia University Press 1980
Mackey, James P., *The Christian Experience of God as Trinity*, SCM Press 1983
Macquarrie, John, *Twentieth-Century Religious Thought*, 1963; Fourth Edition, SCM Press, 1990
——, *Principles of Christian Theology*, 1966; Revised Edition, SCM Press 1977.
——, *In Search of Deity*, SCM Press 1984
——, *Jesus Christ in Modern Thought*, SCM Press 1990
Magee, Bryan, *Men of Ideas*, BBC Books 1978
——, *The Great Philosophers*, BBC Books 1987
Merquior, J. G., *From Prague to Paris: A Critique of Structuralist and Post-structuralist Thought*, Verso 1986
——, *Foucault*, Fontana Press 1985; Second Edition 1991
Moltmann, Jurgen, *The Crucified God*, SCM Press 1974
Montefiore, Hugh, *The Probability of God*, SCM Press 1985

Murdoch, Iris, *The Sovereignty of Good*, Chatto & Windus 1970
——, *Acastos*, Chatto & Windus 1980
——, *Metaphysics as a Guide to Morals*, Chatto & Windus 1992
Norris, Christopher, *Derrida*, Fontana Press 1987
——, *Deconstruction: Theory and Practice*, Routledge, Revised Edition 1991
——, *What's Wrong with Postmodernism*, Harvester Wheatsheaf 1990
Pears, David, *Wittgenstein*, Fontana Press 1971
Phillips, D. Z., ed., *Religion and Understanding*, Blackwell 1967
——, *The Concept of Prayer*, Routledge & Kegan Paul, 1965 & 1968
——, *Religion Without Explanation*, Blackwell 1976
——, *Belief, Change and Forms of Life*, Macmillan 1986
——, *Faith after Foundationalism*, Routledge 1988
——, *From Fantasy to Faith*, Macmillan Education Ltd 1991
Ramsey, Michael, *The Gospel and the Catholic Church*, SPCK 1990
Ruether, Rosemary Radford, *Mary, The Feminine Face of the Church*, SCM Press 1979
Selden, Raman, *A Reader's Guide to Contemporary Literary Theory*, Harvester Wheatsheaf, Second Edition, 1989
Sheppard, David, *Bias to the Poor*, Hodder & Stoughton, 1983
Silverman, Hugh J. ed., *Continental Philosophy II: Derrida and Deconstruction*, Routledge 1989
Soskice, Janet Martin, *Metaphor and Religious Language*, Clarendon Press 1985
Staten, Henry, *Wittgenstein and Derrida*, Blackwell 1985
Stendahl, Krister, *The Bible and the Role of Women*, Fortress Press, Philadelphia 1966
Swinburne, Richard, *Revelation: From Metaphor to Analogy*, Clarendon Press 1992
Vidler, Alec, ed., *Soundings: Essays Concerning Christian Understanding*, CUP 1962
Ward, Keith, *The Concept of God*, Blackwell, 1974
——, *Holding Fast to God*, SPCK 1982
——, *Rational Theology and the Creativity of God*, Blackwell, 1982 & 1985
——, *A Vision to Pursue*, SCM Press 1991
Wiles, Maurice, *What is Theology?* OUP 1976

*(e) Articles by Other Authors*

Clark, Stephen R. L., 'Cupitt and Divine Imagining', *Modern Theology* 5:1, 1988, 45–60
Cowdell, Scott, 'The Recent Adventures of Don Cupitt', *St Mark's Review*, No. 134, 1988, 32–35
——, 'Radical Theology, Postmodernity and Christian Life in the Void', *The Heythrop Journal* 32, 1991, 62–71

Handley, Paul, 'Taking Theology Seriously', (A Profile of Janet Martin Soskice), *Church Times*, 20 November 1992, 8

Hebblethwaite, Peter, 'Feuerbach's Ladder: Leszek Kolakowski and Iris Murdoch', *The Heythrop Journal* 13, 1972, 143–161

Kerr, Fergus, 'Don Cupitt's Philosophy', *The Month* 18, 1985, 87–90

Matthews, Melvyn, 'Cupitt's Context', *New Blackfriars* 66, 1985, 533–543

Mullen, Peter, 'Serial Theology', *Theology* 86, 1983, 25–29

Pattison, George, 'From Kierkegaard to Cupitt: Subjectivity, the Body and Eternal Life', *The Heythrop Journal* 31, 1990, 295–308

Russell, Brian, 'With Respect to Don Cupitt', *Theology* 88, 1985, 5–11

Tarbox, Everett J. Jr., 'The A/Theology of Don Cupitt: A Theological Option in our Post-Modern Age', *Religious Humanities*, Spring 1991, 72–82

Turner, Denys, 'De-Centring Theology', *Modern Theology* 2:2, January 1986, 125–143

Walker, David A., 'Truth and Objectivity: A Response to Don Cupitt', *The Expository Times* 97 No. 3, 1975, 75–79

Williams, Rowan, '"Religious Realism": On Not Quite Agreeing With Don Cupitt', *Modern Theology* 1:1, 1984, 3–24

## (f) Book Reviews

### Christ and the Hiddenness of God

France, Malcolm, *Frontier* 15, 1972, 120

### Crisis of Moral Authority

Frances, Malcolm, *Frontier* 16, 1973, 53–4

Fraser, John W., *Scottish Journal of Theology* 26, 1973, 497–499

### The Leap of Reason

Allen, Diogenes, *Theology Today*, 34, 1977–8, 340–341

Heywood, Thomas, J., 'A Philosophy of Spirit', *The Expository Times* 88 No. 5, 1977, 156

Wiles, Maurice, *Journal of Theological Studies* 28, 1977, 265–267

### Explorations in Theology 6

Baxter, Christina A., *Churchman* 94 No, 2, 1980, 163

Jones, Hugh O., *Theology* 84, 1981, 123–125

*Jesus and the Gospel of God*

Drury, John, *Theology* 82, 1979, 377–379
Turner, Geoffrey, 'The Image of the Invisible God', *New Blackfriars* 60 No. 713, 1979, 416–425

*The Nature of Man*

Carey, George, *Churchman* 94 No. 1, 1980, 77–78
Jones, Hugh O., *Theology* 84, 1981, 123–125

*The Debate about Christ*

Kerr, Fergus, *Journal of Theological Studies* 31, 1980, 282–283
Mackey, James P., *Theology* 83, 1980, 217–218

*Taking Leave of God*

Mark, James, *Theology* 84, 1981, 211–213
Robinson, John A. T., 'Man's Last and Highest Parting', *The Times Literary Supplement*, 5 December 1980, 1376
Slater, Graham, *The Expository Times* 92, 1981, 154

*The World to Come*

Collins, Steven, *Theology* 86, 1983, 46–48
Slater, Graham, *The Expository Times* 94, 1983, 188
Sutherland, Stewart R., 'En Route for the Ineffable', *The Times Literary Supplement*, 28 May 1982, 574

*The Sea of Faith*

Wiles, Maurice, *Theology*, 88, 1985, 232–233

*Only Hunan*

Kolakowski, Leszek, 'It's all relative, except . . .',     *The Times Literary Supplement*, 2 August 1985, 854
Surin, Kenneth, *Theology* 89, 1986, 132–134

*Lifelines*

Phillips, D. Z., 'Have You Missed Your Connection?', *The Times Literary Supplement*, 26 December 1986, 1446
Turner, Geoffrey, *New Blackfriars* 68, 1987, 363–364

*The Long-Legged Fly*

Slater, Graham, *The Expository Times* 100 No. 2, 1988, 72–73

*The New Christian Ethics*

Dyson, Anthony, *Theology* 92, 1989, 538–539
Southwell-Sander, Peter, *The Reader* 86 No. 4, 1989, 140–142

*Radicals and the Future of the Church*

Webster, Alan, 'The Fray of Faith', *The Times Literary Supplement*, 27 October
–2 November 1989, 1188

*Creation out of Nothing*

Race, Alan, *Theology* 94, 1991, 206–207

*What is a Story?*

Wiles, Maurice, 'Valuable Socratic Gadfly', *Church Times*, 29 November 1991,
'Faith' Supp., iii

*The Time Being*

Woodhead, Linda, 'This World Too', *Church Times*, 19 June 1992, p. 12

*Who Was Jesus?* (With Peter Armstrong)

Grayston, K., *Theology* 82, 1979, 60–62

Scott Cowdell, *Atheist Priest?*

Crowder, Colin, *Modern Theology* 6 No. 3, 1990, 301–303
Durrant, Michael, *New Blackfriars* 71 No. 838, 1990, 258–260
Hudson, W. D., 'New Theology or Confusion', *The Expository Times* 100 No. 8,
312–313
Southwell-Sander, Peter, *The Reader*, 86 No. 4, 1989, 140–142

# Index of Names